Picturing the Social Landscape

We live in a visual culture, and visual evidence is increasingly central to social research. In this collection an international range of experts explain how they have used visual methods in their own research, examine their advantages and limitations, and show how they have been used alongside other research techniques. Contributors explore the following areas:

- Self and identity
- Visualizing domestic space
- Visualizing urban landscapes
- Visualizing social change.

The collection showcases different methods in different contexts through the examination of a variety of topical issues. Methods covered include photo and video diaries, the use of images produced by respondents, the use of images as prompts in interviews and focus groups, documentary photography, photographic inventory and visual ethnography.

    The result is an exciting and original collection that will be indispensable for any student, academic or researcher interested in the use of visual methods.

Caroline Knowles is a Reader in Sociology and **Paul Sweetman** is a Lecturer in Sociology at the University of Southampton.

Picturing the Social Landscape

Visual methods and the sociological imagination

Edited by

Caroline Knowles and
Paul Sweetman

Routledge
Taylor & Francis Group

LONDON AND NEW YORK

First published in 2004
by Routledge
11 New Fetter Lane, London EC4P 4EE

Simultaneously published in the USA and Canada
by Routledge
29 West 35th Street, New York, NY 10001

Routledge is an imprint of the Taylor & Francis Group

Typeset in Perpetua and Bell Gothic by
Florence Production Ltd, Stoodleigh, Devon
Printed and bound in Great Britain by
TJ International Ltd, Padstow, Cornwall

British Library Cataloguing in Publication Data
A catalogue record for this book is available from the British Library

Library of Congress Cataloging in Publication Data
A catalog record for this book has been requested

ISBN 0–415–30639–6 (hbk)
ISBN 0–415–30640–X (pbk)

For Daniel, James, Jess, Will and Sophie

And for Sam and Arno

Contents

Notes on contributors

Les Back teaches Sociology and Urban Studies at Goldsmiths College, London. His recent books include *The Auditory Culture Reader* with Michael Bull (Berg, 2003) and *Out of Whiteness* with Vron Ware (University of Chicago Press, 2002).

Howard S. Becker lives and works in San Francisco. He is the author of *Outsiders* (Free Press, 1963), *Tricks of the Trade* (University of Chicago Press, 1998) and *Art Worlds* (University of California Press, 1982).

David Byrne is Professor of Sociology and Social Policy at the University of Durham. His main research interests are in the application of complexity theory to the social sciences and in understanding the nature and experience of post-industrial transformations. Recent publications include *Interpreting Quantitative Data* (Sage, 2002).

Elizabeth Chaplin has been associated with the Open University since 1973, first as a student and later as a member of staff. Her interests include visual culture, photography theory and diaries. Her publications include *Sociology and Visual Representation* (Routledge, 1994).

Cedric N. Chatterley's photography has been supported by the National Endowment for the Arts and state and humanities agencies in Illinois, Maine, North Carolina and South Dakota.

Elizabeth Cleaver is Senior Research Officer at the National Foundation for Educational Research, UK. She is the co-author, with Sue Heath, of *Young, Free and Single: Twenty-Somethings and Household Change* (Palgrave, 2004).

Aidan Doyle is a Senior Research Associate in the Centre for Land Use and Water Resources Research at the University of Newcastle. He is an artist, photographer and sociologist who has had a long-term commitment to documenting experiences of change in the north-east of England, both through visual images and through recording people's own words describing how their lives have changed.

John Grady is the Hannah Goldberg Professor of Sociology at Wheaton College in Norton, Massachusetts. He has produced numerous documentary films, including *Mission Hill and the Miracle of Boston; Water and the Dream of the Engineers*; and *The Collective: Fifteen Years Later*. He has written extensively in the journals *Visual Sociology* and *Visual Studies*.

Douglas Harper is Professor and Chair of the Department of Sociology at Duquesne University, USA. He is the founding editor of *Visual Sociology*, and was a founding member of the International Visual Sociology Association. He has written several sociological studies that feature photography, most recently *Changing Works: Visions of a Lost Agriculture* (University of Chicago Press, 2001). He was also, during the time data were being collected for this chapter, a pretty good bowler.

Sue Heath is a Senior Lecturer in Sociology at the University of Southampton, with a specific interest in the sociology of youth. Previous publications include *Sociological Research Methods in Context* (with Fiona Devine; Macmillan, 1999) and *Young, Free and Single: Twenty-Somethings and Household Change* (with Elizabeth Cleaver; Palgrave, 2004).

Ruth Holliday lectures in the Centre for Interdisciplinary Gender Studies at the University of Leeds. She has published in the areas of work and organizations, gender, sexuality and the body, and visual methods, and is currently working on a book exploring the cultural politics of kitsch.

Caroline Knowles is a Reader in Sociology in the School of Social Sciences, University of Southampton. Her research interests are in urban sociology, race, ethnicity, migration and globalization. Her publications include *Race and Social Analysis* (Sage, 2003), *Bedlam on the Streets* (Routledge, 2000), *Family Boundaries: the Invention of Normality and Dangerousness* (Broadview Press, 1996) and *Race, Discourse and Labourism* (Routledge, 1990).

Alan Latham is a Lecturer in Geography at the University of Southampton. His research focuses on sociality and urban public culture. His work has appeared in a number of edited collections and international journals such as *Society and Space, Urban Studies, Environment and Planning A* and *Area*.

Ana Maria Mauad is an Associate Professor in the History Department at the Universidade Federal Fluminense (Brazil) and a researcher in the Laboratory of Oral History and Image (www.historia.uff.br/labhoi) at the same university. A specialist in the analysis of visual and oral sources in history, her publications in English include 'Composite Past: Photography and Family Memories in Brazil

(1850–1950)', in Richard Cándida Smith (ed.) *Art and the Performance of Memory: Sounds and Gestures of Recollection* (Routledge, 2002).

Alicia J. Rouverol is former Assistant Director of the Southern Oral History Program at the University of North Carolina-Chapel Hill (USA) and former Associate Director of the Northeast Archives of Folklore and Oral History at the University of Maine. She has taught oral history and life review at UNC and Duke University. She is co-author of *'I Was Content and Not Content': The Story of Linda Lord and the Closing of Penobscot Poultry* (SIU Press, 2000). A consultant in folklore and oral history, she is currently at work on her next book, *Trying to Be Good: Lessons from a Penitentiary*.

Charles Suchar received his Ph.D. in Sociology at Northwestern University, Evanston, Illinois, in 1972. He is Professor of Sociology and Associate Dean for Graduate Programs in the College of Liberal Arts and Sciences at DePaul University, Chicago, Illinois. He served as President of the International Visual Sociology Association from 1990 to 1994 and as Book Review Editor of *Visual Sociology* from 1994 to 1998. His current scholarly interests are in the transformation of urban neighbourhoods and in the process of gentrification. He is also interested in the methodological applications of documentary photography and visual sociology.

Paul Sweetman is a Lecturer in Sociology at the University of Southampton. He has published articles and chapters on reflexivity and habitus, contemporary body modification, fashion and subcultural studies, and his research interests as a whole centre on issues of the body, identity, fashion and consumption. He is currently working on a book on *Fashion and Social Theory* which is also to be published by Routledge.

Tony Whincup is Director of Photography in the College of Design, Fine Arts and Music at Massey University, New Zealand, and a Fellow of the New Zealand Institute of Professional Photographers. His photographic work is held in both public and private collections and in numerous publications, including his recent award-winning book, *Akekeia! Traditional Dance in Kiribati* (with Joan Whincup; Tobaroi Travel, 2001). His current research explores the social significance of the canoe (*te wa*) in Kiribati.

Acknowledgements

We would like to thank Elizabeth Chaplin, Graham Crow, Doug Harper, Mari Shullaw, Chuck Suchar and Jon Wagner for their comments on earlier versions of the introduction or the initial proposal for the project as a whole. We are also grateful to Martin Edney for technical assistance here at Southampton, and to the editorial and productions teams at Routledge and all of the contributors for their efforts in helping to bring the project to fruition.

Credits for images and photographs are as follows. 'Introduction' (Caroline Knowles and Paul Sweetman): photographs attributable to Caroline Knowles and Paul Sweetman. 'Working with visible evidence' (John Grady): Plates 1 and 2 from Bill Owens's *Suburbia* (Straight Arrow Books, 1973), Plate 3 from issues of *Wheaton College Yearbook,* Plate 4 from William H. White's *The City: Rediscovering the Center* (Doubleday, 1988). Chapter 1 (Elizabeth Chaplin): all photographs attributable to Elizabeth Chaplin except Plate 1 – composite photograph of Elizabeth Chaplin's diary photographs by University of York Photographic Department. Chapter 2 (Ruth Holliday): images attributable to Ruth Holliday/ participants. Chapter 3 (Sue Heath and Elizabeth Cleaver): photographs attributable to participants in the ESRC shared household project, diagrams attributable to Sue Heath and Elizabeth Cleaver. Chapter 4 (Tony Whincup): photographs attributable to Tony Whincup. Chapter 5 (Douglas Harper): photographs attributable to Douglas Harper. Chapter 6 (Alan Latham): photographs attributable to participants, diagrams attributable to Alan Latham unless otherwise specified. Chapter 7 (Les Back): photographs attributable to Nicola Evans (Plates 1 and 6), Antonio Genco (Plates 4 and 7) and Gerard Mitchell (Plates 2, 3 and 5). Chapter 8 (Charles Suchar): photographs attributable to Charles Suchar. Chapter 9 (David Byrne and Aidan Doyle): photographs attributable to Aidan Doyle, diagram attributable to David Byrne and Aidan Doyle. Chapter 10 (Ana Maria Mauad and Alicia Rouverol): photographs attributable to Cedric N. Chatterley.

Caroline Knowles and
Paul Sweetman

INTRODUCTION

Introduction

RECENT YEARS HAVE SEEN a significant expansion in the use of visual presentational strategies in texts, teaching and conferences, as well as in the use of visual research methodologies and their accompanying commentaries. A number of factors are driving this visual agenda, including an expanding array of digital technologies which are inexpensive and easy to use. From PowerPoint to the digital images which can be made and manipulated through still and video cameras, making everyday visual records has never been easier or more accessible. That sighted human beings navigate the social world visually is by now established as a fundamental fact of social existence. John Berger's (1977: 7) famous comment that 'Seeing comes before words . . . and establishes our place in the surrounding world' supports the fundamental connection between visualization and the organization of human existence, of being in the world. Our knowledge of the world is shaped by our senses, and contemporary bodies in western societies prioritize the visual over other senses (Mellor and Shilling 1997: 6). Non-coincidentally, mass culture is hyper-visual.

It is unsurprising that these establishing facts of social existence should influence those whose job it is to provide social commentaries. Social researchers have used visual means of collecting and recording data since these means were available. But since the mid-1990s social researchers have noticed and focused on the visual particularly. What has shifted and, in combination with other factors, supported the burgeoning interest in the visual, is the subtle shading of the intellectual micro-climates in which social research is produced. What is widely billed as the reflexive turn in social investigation (Jenks 1995: 11) – and which gave us traditional and reworked sources of social knowing in auto/biography, human interaction, ethnography, performance, everyday life and concern with space – has produced a renewed enchantment among social researchers with people and places. People and places, in particular, demand visual representation as researchers struggle with the methodological means of imparting what they *see* in more than words. The growth of cultural studies as a discipline has provided another source of intellectual impetus driving the visual agenda. Visualizing the social world, what we see and how we see it, is like social theory itself. Both seeing and social theory are acts of interpretation: selection, abstraction and transformation (Jenks 1995: 4, 8). Both are socially constructed and culturally located (Jenks 1995: 210). When we write or picture the social world we reformulate it. The new prominence of visual strategies in social research, then, is about new theoretical and technical possibilities, a re-enchantment among social commentators with the texture of social life, the shifting and fragmented frameworks of knowledge in which we all operate and a determination to reach beyond words in producing accounts of the social world. But, as Berger (1977: 7) points out, 'The relation between what we see and what we know is never settled'. It is against the backdrop of this unsettling insight that this text is produced. All of its contributors grapple with the dynamic of seeing and knowing in different research contexts.

Genealogies of visual methods

Histories of visual methods have been extensively recorded elsewhere. It is not our intention to rehearse these narratives in any detail but simply to sketch in some of the basic contours and to indicate where fuller versions can be found. Douglas Harper (1998) and Elizabeth Chaplin (1994) have produced particularly extensive versions of the roots of visual methods. Visual strategies have developed in the context of their disciplines. Significant in the development of social anthropology are the photographs and film footage of Gregory Bateson in his work with Margaret Mead, *Balinese Character: a Photographic Analysis* (1942), in which groups of images are placed together to convey something beyond words about the Balinese (Chaplin 1994: 210; Harper 1998: 25–6). John and Malcolm Collier (1986) discuss their own use of film in anthropology as a technique for producing inventories of material culture and as *aide-mémoire* in depicting the field. Tim Asch's ethnographies of Cape Breton during the 1950s used film and photography in depicting landscape, people and social relationships in that area (see Harper 1994). Ethnography and photo-journalism were the parents of visual sociology (Harper 1998: 24). Auguste Comte and Louis Daguerre – pioneers of sociology and photography respectively – were products of the same set of historical circumstances (Chaplin 1994). Photo-journalist social reformers like Jacob Riis photographed the New York slums in the 1890s, and Lewis Hine, the documentary photographer who trained as a sociologist, campaigned against child labour in the period leading up to and including the First World War. Sociology's famous alliance with social reform was significantly rooted in the use of visual strategies; early editions of the *American Journal of Sociology* (1896–1916) contained photographs, including Blackmar's 'The Smoky Pilgrims' from 1897, a study of two impoverished families in Kansas (Chaplin 1994: 198, 201, 204). This visual heritage was later reworked in texts such as Howard Becker's 'Photography and sociology' (1974) and *Exploring Society Photographically* (1981), Erving Goffman's *Gender Advertisements* (1979), and Douglas Harper's *Good Company* (1982) and *Working Knowledge* (1987). Together, these studies demonstrate that 'when experienced social scientists who are also skilled photographers aim to produce images which have both documentary reach and aesthetic quality, these can – in combination with verbal text – generate a type of social science understanding which is very rich' (Chaplin 1994: 221–2). The principal organizational base of visual sociology – the International Visual Sociology Association – was established in 1981 (Chaplin 1994: 222) and ran the *International Journal of Visual Sociology* under the editorship of Leonard M. Henny. In 1986 *Visual Sociology*, edited by Harper, began to showcase the work of the 'visually driven thinker' (Chaplin 1994: 222–3) and the use of visual methods in social research took a number of steps forward.

Retracing our steps to the nineteenth century, it is important to note that photography moved in a number of other directions apart from ethnography and advocacy in the cause of social reform. Most famously it was deployed in the management of problematic populations – the mad, criminals, orphans and so on (see Tagg 1988) – and in documenting the successful lives of celebrities and the European and American middle class (Hamilton and Hargreaves 2001). John Tagg (1988: 13) argues that photographs operate as a 'politically mobilised rhetoric of truth': they can represent any set of social circumstances and frame them in any number of ways. They are given meaning by the frameworks in which they are deployed (Law and Whittaker 1988: 161). Deployed in support of political regimes, in the task of social critique or in the cult of celebrity, they are infinitely flexible. From other disciplinary bases and cross-disciplinary spaces came other significant contributions to visual strategies. Geography has always used maps and other diagrams, while cultural studies – despite its association with the 'linguistic turn' in social and cultural theory – has also developed in a visual frame because of its close association with popular culture and the popular imaginary. Pierre Bourdieu's (1990) *Photography: a Middlebrow Art* sets out what can be learned sociologically from examining the photographs people take and this has prompted more recent investigation of what it is that people do with photographs. Community studies have often used photographs to help 'place' or 'ground' sociological discourse and add another dimension to the arguments they pursue (Payne 1996: 18–20). Examples are Bill Williamson's *Class, Culture and Community* (1982), Ray Pahl's (1984) Sheppey study and others (see Crow 2000). Often community studies have used visual images in an unselfconscious way without commenting on their visual methods. John Berger and Jean Mohr have, over a number of publications – *Seventh Man* (1975), *Another Way of Telling* (1995) and others – developed a partnership of words and images depicting the social texture of life-worlds, people and places. Berger's (1977) *Ways of Seeing* is a seminal text in visual literacy.

Placing the collection

Recent years have seen the publication of a number of volumes focusing on the analysis of visual aspects of contemporary culture (see, for example, Evans and Hall 1999; Jenks 1995; Mirzoeff 1999) as well as several texts which focus more specifically on the use of visual methods within social and cultural research. Books in the latter category include Marcus Banks's *Visual Methods in Social Research* (2001), Michael Emmison and Philip Smith's *Researching the Visual* (2000), Sarah Pink's *Doing Visual Ethnography* (2001) and Jon Prosser's edited collection, *Image-based Research* (1998). Each of these texts has made a significant contribution to, and itself reflects, the growing interest in visual methods within social and cultural research. As with any such text, each has its limitations, however. Emmison and Smith's (2000) argument that we should expand our understanding of visual material to 'potentially encompass any object, person, place, event or happening which is observable to the human eye' (2000: 4) is interesting and provocative. But, as they themselves acknowledge, it opens up the field – and the attempted scope of their introductory text – to 'the subject matter of the social sciences almost in their entirety' (2000: 19). As an introduction to visual methods, the text is also somewhat perverse in extolling the virtues of its own lack of reliance on visual material (2000: 18) and suggesting that purely textual accounts may make for better 'visual social research' than those that employ photographs or other forms of visual representation (2000: 10).

Banks's *Visual Methods in Social Research* (2001) and Pink's *Doing Visual Ethnography* (2001) focus on the use of visual methods in anthropological research, and the former provides little consideration of specific methods, instead offering a more general discussion of the use of visual material which at times strays into rather basic territory. Parts of the discussion also move away from visual methods entirely: chapter four, for example, devotes a section to television studies, but as this section itself acknowledges, since the shift from text to audience in media studies, researchers like David Morley have been more concerned with what people *do* when they are watching television than with anything that is happening on the screen. Despite its anthropological bias, Pink's (2001) book is arguably the most useful and comprehensive single-authored introduction to visual methods, even if it is a little over-critical of much sociological work in this area, and of work that Pink identifies with what she refers to as a 'scientific realist' paradigm. This includes Prosser's *Image-Based Research* (1998), which provides a useful introduction to the use of visual methods, but as a collection is rather narrowly focused. There is a lot of good background material in Parts 1 and 2, but the contributions to Part 3 – 'Image-based research in practice' – are both few in number and rather limited in scope: of the six chapters that make up this part of the book, four discuss image-based research in education, and these are both practitioner-oriented and tightly focused on specific arguments and debates.

This collection attempts to do something different. While we are sympathetic towards Emmison and Smith's (2000) all-inclusive approach, our understanding of what constitutes visual material focuses on pictorial representation, particularly photographs and film or video, but also including non-photographic illustrations and more formal representations such as maps, graphs and so on. The focus within this collection is particularly on photography, though we also include a chapter by Ruth Holliday which explores the use of video-diaries, while the contributions from Alan Latham, Sue Heath and Elizabeth Cleaver, and David Byrne and Aidan Doyle, each make use of different forms of diagrammatic representation alongside their photographs, with Heath and Cleaver's representations of shared living space having been produced *in situ*, alongside more conventional fieldnotes. Latham's updated version of the conventional time–space diagram, meanwhile, combines photography and handwritten and conventional text in a way that highlights the complexity and changing rhythms of his informants' movements through the day.

As Emmison and Smith suggest, a great deal more could be included in our understanding of visual material, but to adopt an all-inclusive approach would be to render visual material indistinct from most other forms of data, and would also be to neglect the predominant focus on particular forms of visual material within the wider body of literature of which this collection forms a part. In talking about visual methods, then, we are referring to the use of visual material as we understand it within social and cultural research. More specifically, we understand visual methods to include ways of *doing* research that generate and employ visual material as an integral part of the research *process*, whether as a form of data, a means of generating further data, or a means of representing 'results'. Despite the conflation of these two aspects of visual sociology in certain introductory texts, our understanding of visual methods does not, in the main, extend to forms of analysis such as semiotics or content analysis, in which already existing visual material is the focus of research or *object* of enquiry, but, except in so far as it is what is looked *at*, does not play an integral part in the research process itself. While these two areas are closely connected, we are interested here in exploring the use of visual methods *in* social research rather than providing a sociology *of* visual culture, which focuses on the prominence of the image, but does not necessarily employ visual methods as a core component within research. Most importantly this book differs from others in its engagement with the conceptual potential of visual images in the research process.

Conceptual organization

There are, broadly speaking, three key theoretical approaches to visual images within social research. Under the realist paradigm exemplified by early anthropological fieldwork and the classical tradition of photo-journalism, images are regarded as *evidence* – as representations of reality and an uncomplicated record of already existing phenomena or events. From a broadly poststructuralist perspective, however, images help to *construct* reality: they operate as part of a regime of truth, while performing a central role in the surveillance and management of individuals and populations. This second perspective is perhaps best illustrated by Tagg's (1988) discussion of the role of photography in the management and control of 'problematic' groups in the nineteenth century, such as criminals, orphans and psychiatric patients. When viewed from the vantage point of the third key paradigm – semiotics or semiology – already existing images are regarded as texts which can be read to uncover their wider cultural significance and the ideological and other messages they help to communicate, naturalize and maintain.

This book does not fit neatly into any one of these theoretical frameworks. Certain contributions adopt a broadly realist perspective, while others are more critical of the status of the image. Throughout, it is not so much the status of the image that is of concern, but its *conceptual and analytic possibilities*: what it is that visual methods are able to *achieve*. That is not to say that either individual contributions or the collection as a whole represent a form of naïve atheoreticism – each chapter makes claims to the status of the image, even if in certain cases such claims remain largely implicit. What it is to say is that in concentrating on the use of visual material in the research *process*, we are less concerned with the ultimate status of the image than with the *uses* to which it can be put. As editors, we would reject a naïve realism which suggests that images – photographic or otherwise – simply *re-present* objective and already existing realities. At the same time, however, we would argue that a *pragmatic* realism – which accepts that the status of the image can remain largely unquestioned and its representational qualities accepted as given – is *sometimes* an appropriate stance to adopt. Indeed, for much of the work collected here, the theoretical status of the image *is* ultimately unimportant: when research subjects are asked to comment on their own or others' photographs, it is what they *make* of the images that counts.

There are, then, two primary reasons for our refusal to adopt an overarching theoretical perspective for the collection as a whole. First, as an edited *collection*, the book is deliberately intended to highlight the range of possibilities of which visual methods are capable, the range of uses to which they can be put. Second, we are concerned here with visual *methods* and the use of visual material in the *research* process: with the conceptual and analytic possibilities of visual methods rather than the status of the visual image itself. Above all, this is a pragmatic collection, which emphasizes that, while it may sometimes be important to examine the ontological and epistemological status of the image, at other times such questions are less significant, and the theoretical status of the image can remain largely unexplored. That does not mean the collection lacks theoretical engagement, however. Indeed, in emphasizing the *analytical and conceptual possibilities* of visual methods we are also emphasizing their theoretical possibilities, or rather, their capacity to allow for the development of theoretical insight or understanding, and it is this which underpins the organization of the book. In this it is unusual. The conceptual and analytic potential of images is not often directly confronted, beyond the selecting and framing which go into their composition, but remains unexamined in the background. In this book the conceptual and the analytical – the theoretical potential of images – are central rather than implicit.

This raises important questions. What do we mean by theory? Some claim that even the task of *describing* the social landscape involves its arrangement and rearrangement. Is this not social theory? We think it rather depends on the extent of arrangement and rearrangement embedded in description. As Anthony Giddens (1987: 19) points out in relation to sociology – but we can include all the other disciplines which grapple with the social world like cultural theory, human geography and so on – what we have to offer as social commentators is inevitably parasitic on lay concepts and popular understanding. If by description we mean the reproduction of these forms, then this, in our view, is not theory. We do not need social theorists to restate what everybody already knows. Anyone can do this. Theoretical understanding should not simply confirm what is already known or believed to be true. Neither should it be limited to using only the lexicon and the understanding of the agents of social action. Theory or analysis *must* involve the rearrangement of popular forms of social knowing so that hitherto unknown and non-apparent things become visible. Theory must involve discovery: uncovering what is not readily apparent, connections between one thing and another, the underlying assumptions from which we operate.

Giddens's (1987: vii) distinction between *social* theory and *sociological* theory is useful here. As a conceptual term, social theory is more inclusive than sociological theory and applies to the related disciplines on which the contributions in this collection draw. Social theory invokes 'a whole range of issues to do with human action, social institutions and their mutual *connections*' (Giddens 1987: vii, our emphasis). Goffman, who strayed neither into the micro-psychological territories involved in his investigation of the self, nor into an elaboration of the macro connections of his micro-analyses, nevertheless developed, as Giddens (1987: 109–10) points out, a systematic approach to the study of human social life. It was *systematic* – and hence theoretical – in its capacity to take the routine and the mundane and reveal its inner mechanisms. The systematic – and hence theoretical – developments of this insight 'mirror that episodic continuity characteristic of the day to day forms of social life . . . [Goffman] seeks to describe and analyse' (Giddens 1987: 110). It is in this, Goffmanesque, sense that we use the term social theory in this collection. Through the various contributions we explore the theoretical or analytical capacities of visual methods – their 'delicate insights' – as Giddens (1987: 110) says of Goffman's analyses. We are concerned with visual images' capacity to reveal what is hidden in the inner mechanisms of the ordinary and the taken for granted. We are concerned with connections between things of different scope and scale: how small things are connected with the bigger social landscapes in which they are set. In this collection the images are a point of access to the social world and an archive of it. Social analysis reaches beyond and beneath common understanding and makes connections. So do visual strategies. And this collection is arranged so as to show how this can be achieved. C. Wright Mills's 'sociological imagination' (1970) is central in underpinning the conceptual pragmatism of this collection.

In capturing the particularity of social processes, illustrating the general in the particular, and illuminating the relationship between the two, visual methods are particularly well suited to developing what Mills referred to – in what was intended in a non-disciplinary-specific sense – as the 'sociological imagination'. The sociological imagination links the larger historical and social scenes in which lives are set with individual experience and biography (Mills 1970: 12). It activates the capacity to shift from the 'most impersonal and remote transformations to the most intimate features of the human self – and to see the relations between the two' (Mills 1970: 14). The sociological imagination works particularly well through visual strategies, which capture the particular, the local, the personal and the familiar while suggesting a bigger landscape beyond and challenging us to draw the connections between the two. The drawing of connections between things of varied scale *is*, as we suggested above, social analysis: situating 'the personal troubles of milieu' in the 'public issues of social structure' (Mills 1970: 14). Allowing us to understand how the smallest units of social analysis – people, lives, the minutiae of material culture – operate in relation to broader social landscapes and bigger processes, visual strategies offer a way into understanding how the personal is social and the social personal. Visual research strategies comprise a set of techniques which – in concert with others – activate the sociological imagination in the broad sense in which Mills intended it. Visual techniques, in other words, are an analytically charged set of methodologies which incline researchers towards the tracing of connections between things of quite different social scope and scale.

The essays in this collection share this conceptual landscape – not a single theoretical position – as a basis for methodological engagement in a variety of fields and areas of concern. They share a concern to understand the interaction of human agency with its broader social scenes: the intersections between people and place, the placing of people and the peopling of place. In this framework people are the architects of social scenes, relationships and processes, which in turn fabricate their lives and their being in the world. The chapters in this collection share a concern to understand the ways in which people *make* the social fabric with which their lives are bound up. They are concerned with different types of social processes, with different types of performance and with different kinds of social space. The contributions in this collection share this conceptual ground but they move out from it in quite different directions. They do not share a single theoretical position, but display the diversity of which the sociological imagination is capable. As well as having quite different concerns from each other, they move in different directions and work with different degrees of magnification and scope. Between them they show creatively what visual strategies can achieve in different research contexts.

The collection is organized so as to move from small to larger social contexts. Following John Grady's 'invitation' to visual methods, the chapters in Part One – 'Picturing the self, identity and domesticated space' – focus on smaller-scale processes, spaces and places: the more intimate nooks and crannies of the social landscape as a whole. By comparison, the chapters in Part Two – 'Picturing the city, sociality and post-industrial change' – move things up a notch on the scale, focusing on public spaces and less *apparently* individualized issues and concerns: the broader vistas, crests and valleys of the urban landscape and wider processes of social change. In each case, the shift in scale from Part One to Part Two is also reflected in the organization of the chapters within the two sections, moving from the intimacy of Elizabeth Chaplin's visual diary, and the concern with objects, selves and interior spaces in the chapters by Ruth Holliday, Sue Heath and Elizabeth Cleaver, and Tony Whincup, through to the public/private space of Doug Harper's bowling alleys in Part One, and from the bars and restaurants of Auckland, via urban encounters in London's Brick Lane and processes of gentrification in Amsterdam and Chicago, through to the post-industrial landscape of north-east England, and the impact of global processes of restructuring in Part Two.

While organized in part around progressive shifts in scale – or by different magnitudes and magnifications of space – however, the contributions to this collection are also arranged to showcase the different ways in which visual strategies operate in research contexts. Visual methods are rarely used alone and the book's chapters are arranged to show visual methods in combination with various other research methodologies, as well as to demonstrate the range of resulting output which visual methods are able to achieve. Finally, the collection is also arranged so as to highlight two comparative dimensions: one disciplinary and the other to do with social contexts. Beneath the surface of the text are a series of dialogues between different disciplinary concerns and approaches, and between different social contexts and places dealing with similar issues in different ways. The collection is cross-national and cross-disciplinary.

Part One – 'Picturing the self, identity and domesticated space' – is concerned with the intimate and the personal and with the social arenas and social categories through which people reach out beyond the self and its auto/biographical scenes and connect with others. This section focuses on the social processes of self/other connection and the intimate places and spaces of shared living. Contributors to this section make connections between clothing, ornaments, décor and the micro-social aspects of domestic life on the one hand, and forms of social distinction on the other.

Elizabeth Chaplin's 'My visual diary' deftly displays the scope of visual autobiographical work. In this chapter the autobiographical subject is the point of access to an archive of social activities which challenge the boundaries between 'ordinary' and 'exceptional lives'. Chaplin shows how our ordinary, routine selves are intricately connected with wider social issues and social relationships, and she encourages researchers to begin their journeys of social understanding from the vantage point of their own lives. In Ruth Holliday's 'Reflecting the self' young men and women connect themselves through video performances of fashion and style with queer sexual identities: a connection with broader social landscapes which is simultaneously intimate and impersonal. Video diaries provide complex and multi-layered texts which convey the self and identity in ways that challenge notions of stability and conventional boundaries.

Shifting focus slightly from individual identities to the interconnections between people and the intimate spaces of domestic life, Sue Heath and Elizabeth Cleaver's 'Mapping the spatial in shared household life' interrogates the use of visual methods to speak about events, social relationships and personal space among young people in shared UK households. Emotional closeness and distance have spatial, material and aesthetic expression and are captured with the help of fieldnote diagrams and informants' photographs.

The aesthetic arrangement of domestic space resurfaces in Tony Whincup's 'Imaging the intangible' where we see individuals connecting themselves – through artefacts of domestic décor – with others: making connections through aesthetics and style with forms of social differentiation that are considerably more subtle than class. Domestic objects become a photographable archive of the intangible through their symbolism and meaning. Douglas Harper's 'Wednesday-night bowling' moves us up a level in scale to a more public form of domesticated space in its focus on the intimate interactions and rituals of the upper New York State bowling alley. In this respect this chapter is the bridge between the two sections of the book. It shows men working on versions of identity and the meaning of their lives and work through involvement with their local bowling team in a rural context. Here we see men connecting with other men and in the process actively constructing, reconstructing and *performing* a localized, practical version of masculinity.

The social landscapes in this section are *placed* – in the New York State bowling alley, in residential spaces in the south of England, suburban New Zealand and so on – but they also reveal ways of being in the world. These social landscapes reveal their texture, their social categories, collective ways of grouping the self through sexuality, masculinity and forms of social differentiation as well as the social relationships composing the substance of human connection. Hence the chapters in this section are about the connection between the self and others, the meaning of subjectivity and the fabric of social life itself.

A shift in scale towards more panoramic social concerns occurs throughout Part Two, 'Picturing the city, sociality and post-industrial change', without losing sight of the individual actors involved. These contributions are wider in scope and concern the ways in which individuals connect themselves not only with the urban landscape but also with some of the most significant and pervasive developments currently affecting all of our lives, the profound realignments involved in deindustrialization and globalization.

Alan Latham's 'Researching and writing everyday accounts of the city' explores experiences of everyday life in Auckland by piecing together aspects of urban public culture in the ways in which people use cafés, restaurants and bars, each of which can be regarded as illustrations of embodied practice and as compositional of routes through urban space. Latham demonstrates how respondents' photographs can be combined with other forms of data to produce richly layered accounts of the complex 'banalities' of everyday sociality and everyday life. Les Back's 'Listening with our eyes' raises important questions about photography and the urban landscape in the context of a street photography project in the East End of London. In Back and his photographer collaborators' *About the Streets Project*, a space opens for a dialogue between researchers/photographers and those whose lives form the texture of the street and who in turn offer their image to the lens. The camera acts as a window that opens out onto the street and through which the street looks back in, allowing for the recognition of those who are usually not recognized.

Moving up a level and exploring the transformation of the urban landscape through processes of gentrification, which reflects post-industrial restructuring while at the same time allowing comparison between different urban environments and the policy context in which they are shaped, Charles Suchar's 'Amsterdam and Chicago: seeing the macro-characteristics of gentrification' brings several strands of local particularity into focus as features of global realignment. Suchar's photographic inventory offers a visual survey and documentation of macro-processes that display the texture of urban social transformation. Taking a more collective approach to biography than in the first section of the book but exploring a similar set of global processes to Suchar from a different locale, David Byrne and Aidan Doyle's 'The visual and the verbal' documents the ways in which the closure of the Durham coal field in the UK shifted people's relationships to the landscape and its social and cultural practices. Various photographs – including a sequence of images that is partially reproduced in this collection, and which itself formed 'a very slow movie in six frames' – were used to elicit responses from members of different focus groups. Alicia Rouverol and Ana Maria Mauad's 'Telling the story of Linda Lord through photographs' explores the use of Cedric Chatterley's photographs to capture the impact of the closure of a chicken-processing factory in Maine on the life of one of its workers. Through the biography of Linda Lord we see how global shifts impact on individual lives and the ways in which people accommodate these dramatic changes in circumstance.

Despite the shifts in scale as we move through the collection, each contribution shows how a focus on the particular can be used to explore more general themes: how – whatever the scale or degree of abstraction of the issue under investigation – it is possible to focus on the local and the specific as a means of drawing connections between the individual and society, biography and history, agency and social structure. It is in this sense that each contribution – despite the variety of theoretical positions adopted – demonstrates what Mills refers to as the sociological imagination. And it is in this sense that the ordering of the collection – and the shifts in scale from intimate scenes to global processes – should not be regarded as a shift from micro- to macro-social phenomena or concerns. Indeed, it is one of the intentions of this collection to demonstrate the way in which visual methods – in particular – can be used to problematize this distinction, and show how the most intimate scenes connect to wider processes and events, while global shifts impact upon real people at a local scale.

Through this volume's conceptual organization runs another principle, and that is that methods should be judged by what they are able to achieve. What are they able to tell us that we didn't already know? Each chapter shows what can be learned through the interface between forms of agency, landscape and social processes in a context which makes methodological decisions transparent. Despite its conceptual ordering, this is a book about the use of visual methodologies in social research contexts, and each contribution is intended to show how the visual can be deployed in a particular research setting. The variety and scope of visual methods and their various achievements in research contexts are apparent in the arrangement of the chapters. Different researchers use visual methods in different ways and in different combinations with other methods, and visual images occupy different positions in research schemes. Sometimes visual material is the primary form, or source, of data in the research, sometimes it shares the stage with other forms of data and methods of enquiry. Sometimes images are the material under investigation and sometimes they are used to generate other forms of – non-visual – material. Generally, those who have well-developed image-making skills deploy them in their research. Those who are less technically accomplished either employ their own, more rough-and-ready images, or make use of those produced by their informants. Still others establish collaborations with skilled image makers. All end up in the alchemies of words and images used in the making of social analyses.

Although the comparative dimensions of this collection are not central, neither are they insignificant. Inevitably there are comparisons which work across disciplines, reflecting their different concerns and approaches. But the text is arranged so as to highlight dialogues across national contexts as well. Harper's blue-collar masculinities being made at the bowling alley illustrate the peculiarities of their rural US location, just as Holliday's queer performances reconstruct femininity and masculinity in British urban locations. Whincup provides a sense of New Zealand aesthetics and social distinction as a counterpoint to the domestic landscapes featured in shared British households by Heath and Cleaver. The urban landscapes featured are London (Back), Auckland (Latham) and Chicago and Amsterdam (Suchar): placing the present against the past and the classic formulations of urban theorists. When it comes to social processes, deindustrialization in the United States is contrasted with the north of England's loss of coal mining and the way such developments are played out, both in terms of people's understanding and experience, and in the course of their everyday lives.

The benefits and limitations of visual methods

In advocating the use of visual methods within social and cultural research, we are not suggesting either that such methods are always useful or applicable, or that they are without their limitations. There are a number of key difficulties with visual methods, not least their association with morally and scientifically dubious projects in the past and their past and present association with surveillance, although as Les Back's contribution to this collection reminds us, such concerns can be misplaced. More mundane considerations include the problem of ascribing anonymity or confidentiality to research subjects who have been photographed, equipment costs associated with the use of photography and video, difficulties with dissemination – particularly where images are in a moving form – and issues of copyright where already existing images are to be employed. Use of the internet has helped to solve some of the issues surrounding the dissemination of visual material. Unless rendered tactile or made redundant through written or verbal description, however, visual material is also inaccessible to many among the visually impaired.

Perhaps the most interesting and long-standing objection to the use of visual material within social and cultural research, however, concerns the apparent ambiguity of most visual material when compared with texts that take a written or verbal form. Critics have suggested that the inherently polysemic nature of most forms of pictorial representation renders analysis of such material highly subjective, and within certain traditions this is regarded as problematic. Indeed, as Sarah Pink (2001) points out, many existing texts on visual methods have gone out of their way to defend the approach against such accusations, and to suggest ways in which a sufficiently rigorous method can be adopted so as to minimize such pernicious effects. A further and related criticism is that pictorial representations are highly selective, and can easily be manipulated to present the desired effect.

While such criticisms undoubtedly have some validity, they show a remarkable tendency to overlook similar difficulties with other forms of data and other methods of research: writing is also inherently polysemic, and it is as easy to select a particular quotation that supports the point one is making as it is to manipulate the framing, lighting or tone of a photograph to present the desired effect. Indeed, in their ability to convey the emotional tone of an event, photographs are potentially *less* ambiguous – or even misleading – than other forms of qualitative data. The selection, transcription and subsequent recontextualization of a fragment of recorded conversation, for example, can strip it of all traces of irony, humour or other verbal inflection, allowing the *literal* meaning to assert priority in a manner which conceals, refuses or overturns the original meaning of the spoken word. In a photograph, on the other hand, the smile, laugh or scowl remains.

As Howard Becker has pointed out, then, when considering the standard criticisms levelled at visual material it should be remembered that 'every form of social science data has exactly these problems, and . . . none of the commonly accepted and widely used sociological methods solves them very well either' (Becker 1998: 91). It should also be noted that such criticisms overlook the high degree of visual literacy demanded within contemporary culture, and the way in which visual representations such as advertisements, however ambiguous, 'draw upon the same corpus of displays, the same ritual idiom, that is the resource of all of us who participate in social situations, and to the same end: the rendering of glimpsed action readable' (Goffman 1979: 84). Equally, if not more importantly, the apparent ambiguity of pictorial representation is only really a difficulty if one is working within a realist paradigm, and seeking to establish truths rather than interpretations. It can, in fact, be regarded as a positive advantage if one is seeking to allow for multiple interpretations, whether during the collection of data or during the presentation of results (Pink 2001). Pictorial representation – like seeing and social theory, referred to earlier – is, like all other forms of representation, about selection, abstraction and transformation (Jenks 1995: 4, 8).

As analytical and practical devices, visual data both connect and refract, capturing the specificity of social processes and phenomena, and thereby illustrating the general in the particular, while also offering a particular means of illuminating and exploring the relationship between the two. As communicative devices, visual data can also be particularly emotive and evocative, while visual methods are inclusive in the sense that the data are both accessible and can often be produced by both researcher and researched alike.

Conclusions

The routes by which each of the editors came to visual strategies offers a final comment on the renewed interest in and routes into the visual turn and some clues about the origins of this collection. We both have a newly established interest in researching visually. Caroline Knowles began using images – taken by photographer Ludovic Dabert – out of a sense of methodological frustration in researching the interface between released psychiatric patients and the city of Montreal. Her methodological tool-bag, which included taped life-story interviews, observation, and the mapping and analysis of space, came nowhere near to conveying – aesthetically or analytically – the people, lives and places she was trying to describe. Dabert's photographs of 'schizophrenics' in soup kitchens, homeless shelters, boarding houses, inner-city rooming houses and various street locations breathed new life into the voices and experiences she wanted to present in the tapestry of 'community psychiatric care'. A kind of critical realism, this study took local providers of community services to task for their orchestration of a system of human warehousing and neglect. The visual narratives employed within the resulting text (*Bedlam on the Streets*, Knowles, 2000) served both to illuminate and to enliven the verbal narratives of people and place. This work led to the International Visual Sociology Association Conference in Portland, Maine (2000), and Knowles subsequently organized the 2003 IVSA conference – *Images of Social Life* – at the University of Southampton. As well as developing her own skills as a photographer (Plate 1), Knowles has also recently been involved in further collaborative work, with Douglas Harper – a contributor to this collection – providing photographic documentation for the *Landscapes of Belonging* project, which explores the experiences of British 'lifestyle migrants' in Hong Kong.

Paul Sweetman had his first exposure to visual methods as a student of Elizabeth Chaplin, another contributor to this volume, at the University of York. This interest developed during his subsequent Ph.D. research on contemporary body modification, which employed a number of qualitative methods, including participant and non-participant observation at tattoo and piercing studios, tattoo conventions and other related settings (see Sweetman 1999a, 1999b, 1999c). He took numerous photographs during this research, both as a form of fieldnotes, and as a means of illustrating conference papers and other presentations (Plate 2). Asking people if they would mind having their picture taken also turned out to be a very helpful way of providing an initial introduction to potential respondents. That is not to say that the strategy always worked, however. Having forgotten to take his camera to his first tattoo convention, Sweetman decided to cut his losses and buy a disposable as a replacement. At least one potential interviewee disappeared from view when a conversation with a professional photographer turned to the question of Paul's photographic equipment. Since completing this project, Sweetman's interest in visual methods has developed alongside his more substantive interests in the body, identity, fashion and consumption. For both editors the visual has operated as a means of collecting data and as a presentational strategy in teaching and conferences. Neither of us could have done our recent research effectively without images.

The editors of this collection, like a number of its contributors – Back, Byrne and Doyle, Heath and Cleaver, Holliday, Latham, Rouverol and Mauad – are part of the *new* interest in visual methods, arriving at visual strategies because of the

Plate 1 Filipina maids, Sunday, central district of Hong Kong.

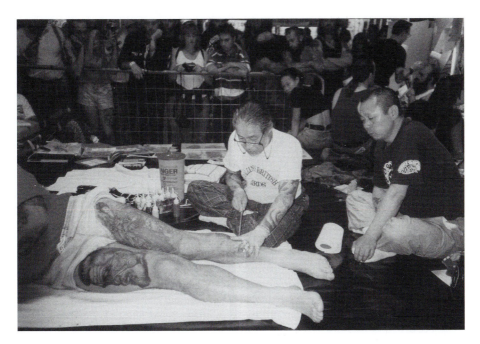

Plate 2 Horiyoshi 3, Tattoo Expo, Dunstable, 1996.

nature of our research, its framing, and because it was possible either to develop our own visual literacy or to deploy the visual literacy of others in research collaborations. Other chapter authors – Harper, Chaplin, Grady, Suchar, Whincup and Becker – have made a sustained contribution to the production of visual research and its commentaries. They are practised visual researchers, and have brought these skills to the task of social analysis. These contributors frequently came to social analysis with image-making skills, while the rest of us have tended to travel in the opposite direction. The resulting volume is a fusion of sustained and more recent interest: a dialogue around the halfway point at which we meet.

The rationale for the arrangement of this text is analytical, methodological, comparative and empirical. It is written for students and researchers in areas such as sociology, social policy, cultural studies and human geography, who want to explore the uses of visual methodologies in particular research contexts. Its editors and contributors are drawn from these and other disciplines, as well as from schools of photography. Texts such as this are inevitably multidisciplinary because visual strategies attract a range of researchers. Not a nuts-and-bolts, 'how to do it', introduction to visual research, this is intended as a guide to conceptualizing the visual dimensions of research and combining visual methods with other research techniques. The contributors showcase what visual methods can accomplish in particular research settings, as well as making transparent the processes by which these strategies operate in tandem with others to produce particular outcomes. This collection addresses issues of scale and abstraction in research settings. Its concerns range from the smallest unit of analysis – an individual person or thing – to the largest units – the global system – that researchers deal with. It shows how visual methods can be deployed to investigate abstract as well as concrete phenomena, social relationships as well as people and places. Finally, it invites a commentary on its efforts by Howard Becker, and an invitation and some practical hints on still and moving image making by John Grady, both of whom have a wealth of experience in visual research and are in a good position to advise and reflect on our progress.

References

Banks, Marcus (2001) *Visual Methods in Social Research*, London: Sage.

Bateson, Gregory and Mead, Margaret (1942) *Balinese Character: a Photographic Analysis*, New York: New York Academy of Sciences.

Becker, Howard (1974) 'Photography and sociology', *Studies in the Anthropology of Visual Communication* 1(1): 3–26.

—— (1981) *Exploring Society Photographically*, Chicago: University of Chicago Press.

—— (1998) 'Visual sociology, documentary photography, and photojournalism: it's (almost) all a matter of context', in Jon Prosser (ed.) *Image-Based Research*, London: Falmer Press.

Berger, John (1977 [1972]) *Ways of Seeing*, London: Penguin.

Berger, John and Mohr, Jean (1975) *Seventh Man*, London: Penguin.

—— (1995 [1982]) *Another Way of Telling*, New York: Vintage International.

Bourdieu, Pierre (1990) *Photography: a Middlebrow Art*, London: Polity.

Chaplin, Elizabeth (1994) *Sociology and Visual Representation*, London: Routledge.

Collier, John and Collier, Malcolm (1986) *Visual Anthropology: Photography as a Research Method*, Albuquerque: University of New Mexico Press.

Crow, Graham (2000) 'Developing sociological arguments through community studies', *International Journal of Research Methodology* 3(3): 173–87.

Emmison, Michael and Smith, Philip (2000) *Researching the Visual*, London: Sage.

Evans, Jessica and Hall, Stuart (1999) *Visual Culture: the Reader*, London: Sage.

Giddens, Anthony (1987) *Social Theory and Modern Sociology*, London: Polity.

Goffman, Erving (1979) *Gender Advertisements*, London: Macmillan.

Hamilton, Peter and Hargreaves, Roger (2001) *The Beautiful and the Damned*, Aldershot: Lund Humphries/National Portrait Gallery.

Harper, Douglas (1982) *Good Company*, Chicago: University of Chicago Press.

—— (1987) *Working Knowledge*, Chicago: University of Chicago Press.

—— (1994) *Cape Breton 1952: the Photographic Vision of Timothy Asch*, Louisville, Ky: IVSA.

—— (1998) 'An argument for visual sociology', in Jon Prosser (ed.) *Image-Based Research*, London: Falmer Press.

Jenks, Chris (1995) 'The centrality of the eye in western culture: an introduction', in Chris Jenks (ed.) *Visual Culture*, London: Routledge.

Knowles, Caroline (2000) *Bedlam on the Streets*, London: Routledge.

Law, John and Whittaker, John (1988) 'On the art of representation: notes on the politics of visualization', in G. Fyfe and J. Law (eds) *Picturing Power*, London: Routledge.

Mellor, Philip and Shilling, Chris (1997) *Reforming the Body: Religion, Community and Modernity*, London: Sage.

Mills, C. Wright (1970) *The Sociological Imagination*, Harmondsworth: Penguin.

Mirzoeff, Nicholas (1999) *An Introduction to Visual Culture*, London: Routledge.

Pahl, Ray (1984) *Divisions of Labour*, Oxford: Basil Blackwell.

Payne, Geoff (1996) 'Imagining the community: Some reflections on the community study as a method', in Stina Lyon and Joan Busfield (eds) *Methodological Imaginations*, London: Macmillan.

Pink, Sarah (2001) *Doing Visual Ethnography*, London: Sage.

Prosser, Jon (ed.) (1998) *Image-Based Research*, London: Falmer Press.

Sweetman, Paul (1999a) 'Anchoring the (postmodern) self? Body modification, fashion and identity', *Body & Society* 5(2–3): 51–76.

—— (1999b) 'Only skin deep? Tattooing, piercing and the transgressive body', in M. Aaron (ed.) *The Body's Perilous Pleasures: Dangerous Desires and Contemporary Culture*, Edinburgh: Edinburgh University Press.

—— (1999c) 'Marked bodies, oppositional identities? Tattooing, piercing and the ambiguity of resistance', in S. Roseneil and J. Seymour (eds) *Practising Identities: Power and Resistance*, Basingstoke: Macmillan.

Tagg, John (1988) *The Burden of Representation: Essays on Photographies and Histories*, Amherst: University of Massachusetts Press.

Warburton, Terry (1998) 'Cartoons and teachers: mediated visual images as data', in Jon Prosser (ed.) *Image-Based Research*, London: Falmer Press.

Williamson, Bill (1982) *Class, Culture and Community: a Biographical Study of Social Change in Mining*, London: Routledge and Kegan Paul.

John Grady

WORKING WITH VISIBLE EVIDENCE
An invitation and some practical advice

Introduction

THERE ARE AT LEAST FIVE reasons why a more visual social science
– making arguments with images and other types of visible evidence of human
intent and action – has much to contribute to the study of society and culture. First,
the visual media and their messages have come to dominate mass communications
in contemporary society. Thus, *studying how these messages are produced, what they
encode, and how they are consumed opens up a vein of data that richly complements the types
of information social scientists usually mine.*

Second, the image is a unique form of data that stores complexly layered
meanings in a format that is immediately retrievable. On the one hand, the image is
tangibly objective. What you see is what the camera got, so, everything else being
equal, the image is a physical record of something that happened at some time or
other.[1] On the other hand, the image is irreducibly subjective. It invariably reflects
the focus of attention at a particular moment of the one holding or directing the
camera. The image may also capture important aspects of the experience of those
portrayed in the image. Thus, images usually represent complex subjective processes
in an extraordinarily objective form and require careful interpretation. *Image-based
research encourages social scientists to pay careful attention to the explanatory potential of various kinds of data and not just to the techniques for manipulating and interpreting those data.*

Third, *thinking, writing and talking about images can make arguments not only more
vivid but more lucid as well.* Quantitative social scientists have long known that the
clearest way of organizing material is to lay tables and charts out in a sequence and
then write an account that explains what is in each one, beginning with the first and
ending with the last. The same logic applies to maps, photographs and film clips.

Fourth, *documentary production — whether with still or with moving images — is a means of communication that can easily be modified by social scientists for their own purposes.* Sociologists, for example, have joined ethnographic filmmakers and documentary photographers in producing narratives that are as rigorous as they are engaging. Also, more conventionally organized reports can be enriched by incorporating a variety of images into the argument, as Douglas Harper so ably demonstrates in *Changing Works* (2000).

Finally, *working with images is ideally suited for teaching about social and cultural processes and issues in the classroom.* Images can be publicly displayed and interpreted collectively in an interactive setting. In this sense, image work enables the instructor to go beyond the lecture and discussion mode and transform the classroom into some-thing like a laboratory or workshop, encouraging a form of instruction that more soundly grounds students' understanding of social and cultural concepts and analysis. In addition, and perhaps of greater importance, projects in the classroom can also provide on-the-job training for social scientists wishing to hone their skills in managing visible evidence. Well-designed projects may provide not only rewarding learning experiences for students but also valuable research programmes for faculty.

The past decade has witnessed a steady growth of interest in a more visual social science. Nevertheless, many conventionally trained social scientists are wary of working with images as data. Ironically, it may be that their very familiarity with technologically sophisticated products of contemporary mass communications undermines their confidence in becoming visually fluent. This apprehension, of course, has a basis in two unavoidable facts. First, working with images requires sustained attention. Cameras have to be pointed at the right thing and clicked at the right time to produce meaning, while interpreting others' images requires a rigour not unlike that practised by scholars of antiquity. Second, image work is technology intensive and whatever can go wrong often will. These sorts of challenges, however, are not insuperable. In fact, this chapter will argue that conventional social scientific training is not only transferable to but also an essen-tial component of image-based research. Realizing that image work is a craft that improves with practice should encourage many more social scientists to incorporate work with images into their professional repertoire.

Social science and image work

At the centre of concern with visual research and analysis is the 'image', which is no more than a picture, however manufactured, of something that has human significance. Generally most images represent a person, object, place or event in the image maker's psychic landscape. Thus, whatever else they may be – ideology, personal statement or even accident – images can always constitute data for one purpose or another.

All images have complex histories. Somebody, some group or social network produces them with a given technology under varying conditions for different purposes. In addition, images are often consumed by other groups of people who may have a completely different set of interests and expectations. As a rule, the more we can learn about how specific images have been made and used, the more informed will be our understanding of the many meanings that an image can sustain.

Consequently, images are forms of data that require the same kind of care in their production and interpretation as surveys, interviews, ethnographic observations and archival records do. It is important, therefore, for the visual novice to appreciate that the skills and techniques used to produce and interpret other kinds of social and cultural data can, and must, be transferred to the study of images. Once we know what images were made and used for, we can define what they could be data for. At that point, we can start doing what we always do with data: sample, count and compare, being ready, of course, to modify technique to whatever kinds of information might be extractable from the images themselves.

Pictures are valuable because they encode an enormous amount of information in a single representation. This information is framed contextually in space and time on a flat surface and so all the bits of information produce, in combination with each other, a synergistic effect that generates even more information. As an inevitable by-product of the material properties of an image, it is possible for a picture to contain many meanings and sustain multiple interpretations. In a sense, images cry out to us to imbue them with meaning and it is this, above all, which provides them with their unique capacity to engage us.

Unfortunately, because images so completely capture our attention, researchers often only use them for illustrative purposes: to make a presentation come alive, while teachers display dramatic images to strengthen arguments that reason often cannot otherwise sustain. What is less well known is that research programmes can be compromised by using an image to establish a meaning in one context (that of the author's rhetorical intent) while neglecting what it might otherwise have to offer. Images used in this way function as a highlighter, vividly enhancing those points in the argument that the analyst wants to underscore. But, like a highlighter, this use of images pushes those unilluminated parts of the text out of focus.

Relying on images only to illustrate arguments can be problematic, then, because it devalues the very thing that makes the image important as data, which is the simultaneity of the relations that exist between the various elements represented in the frame. It is the fact that it is information that is contained in the image which ultimately accounts for its power to engage us. And while the emotional response to that power may be compelling, it is, at best, an unsure guide to identifying that which makes the information significant.

Plate 1 depicts a ceremonial occasion in American suburban life: a neighbourhood barbecue. Tables have been set up, grills lit, swing-sets pulled from the backyards, and people are socializing in small groups in a residential cul-de-sac. A focus on this social event provides data that should be considered in a discussion of the public life of suburban communities. Such a discussion would undoubtedly mirror what has caught the attention of the photographer, and restrict itself to what is depicted in the foreground, thus probably not considering the material infrastructure that provides a staging ground for the drama we are witnessing. Nevertheless, while it may be unnecessary to consider the nature and quality of the housing stock, the automobiles and their garages, and the absence of pedestrian traffic on the sidewalks in a study of neighbourhood sociability, the trained social scientist should still notice all this. These elements of the image might become, for example, useful variables in a comparison between suburban barbecues and urban block parties and festivals.

Plate 1.

Like an interviewer's transcript or an ethnographer's fieldnotes, the photograph is a record of that to which attention has been paid. But the photograph also includes extraneous material that, because it is an actual part of the fabric of its subjects' lives at the moment of record, might turn out to be less extraneous the more that world is studied. A dramatic example of how much more information is embedded in the image than we might think is found by contrasting Plate 1 and Plate 2.

When students inventory what they see in Plate 1, they make lists of the people and things that are visible in the foreground of the photograph. For Plate 2, however, they first identify the horizon line and the shadows that are cast by various objects, which they never mention when viewing Plate 1. In other words, they notice what Gibson (1979) calls the ecological properties of the 'ambient array', or the visually experienced world: mostly shapes, textures and different intensities of reflected light. This information was in the image all along, of course, but so taken for granted that it only becomes evident when we display the inverted image.

Displayed in the classroom and in commercial journalism in the traditional manner of the audio-visual aid, images arguably deserve the scepticism with which they are regarded by certain academics. Mere illustration simplifies complex subjects, trivializes events and issues, and may induce a cognitive passivity that precludes the exercise of analytic reason. Viewed as data, however, images provide material that encourages analysis, especially in conjunction with data from other sources and, of course, texts that work through the data. So, the first, and most important, step to becoming a more visual social scientist is to realize that images are data and should always be acknowledged as such in both research and the

Plate 2.

classroom. Conventional social science also possesses a treasure trove of techniques and experience that provide useful models for using visual materials as data. These include defining research questions, operationalizing variables, and developing effective methodologies and ways of providing insight.

Defining questions

Imagine idly thumbing through a college yearbook, looking at images that are as banal as they are prolific. These include photographs of each member of the graduating class and various categories of formally defined events, as well as ostensibly 'candid' shots which usually focus on students' leisure-time activities and sometimes hint at mildly illicit pursuits. Consider what might be displayed in many of these shots. How are the graduates represented: close-ups or full-body shots; with an indeterminately generic background or posed somewhere around the campus? Are they smiling or not? What kinds of events are displayed? Who is in the shot and what are they doing? How are students' rooms decorated and with what? How are students shown using their rooms and so on?

   A college yearbook is actually an idealized representation of a complex, yet bounded, social world that, when examined carefully, reveals much about what those who put the book together value. In addition, yearbooks are also catalogues of that world's mores. Students wear wristwatches, have certain kinds of hair-dos, are clothed in certain styles, and either have or don't have members of the opposite sex in their rooms. They may display certain items on their walls and on their desks but not others.

For social scientists, therefore, the visual images in something as mundane as a college catalogue can provoke a myriad of questions (Plate 3). Some of these may be comparative and historical. Others may be suggested by anomalies visible in the images. Why do some students appear to decorate their rooms differently from other students? Is it because they are first-year students and not upperclassmen?

But why are we interested? Because as social scientists we're concerned with things like the life cycle and identity formation, occupational cultures, the quality of gender relationships, the lived significance of symbolic forms and the like. With the kinds of questions we routinely entertain, we should be able to find fascinating, useful and important information even in seed catalogues. Imagine how much information can be extracted from, and produced by, visual representations of social worlds full of people and their products. In other words, just about any question for which an observation might provide an answer can be elicited from a visual image, as William Whyte (1988) has so often proved in his various studies of the urban landscape (cf. Plate 4).

Operationalizing variables

All questions entail a hypothesis, or suspicion, about the nature of the relationship between one thing and another. All answers are stories telling us what that

Plate 3.

Plate 4.

relationship may be. Social scientists are seldom surprised that most human narratives concern loss or gain and that certain factors affect how likely it is that people will experience one outcome rather than another. Gender, race, class, age, size, strength, beauty, birth order, group cohesion and so on are all variables that we use both in interpreting behaviour and in explaining social organization. Social distance can be measured, norms of deference identified, settings categorized, and all of these can be correlated with certain mores as opposed to others.

Never be surprised at how much social scientific knowledge can reveal about the images we see or produce. Experienced interviewers often find themselves noticing layers of meaning in a filmed interview that a journalist or filmmaker might overlook. More importantly, what is noticed often suggests other factors or issues that should be explored.

One of the most insightful examples of what social science can do with visual imagery is demonstrated in Erving Goffman's *Gender Advertisements* (1979). This book is social science's most important contribution to the study of advertising and is also a penetrating examination of the ways in which gender expectations shape how we live in our bodies. Goffman argues that advertising as well as vernacular photography 'idealize' conduct. While it is unclear how closely people approximate these idealizations in everyday life, they certainly would like to. So the fact that these poses are exaggerated does not mean that they are unrelated to what we do. Rather, they serve as models, prototypes, for what we are trying to become. In this context, Goffman points out the significance of what he calls 'the feminine touch', which refers to a tendency to depict women holding their hands in a way that accentuates an insufficiency for decisive action. In addition, Goffman noticed a tendency for women to be displayed in a way that suggested that they are not consciously connected with the action in the scene where they are depicted. He named this variable 'licensed withdrawal' and suggested that it is a costly privilege that women are afforded by protective males who are, of course, displayed as far more alert, hands ready for action. I have talked about *Gender Advertisements* at some length because Goffman constitutes a model of what a good social scientist can find in the visual image.

Methodology

If anything characterizes the social scientific approach to research it has been its attention to methodology, to devising ways of collecting reliable and valid information. At its simplest, a research method should be envisioned as a three-stage process: defining a universe of meaning, sampling that universe, and coding the data.

Perhaps you or your students wonder whether the rules of gender representation that Goffman has identified in *Gender Advertisements* are historically specific. Maybe these rules have changed in the twenty years since his book was published? Perhaps men and women were displayed differently in the distant past? Either is a testable proposition. The first step would be to *define* the kinds of venues to be examined. Magazines? If so, what kind? Those aimed at homemakers? At young women? High fashion? Mass circulation family magazines like *Life* or *Look*? Various kinds of men's magazines? Perhaps newspapers, illustrated books, catalogues or posters might be more appropriate? The crucial issue in defining an appropriate universe of meaning, in this case, would be to determine what markets these venues exploited. In the absence of a particular research imperative, a cross-section of those magazines with the widest circulation will usually do.

The second step is to extract a representative *sample* of the images contained in the selected magazines. The easiest way to do this is to establish parameters. Thirty, fifteen or ten images from one, two or three specific issues a year, chosen at ten-year intervals would provide a sample of 300 images covering one magazine over the course of a century. Random sampling of an issue's images can be restricted to those of a certain size – larger images provide more space for thematic embellishment – or to other specifications required by your hypothesis. After counting the total number of acceptable images in any given issue, it is merely a question of using an appropriate technique to select the images for the sample.

Sampling, of course, is also important in case studies, as Howard Becker so ably establishes in *Tricks of the Trade* (1998: 85–8). Videographed interviews for a documentary about a certain event must encompass all of the major social roles which contributed to that event: not just union leaders and managers in a strike, but also rank and filers, non-union members, foremen, the wider community and so on. The concept of a shooting script, first developed by Roy Stryker in collaboration with Robert Lynd as a guide for Farm Security Administration photographers during the Great Depression, also constitutes a kind of sampling procedure. It served as an inventory of basic shots that a photographer needed to take in order to establish a context for whatever is chosen as a focus (Suchar 1997: 36).

The third methodological step is *coding* the data. It is advisable to develop a coding sheet in advance of the sampling process, but categories can be added or modified during the process of research. Goffman provides the reader with some explicit advice on what should be considered in coding rules of gender representation. Nevertheless, he tells us little about other things that might concern a student interested in gender issues, for instance variations in the kinds of activities men and women are depicted in, or the settings they occupy, and whether they are 'eroticized' or not. The key in coding images is to identify just what the presence or the absence of some element in an image may indicate. Length of hair and hem may be significant variables in one investigation but not in another. The strength of any research project depends on the significance of what is coded and how well the actual coding can be replicated.

If, for example, there is concern that the image of women is being increasingly eroticized as most contemporary feminist criticism suggests, then 'nudity' should be a good indicator of the erotic. But what constitutes nudity? In contemporary western culture we should begin with any unclothed display of primary and secondary sex characteristics. These would include genitals, buttocks and breasts. But what about a photograph of a woman taken from the waist up who is unclothed, yet facing away from the camera so that her breasts are not visible? I would argue that this is a 'nude' shot because we can easily imagine what should be on the other side. It would follow, therefore, that my criteria for coding 'nudity' should include *no evidence of clothed primary or secondary sexual characteristics*. While this coding instruction might be arguable, it is easily replicable.

Providing insight

Social scientific training also provides rich resources for interpreting images. Not only is the history of social and cultural theory a repository of insights, but that quality of mind we prize and develop in students is, at its simplest, an alert consciousness poised for insight. As Everett Hughes has said:

> The essence of the sociological imagination is free association, guided but not hampered by a frame of reference internalized not quite into the unconscious. It must work even in one's dreams but be where it can be called up at will. When people say of my work, as they often do, that it shows insight, I cannot think what they could mean other than what-ever quality may have been produced by intensity of observation and a turning of the wheels to find a new combination of the old concepts, or even a new concept.
>
> (Hughes 1971: vi)

Social scientists commonly 'see', 'observe', 'illuminate', 'view', 'display', 'uncover', patterns, processes and structures. Sight, more than any of the other senses, puts the thing perceived in the context of its environment. Sight, therefore, situates objects, much as analysis seeks to do with propositions. It shouldn't surprise us, then, that images invite insight. Why are those people close together, while those are apart? Why are some people smiling and others not? How are the people in the frame related? What roles do they play in the event that has been photographed? Trained social scientists will find themselves brimming with ideas that might explain what is going on in an image.

It is also possible to explicitly create, or search for, images with social and cultural concepts in mind. For example, areas of racial and ethnic transition are often flash points of conflict between different groups. Yet interviewers often find that people in these areas may accentuate positive aspects of relationships and stress instances of civility and neighbourliness in their responses. Various photographic research strategies might provide a richer and more complex picture of the situation. One approach would be to take photographs of specific public places at significant time intervals. Public streets, parks or coffee shops are all places where people go about their business and, as a matter of course, do things together with other people. The photographs should reveal who those others may be and something of the quality of the exchanges. Another approach would be pictures of various kinds of thoroughfares and access points in the neighbourhood, like sidewalks, yards, doorways, windows and so on. Are they inviting, or do they warn the stranger off? Fences, locks, 'no loitering; police take notice' signs, 'neighbourhood crime watch' stickers and bars on windows are all measures of social control whose incidence can be compared with those in more stable or homogeneous neighbourhoods. The photographs not only constitute data in themselves but can be used in conjunction with interviews to elicit testimony about the neighbourhood that residents otherwise might not talk about easily.

Hughes continued the quote above by saying: 'I think I even do my reading by free association: "Didn't Simmel, or Durkheim, Weber, Mead or Marshall, or someone say something on that point?" I do a great deal of my reading by starting with the index' (1971: vi).

The visual social scientist does the same thing with images. Something in the picture, or something glanced at in passing that could be pictured, will suggest an idea or hint at a link to a theory. It is from such moments that insight is born and from such insights that full-blown interpretative and research strategies can be constructed.

It should also be noted that other kinds of visual narratives can be mined for insight. Theda Skocpol tells us that:

> I learned a lot from the hundreds of political cartoons that I collected during the health reform debate. . . . To make people laugh, cartoonists have to capture social truths – and pinpoint political ironies. So cartoons are an excellent source for a scholar trying to understand and write vividly about the deeper meanings of current events.
>
> (1997: xiv)

Skocpol's point can be extended to popular culture generally and to its increasingly pervasive visual products in particular.

Every day television programmes, movies, comics, commercial advertising and the like offer meditations on contemporary society that may be anxious or bemused, richly expressive or banal. In all cases, however, popular culture addresses widespread preoccupations of one sort or another. These preoccupations are worried through in dramas of varying complexity where situations are resolved by fictional beings representing multidimensional personae and not just role models. Explicit messages can be extracted from the stories told in popular culture and certainly messages are often inserted in them. But in a real sense what makes the products of popular culture so enthralling are the situations that the protagonists address and the moral issues that are posed by how these situations are resolved.

Becoming visually proficient means learning a craft

Many of the first visual social scientists were closet photographers. They loved the craft of producing pictures as much as what the pictures themselves represented. For those who are not photographers, however, the technical challenges of making good, or even adequate, images constitute the biggest obstacle to developing a more visual social science. In recent years the development of increasingly user-friendly technologies has, for all intents and purposes, removed this obstacle. Nevertheless, it is extremely important to remember that, idiot-proof as these new technologies may be, working with images is still a craft and many of the rules of any system of good working practice apply in full. Beyond this stricture, there are three important practices that can develop skill in learning how to produce and analyse images: being methodical; producing images; and comparing and contrasting these with others' work. The most important rules of thumb that should guide the novice are the following.

Respect and care for tools

These include cameras, camcorders, scanners, computer software, developers, film and video stock, computers, printers, projectors (slide or digital) and so on. This equipment either works well or does not, and that usually depends on how well it is cared for and how appropriately it is used. Proper maintenance, good carrying cases and many other details are all necessary concerns and require space in office or home and, always, in mind.

One corollary of this rule is always to check equipment to make sure it is all there and in working order. A checklist is always helpful, as is replacement equipment. Having enough batteries and film is always a concern. This rule also applies to the equipment used to display images. Few situations are more embarrassing – and discrediting – than planning a lecture around viewing slides or video clips and then discovering that the projector or monitor doesn't work.

Take one step at a time

Every craft process has its logic and rhythm and involves a sequence of steps. Knowing what the major steps are and then executing them deliberately will minimize most frustrations. For example, load the camera before asking permission to photograph. People do not appreciate standing around while the researcher fumbles with the equipment. Not having equipment ready is also an invitation for disaster, because the investigator's attention is preoccupied with technical details rather than the analytic complexities of a photo opportunity. The more these steps can be anticipated and executed in sequence, the easier the process will be. If there is a corollary to this rule it is this: always allow more than enough time. A useful rule of thumb here is to make a reasonably conservative estimate of the time needed to complete a process and then double it.

The most important reason, however, for taking one step at a time is that each step is not just a part of a mechanical sequence, but is also very often a point for making important choices. The kind of film used, the location of the interview site, the types of establishing shot made, have significant consequences for the final product.

Everything proceeds by trial and error

Be prepared to fail at even some of the simplest tasks. Not noticing that your subjects were so backlit by a bright sun that they have become little more than silhouettes could ruin an entire roll of film and a shooting opportunity. That happens! That's why it is important to practise with new equipment and to allow plenty of time to set up shots. Some failure is not only inevitable but also an opportunity to learn from those mistakes. Nevertheless, the more important a particular operation is, the more attention needs to be paid to the details of a shoot.

As social scientists, however, we should be familiar with this rule of thumb. It's no different from the one that mandates that surveys be pretested. Practising shooting and then carefully viewing the results is an important way of identifying flaws. If work in a classroom, for example, entails displaying student work, be sure to have a 'critique' of how well technique is realizing content as a component of any discussion. Identifying what it is that makes some students' work strong, and having them talk about what they did, is one of the very best ways of helping the rest of the class improve their performance. The same practice should be used in research groups.

Start simply

While there is much to be said for shooting lots of film, only do so if it does not distract from the substantive goal of the project. As a rule it is probably better to aim for ten good photographs rather than one perfect one or a hundred hasty ones. The important thing is to allow enough time to shoot at least several photographs for each item on a shooting script. For public presentations, it is also often better to display a few good images rather than overdo things by showing too many.

Learning how to use modern representational technology – cameras, scanners, databases, display alternatives and the like – is best done methodically and in a step-by-step process. Most of these technologies have instruction manuals that are extremely clear and useful. In addition, a number of visual social scientists have written at greater length and in more detail about achieving representational goals (Barbash and Taylor 1997; Grady 2001; Rieger 1996). Suffice it to say that one of the most useful ways of proceeding is to have a small and very manageable project and learn the technology needed to achieve it. This might be as simple as wanting to show a particular image to a class. Learning how to shoot that image, scan it, and then display it in the classroom shouldn't take more than a day's worth of work and might be even quicker with professional assistance. Once carried through to completion, creating a small slide show might not require that much more technical effort.

Those whose interest in a more visual social science is restricted to analysing images produced by others should still produce their own images on a fairly regular basis. There are three reasons why this kind of experience is important. First, photographic experience provides a basis for understanding what the limits of the medium may be and for appreciating the accomplishments of others. Practice in shooting in an intentional and focused way increases awareness of the choices that go into the production of images. Second, producing images trains and refines the photographer's 'eye' so that more is seen in other's prints. Third, even simple exercises can provide material that can be used to compare with what others have produced. Many studies by visual sociologists and documentarians can be replicated in other locales. In some cases they provide models, or implicit shooting scripts, for photographing a setting or subject that is being studied non-visually, providing material that can be used in research or the classroom. Reduced to a nutshell, the rule of thumb is: the more you shoot, the more you see.

Looking at, and working with, images that others have produced is useful for several reasons. First, it can provide ideas for improvement. Lessons can be learned about composition, lighting, cropping and editing by noticing what the experts have done. Visual sociologists tend to be aesthetic minimalists and limit their choice of effects to those that emphasize social meaning. But making aesthetic consideration secondary is not a licence for a poor approach to one's craft. Everything else being equal, the more arresting an image the better, and there is no better way of learning how that is achieved than by looking at the work of really good photographers and filmmakers.

Second, studying the work of others stimulates the imagination. Photojournalists and documentarians are particularly interested in exploring the diversity of human experience and have done remarkable studies of ethnic groups and institutions, deviant communities and social issues. They have also been quite interested in exploring the taken-for-granted world, as well as little-known aspects of contemporary history and culture.

Conclusion

The largest obstacle to a more visual social science is unfamiliarity with managing images as data and with the technology of image creation, storage and display. Social scientific training – once the particular affordances of images are taken into account – provides an excellent preparation for conducting visual research. In addition, just realizing that working with images is a craft that is best learned through practice should help novice visual social scientists adjust their expectations and reduce frustration. In many ways, the more visual technologies are digitized, the more the craft aspects of image work – and its frustrations – will be familiar to scholars who have realized that computer literacy is a process of life-long learning.

There are also many opportunities that should serve as incentives for social scientists to explore visual research. First, it is increasingly possible – technically and financially – to reproduce visual materials in scholarly publications and to use digital databases to make research findings available to other scholars. Second, and perhaps most exciting, is that classroom instruction – how a significant number of social scientists earn their living – is ideally suited to developing research and interpretative skills in a receptive environment.[2] Not only does visual work have much to contribute to good teaching, but it can also foster collaborative research with students that can lead to viable research programmes.

Notes

1   'Everything else being equal' is, of course, never the case. The image is always a representation that is mediated by the camera holder, the condition and capacity of the medium and equipment, conditions (natural, social and personal) at the time of the shooting, the response of the subject to those conditions, and how the image is made visible and prepared for display. There is also much room for mischief at each phase of the process. The distortions and misinterpretations that most concern social scientists usually involve taking a photograph out of context, or not bothering to understand the context of the photo opportunity in the first place. More technical distortions can often be identified 'internally', by an informed critique of the photo-graph itself. Most questions concerning the adequacy of a representation can be resolved with a little elbow grease in the form of scholarly attention and technical skill. It is important to note, however, that the reason why there is such concern about distortion is due to the power of the image. This power is rooted in its capacity to represent something other than itself on something that is experienced as close to that other's own terms.

2   I have discussed this matter more practically and at length in Grady (2001).

References

Barbash, Ilisa and Taylor, Lucien (1997) *Cross-Cultural Filmmaking*, Berkeley: University of California Press.

Becker, Howard (1998) *Tricks of the Trade*, Chicago: University of Chicago Press.

Beeghley, Leonard (1996) *What Does Your Wife Do?: Gender and the Transformation of Family Life*, Boulder, Colo.: Westview Press.

Gibson, James (1979) *The Ecological Approach to Visual Perception*, Hillsdale, NJ: Lawrence Erlbaum Associates.

Goffman, Erving (1979) *Gender Advertisements*, London: Macmillan.

Grady, John (2001) 'Becoming a visual sociologist', *Sociological Imagination* 38(1–2): 83–119.

Harper, Douglas (2000) *Changing Works*, Chicago: University of Chicago Press.

Hughes, Everett (1971) *The Sociological Eye: Selected Papers on Work, Self, and the Study of Society*, Chicago: Aldine-Atherton.

Lieberson, Stanley (1985) *Making It Count: the Improvement of Social Research and Theory*, Berkeley: University of California Press.

Lofland, Lyn (1998) *The Public Realm: Exploring the City's Quintessential Social Territory*, New York: Aldine de Gruyter.

Owens, Bill (1973) *Suburbia*, San Francisco: Straight Arrow Books.

Rieger, John (1996) 'Photographing social change', *Visual Sociology* 11(1): 5–49.

Skocpol, Theda (1997) *Boomerang: Health Care Reform and the Turn Against Government*, New York: Norton.

Suchar, Charles (1997) 'Grounding visual sociology research in shooting scripts', *Qualitative Sociology* 20(1): 33–56.

Whyte, William H. (1988) *The City: Rediscovering the Center*, New York: Doubleday.

PART ONE

Picturing the self, identity and domesticated space

Chapter 1

Elizabeth Chaplin

MY VISUAL DIARY

Introduction

MANY PEOPLE KEEP A WRITTEN DIARY at some point during
their lives – one thinks of teenagers, anthropologists, politicians. And nowa-
days video-diaries are increasingly common – one thinks of 'docu-soaps', blogging
and various forms of reality TV. A few visual artists have produced sequences of drawings or paintings in diary form (Kitson 1982; Kelly 1983). But photographic diaries
are very rare, despite the fact that 80 per cent of the UK population owns a camera.[1]
As a social scientist, I have kept a daily photographic diary for fifteen years. This chapter describes that experience and discusses the advantages of keeping such a diary.

Most diarists focus on events that stand out in their minds from the basic routine
of their everyday lives; but a few, like the eighteenth-century village shopkeeper,
Thomas Turner (Vaisey 1984), dwell on the detail of that routine itself. For social
scientists and historians this latter type of diary is important, because everyday
routine is, by definition, what much of our lives consist of – and it tends to get
forgotten. My diary aims to be of this type. But the still visual diary, unlike video
and written diaries, does not present a flow of events over time. Instead, it consists
of a sequence of (possibly captioned) frozen moments, each of which becomes
exceptional by the very fact of being singled out. So, in the short term, a photographic diary may record a series of 'heightened' ordinary moments. But viewed
over a longer period – say, a year – some of those heightened moments may begin
to recur regularly, though in a slightly changed form; and patterns of continuity –
and even routine – may become apparent.

The idea of keeping a photographic diary did not come to me out of the blue;
it has a prehistory. As a social science undergraduate, I was advised to keep an

intellectual diary: to save newspaper cuttings, and jot down notes on a fairly regular basis, about issues, topics and ideas that concerned me. This became a long-term habit; and in one sense the photographic diary grew out of that habit. But there were other reasons for embarking on it as well. In the late 1980s, I was researching some British visual artists, and felt the need to 'get closer' to them: to share their experience of making aesthetic visual artefacts.[2] The idea of a keeping a photographic diary seemed to fit the bill. Besides constituting a formal visual project on the world, it would record my contacts with the artists. In addition, Goffman had made some intriguing remarks (1979: 20) about a photograph being unable to record routine, which I wanted to explore. I started my photographic diary on 7 February 1988. Apart from the occasional missed day, and some slightly longer periods when its immediate purpose had become rather unclear, I have kept it up ever since.

I soon found that photographs lead to the heart of social science theory. For while they do record – indeed they discover things our minds have failed to consciously register as we go about our lives – they never record neutrally. A photograph is 'taken', but at the same time, 'made'. It does constitute a trace, but how that trace is visually presented is the result of many subjective – often 'aesthetic' – decisions. And how that photograph is viewed is not a simple matter either. A photograph is almost never viewed purely 'as a photograph'; we tend to focus on the content of the image, and 'what it means' seems to vary according to the context in which it is viewed. And again, the notion of 'context' itself conjures up a veritable range of theoretical possibilities.[3] Thus, when social scientists take/make photographs on a regular basis, they become unavoidably implicated in a theoretical maelstrom. And involvement in that maelstrom is no purely academic matter when fuelled by a fascination with photography and photographic images, because what is also unavoidably involved is a consideration of that most powerful of social institutions, the media.[4]

The career of my visual diary

Year 1: 1988

Goffman has remarked that routine behaviour and action cannot be shown in a photograph. On the other hand, keeping a diary is a matter of routine. My original project was to attempt to show routine via a *sequence* of daily photos. But I soon realized that that my 'visual diary' would – more accurately – need to consist of a daily photograph accompanied by a short descriptive verbal passage. Photographs do not speak for themselves, and at a basic contextual level it is words which give meaning to images (Burgin 1986). So I decided to produce one captioned photograph per day for a whole year, with the aim of exposing traces of routine in my life. However, soon after I started I found it necessary to construct a rule about what to photograph and when to photograph it – another verbal intrusion into the 'visual diary'. And as the months passed, I became increasingly taken up with inventing rules which narrowed down the choice of what to photograph. Plate 1 shows August 1988, when the photograph was taken 'straight ahead' at 12 noon each day, but any rule seemed to contain an element of arbitrariness (for example, 'straight ahead' does not specify the height at which the picture is to be taken).

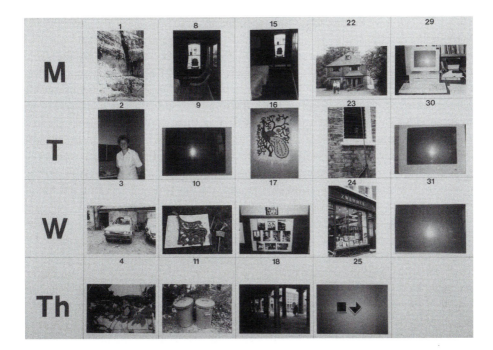

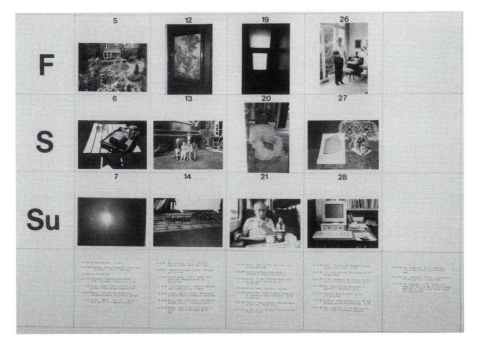

Plate 1 August 1988. Visual diary. Coloured photographs mounted on board.

However, half way through the year, the offer of an exhibition of the year's visual diary at Leeds University art gallery turned the project into an aesthetic one. So now I really was 'getting closer' to my research subjects, although, by the same token, this development pushed the already modified Goffman-related question slightly out of focus. I produced a set of twelve boards, each containing a month's photographs and captions, together with the monthly rule. Having been shown for three months as art, the same set of boards was then displayed as visual anthropology at the annual social anthropology conference. The change of context gave the work an entirely different meaning: the daily captioned photographs were now seen as 'anthropology at home'; this – despite the newly acquired social scientific context – was not quite the same thing as a focus on routine. The importance of contextualization would stay with me into Year 2.

Year 2: 1989

This year I was working closely with the artists. I wanted to produce photographic images which were visually analogous to their geometric abstract work but also explored the notion of context. The fall of the Berlin Wall was a prominent news item, and photographs of the wall were in all the newspapers. This triggered the idea of photographing a different wall each day. I started to produce a daily close-up of a wall, and, in addition, a contextualizing view of it. The close-ups of walls helped me to address some of the artists' concerns because I was producing images similar to their geometric abstract work, yet with a rather different theoretical underpinning. The contextualizing views showed the work that 'background' does in supplying meaning for a foreground object, transforming it from an aesthetic composition to a social situation. But after nine months, I began to miss recording people and social events, and viewers evidently felt the same, because they just flicked through the prints. So I stopped photographing walls, and began to address other current concerns: the position of the researcher in the research, and the feminist concern with voyeurism. My photographs became much more self-consciously made, as I attempted to show a trace of myself, the photographer, in each photograph that I produced. This trace consisted either of a shadow, a footprint, a reflection (in water or a mirror) or an actual hand or foot. The photographs became rather elaborate and unconventional: I found I was stepping over the borderline between record and aesthetic composition in a different way from in the previous year.

Year 3: 1990

This year I acquired a new camera with the date built in; so one aspect of the daily recording process was transferred into the technology of the camera. I became increasingly dissatisfied with the part played by the commercial processors in producing the daily image. I wanted greater control, so I changed from colour to black and white film, and started processing it myself. Once I had set up my darkroom, and was liberated from the expense of having the film commercially processed, I took several photographs each day. But I then faced the problem of which negatives to print and which to ignore, since printing was very time consuming. For a while, the project consisted of selecting negatives to print on a random basis; then of selecting according to a rule (e.g. every fourth negative). But the lure of the 'good' negative soon overcame this, and I began to print up the most promising ones. The subject matter became more various: family, research project, holidays, curiosities, visual compositions. In fact, more time was now being spent on learning how to produce black and white photos than on sociological concerns. However, I exhibited a visual and verbal analysis of the diary to date at the annual British Sociological Association conference, and my daily photograph of 4 April 1990 was a record of that display.

Year 4: 1991

I carried on working in black and white, but focusing on improving technical skills was still taking precedence. I had some of the current diary exhibited at York University Library, alongside the work of my artist research partner. This daily photograph (Plate 2) shows a student looking at the exhibition. Later in the year, I reluctantly changed back to colour and commercial processing (for good), because

Plate 2 8 October 1991. Visual diary. Student looking at visual diary exhibition in J. B. Morrell Library, University of York. Black and white photograph.

the processing was taking up too much time. 'Year 1' was exhibited at Wakefield Museum, alongside an artist's visual diary drawings of the same year. The exhibition thus consisted of a double-entry visual diary.

Years 5–7: 1992–4

During this period, I became involved with the British Constructivist artists' women's group, and documented preparations for our exhibitions at the Mappin Gallery, Sheffield, and at Warwick University. One of these exhibitions included my own artwork postcard (Plate 3) – a collage of various diary entries. In Year 7 (1994) I made an artwork, 'Postcard Rack', which displayed items from my photographic diary. This was again exhibited with the women artists' work. I had become accepted as an artist, as 'one of them'; and my photographic diary had become the raw material from which my artwork was constructed. I used the project for my teaching on an M.A. course at the University of York, UK (as I had done each year until now), and photos of the students at seminars became part of 'Postcard Rack'.

Year 8: 1995

I loosened ties with the artists, and helped produce the Open University course, Culture, Media and Identities. As a result, semiotics and cultural studies began to influence my approach: for example, I acquired a certain self-conscious awareness of the semiotic significance of the image. But the actual day-to-day visual diary was becoming less important – which indicates that a semiotic approach, though

Plate 3 The Countervail Collective, 1992. Montage of visual diary colour photographs.

appropriate to the analysis of *found* images, may present problems when applied to one's own current daily photographs. Mine tended to dry up. Theory took precedence, and the image receded into becoming a judiciously chosen illustration.

Years 9–11: 1996–8

During this period, my visual diary merely ticked over. I was 'just' photographing items of daily interest, sometimes several a day, and I sometimes forgot a day. This was partly because I acquired a digital camera in Year 9 and was beginning another visual project which did not seem to relate to the diary. It was also partly because I was no longer researching the artists, and writing about semiotics had dampened the project. At this stage, having kept the diary up for so long, it just seemed a shame to stop. I exhibited and discussed 'Postcard Rack' at a visual anthropology conference at the University of Kent.

Year 12: 1999

In early 1999, preparations for a public seminar obliged me to reassess all the work I had done so far. At last I put my finger on the visual diary's key purpose: it is a *tool* which can be used to help you think about whatever concerns you at the moment. I decided to use it to look again at the concept of routine, for in Year 1 my exploration of this topic had eventually been overlaid by a concern to produce an exhibition. Now, besides noting that a photograph can only establish that what it displays happened once, Goffman (1979: 21) also remarks that: 'The clothes worn on the occasion when the photograph was taken do give an indication of similar occasions when the same garb will have been worn.' Put more generally, the idea is that what is shown in a photograph relates to what is *not* shown in it. So might not a sequence of daily images of the same judiciously chosen subject hint at a routine (and changes in it) taking place beyond the framed view? I decided to photograph our hall table by the front door, since it remains pretty static but is also used as a picking up and putting down point. The changing items on, below and above it would at any rate give some daily indication of what was coming in and going out. I started to photograph the table every day at about 9 a.m. Each day the picture, with the help of the verbal entry, pinpointed what was there. By the end of the year I had produced over a hundred 'frozen moments' of the same subject in which, on a daily basis, objects were depicted, changed position, were accompanied by other objects, or vanished. Reading such a sequence suggested some of the routines, and changes in routine, which were taking place 'behind the scenes', unphotographed, in our daily home lives over a prolonged period.

Year 13: 2000

The 'Hall Table Project' continued throughout Year 13. Eventually I produced over 500 photographs of the hall table. These are best viewed as a 'flick-book'. When read at speed, they do indicate aspects of our routine, and changes in it: from how often I vacuum the carpet, to preparations for Christmas, and redecorating the wall

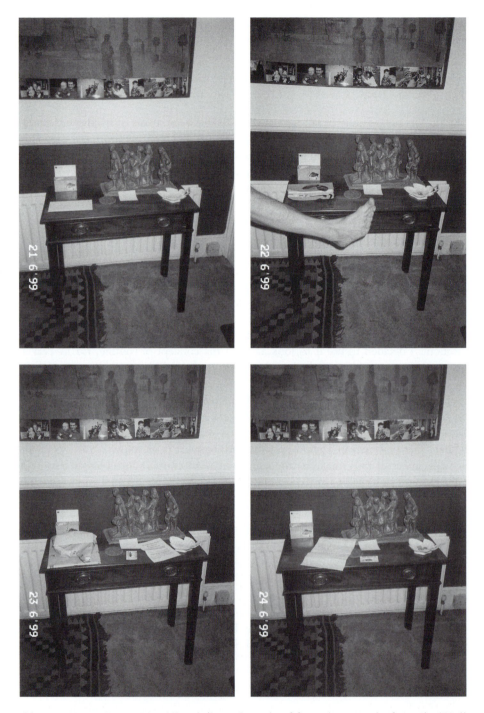

Plate 4 21–24 June 1999. Visual diary. Sample of four photographs from the 'Hall Table' project.

behind the table. Meanwhile, in May of this year, as part of the Open University's National Everyday Cultures Programme, I undertook a photographic survey of all the residents of my road.

Year 14: 2001

I started to use my diary to supplement and deepen the photographic survey of the residents by photographing daily happenings in the road. But after two months, I abandoned this because I thought it could undo the goodwill I had established with the residents (i.e. people would think me nosy if I was always photographing in the road). I went back to photographing 'anything and everything', i.e. no particular plan, but not many forgotten days.

Year 15: 2002

Family was becoming increasingly important. I had four grandchildren by now, and photographed them growing up. But on days when I didn't see them, I focused more on pictures of ordinary things, like wastebins, feet and shopping: subjects which were notable because they were not normally thought worthy of photographing. Perhaps this year's photographs reflected the fact that I was gradually retiring from professional life, and in particular from a tendency to generate my diary photographs from complex theories.

Some commonly asked questions

Why keep a daily photographic diary?

Keeping a daily photographic diary, for whatever reason, makes you look at life around you differently from how you would if you weren't keeping the diary. It is often remarked that we tend to take in the visual scene before us quickly – indeed, in a flash. We only look again, more carefully, if we sense that we need to – in order to avoid danger (at a level crossing), to get to where we have to go (is that a bus coming in the distance behind the trees or is it something quite else?): in other words, as Wittgenstein put it, in order to be able to go on. Knowing that you will be photographing something during the day forces you to step more often out of that 'in a flash' mode, and to take a longer look, because you are thinking: Shall I photograph that? Would it make a good picture? Why would it? How would it relate to the pictures I've already taken? Keeping a daily photographic diary teaches you, for example, to look critically – to consider the wider significance of what you are seeing (as Foucault, 1977, did in his study of Panopticism). It also helps you to relate one visual shape or colour to others and thus to think abstractly in visual terms (as many artists do). It enables you to look back, take stock and reflect on how your life and interests have changed over a given period of time. It gives you the experience – on a regular basis – of marvelling at, deploring, judging what is in front of your eyes (developing an aesthetic sensibility).[5] In other words, keeping a daily photographic diary stops you from taking what you see for granted. And that, in general terms, is just what social scientists aim to do.

How, more specifically, can keeping a photographic diary help us to 'do' social science?

The social scientist's visual diary is probably best thought of as a tool to help address whatever issue you're focusing on at the time; it is as likely to be an aid to research, an adjunct to a project, as it is to be 'the project itself'. Thus over the years, its use will probably change. During a period of fifteen years, I have used my visual diary to help think about (theorize) the topics of routine, reflexivity, voyeurism and autobiography.[6] I have also used it to record a particular research process; to find out what it's like to have a formal visual project on the world; to expand a project by providing additional ethnographic material (i.e. visual evidence); and as an integral part of a longitudinal study. In addition, for the first seven years of its life, I used my visual diary as a teaching resource in methodology workshops for M.A. students at the University of York.

Does it have to be a daily diary?

The diary doesn't have to be daily.[7] You could take a photograph once a week, say; or at irregular intervals – for example, whenever you have contact with the people or items you want to photograph. Clearly the interval between each photograph will depend on what you're trying to achieve, and, indeed, on your financial circumstances (see below). In one sense, the point is the rationale according to which the series of photos is taken. But the longer the period between taking photos, the less you will be in the habit of looking actively, which is one of the main points of keeping a visual diary.

Assuming that you keep a daily diary, what if you miss a day?

If your visual diary is underpinned and informed by a clear rule – like taking a photo on the dot of 3 p.m. each day, in which case you could preset your watch alarm – the problem of missing a day may not arise. But in the long term, days do get missed, whatever the underlying rationale for taking the photo. When the month's photos are laid out, or exhibited, an occasional miss might become significant – rather as an interview refusal does. But several missed days might, in retrospect, indicate to you that you are 'losing the plot' and need to reassess the purpose of your visual diary. As with cleaning your teeth, or practising a musical instrument, the benefits come from doing it regularly.

What if you take a photograph, and then later in the day find a better subject?

This question is often asked, and it points to the fundamental difference between making one written diary entry per day, and taking one photo per day. I think it's a mistake not to take a photo simply because you've already taken one that day.[8] If you mount your photos in clear pockets in a loose-leaf album, you can choose which one to put in the front of the daily pocket, and which ones behind. Or you might be able to 'save' the second subject for the next day. In the long term, expense will probably curb your enthusiasm.

Practical stuff

The camera

In descending order of importance:

1   It must be very reliable, as it will be in continual use over an extended period of time (choose a metal rather than plastic case).
2   It must be small enough to carry around in a pocket wherever you go.
3   An auto focus (zoom?) camera with built-in flash is best: this allows pictures to be taken quickly – there may be no time to make aperture adjustments etc.
4   Use a model which stamps the date on the front of the print. In this way, the image becomes 'diarified': your camera is a diary-producing tool.
5   It should have a reasonably high-quality lens.

In other words, you are looking as near to the top end of the 35mm compact or digital camera range as you can afford.

Taking photographs of people

It may take courage to ask a stranger or neighbour if they are willing to be photographed (always ask permission *before* photographing someone, and always get written permission *before* publishing the photograph) because you know you are intruding into their lives; you are asking to extract, as it were, part of their identity, and to keep it for yourself. But in my experience, most people are delighted to oblige, and furthermore are unlikely to ask what the photo will be used for. On the other hand, you will get the occasional refusal, and this may be strongly expressed. This is because asking to photograph someone can bring to the surface things that matter to them deeply; and they will be well aware that a photo commonly counts as evidence. This is why refusals can be so significant. Once you have asked to photograph someone, you have established a relationship (which may be greatly extended since the very act of asking often prompts further conversation). This relationship between photographer and photographed becomes a variable, an influence, on your project. Methodologically, taking photographs itself influences a project. I always offer a copy of the photo – notwithstanding the post-colonial argument that it is condescending to offer the equivalent of glass beads to the natives. I have never known anyone say they positively don't want a copy of 'their' photograph. A few say they are 'not bothered', but most positively want a print, and some ask for more than one copy.

Processing the film (and buying it in the first place)

If you are using a conventional as opposed to a digital camera you will have to decide whether to develop and print the film yourself, or whether to get it commercially processed. For the former (presumably black and white images) you will need a darkroom. Developing and printing is a lengthy business and a skill that takes time to acquire. But if gaining control over as much of the process as possible is important to you, then you may choose this option. However, home processing presents you with all sorts of choices about how to *create* the photograph, about how it will finally look. Do you want to be in a position where you have to make these choices? I found, reluctantly, that I did not, because it complicated and extended the whole process of keeping a diary to the point where I was in danger of giving it up. I argue, instead, that the diary photos are, on the whole, of ordinary everyday life, taken with a fairly ordinary camera, so it seems reasonable to get them ordinarily processed at a high street store. And, of course, commercial processing is quicker, less effort; and colour is, on the whole, more informative than black and white (and the film is cheaper and more readily available). At the time of writing, taking colour photographs at the rate of one a day and getting them commercially processed costs £7–8 a month. Alternatively, try getting Kodak to sponsor you!

Storing and displaying the photographs

1   Scan them into a computer, and keep a year's visual diary on CDs.
2   Get yourself an exhibition in a gallery at the end of the year, with each month's photographs mounted on a board, and any captions (see next section) set alongside. In this case, you temporarily turn into an artist, which experience is, in itself, not without sociological interest.
3   Slot each daily photograph into a pocket in a transparent storage page (for example there are pages designed for 6″ × 4″ photos which house four on each side of the page); keep the pages in a loose-leaf album, and keep the captions in a separate book.

I have tried all three methods, but routinely use the third.

Captioning images

John Berger (1982: 92) has remarked that 'the photograph [is] irrefutable as evidence but weak in meaning'. For this reason, and as previously discussed, I have always supplied a short verbal caption for each of my images. Consequently – alongside my album of daily photographs – I keep an exercise book, in which every photograph receives a dated one-line caption. Very occasionally, I use more than one line. When the focus is predominantly on theoretical issues, the words tend to lead, and the images tend to display examples. When primarily documenting events, the situation changes: the image serves as witness, as evidence of what the words describe, and of more that they don't. When an aesthetic focus is being created, the image tends to lead, with words providing very active support for that aesthetic. Almost every one of my combined visual diary entries embodies each of these three elements, in combination, in tension, but each to differing degrees. It's a case of which element – the theoretical, the documentary, the aesthetic – has the strongest pull.

Concluding remarks

Photographs exhibit a tension which lies at the heart of social science theory. Cultural studies emphasizes that an image cannot be a record of something 'out there' because it is polysemic: its meaning floats, and can never be finally settled. But many photographers and theorists of photography argue that photographs are a special kind of image in that the mechanism of the camera – that which actually defines it as a camera – produces a trace, therefore a record, of what has been photographed (the photographer sometimes presses the button without knowing it, and the camera records an image of what it happens to be pointed at). Some people regard this clash as unresolvable; and on theoretical grounds it probably is: 'meaning' and 'showing' are as difficult to integrate as oil and water. Others, including me, take a practical stance, arguing that the photographic trace is a record of something which could, on the other hand, have been recorded differently; and is, furthermore, open to many different interpretations. Indeed, it seems clear that the degree of objectivity and subjectivity involved in each photograph varies from image to image. The social scientist/photographer can experiment with producing photographs which are primarily records or which are primarily constructions, with the caption either giving back-up description or taking the theoretical and/or aesthetic high ground. In other words, the camera can be used as a tool to think with, over a range of theoretical positions. As far as the photographic *diary* is concerned, the camera helps you to see actively, to pinpoint the taken for granted on a regular basis. And revisiting your diary is a very useful memory prompt, and aids reflection. I've kept my diary up for a long time. But if you are wondering about keeping a visual diary, don't let that put you off. I didn't know when I started that I would be keeping it up for so long. Try it for a month, if you think it could help you with whatever social science issue concerns you at the moment. Then see what happens.

Notes

1   This article was written just before the advent of multimedia message system (MMS) mobile phones which include a digital camera, and which, according to the *Guardian*, 2 January 2003, may encourage people 'to create their own visual diaries'. So this article may fast become a historic record, and a relic, of a pre-MMS age.

2   In brief: I had embarked on a joint project with the Constructivist artist, Malcolm Hughes. He wished to use my knowledge of recent developments in the sociology of science in order to make the theoretical basis of British Constructivism 'more solidly scientific'; in return he offered me access to twenty-three British Constructivist artists. I interviewed each one of these artists. My aim was to document their contacts with each other over a period of time, and to explore how these contacts were affecting the development of their visual work. I also tried to understand how their political views became translated into abstract visual artworks. The project then developed in several directions during the course of five years. In particular, I became part of the Constructivist women's group (see below, 'The career of my visual diary, Years 5–7').

3   e.g. realist, semiotic, Foucauldian, Althusserian, psychoanalytic.

4   Take, for example, an article in the *Guardian*, 25 July 2001. Its headline, 'Student's video "catches police attack"', and its first sentence – 'A burly policeman caught on video as he apparently punched and kicked a defenceless man after a row faces dismissal if complaints by the victim are upheld' – both indicate the take/make, show/mean dichotomy involved in photography, and hint at the implications of adopting one side to the exclusion of the other.

5   Barbara Story of Leeds routinely photographs the view from the bus window on her journey from Leeds to Ilkley. She told me that the experience has immeasurably sharpened her appreciation of the Dales landscape.
6   For the idea of autobiography as theory, see Finnegan (1997).
7   The word 'diary' comes from the Latin *dies*, which means day.
8   Perhaps you have taken a photo which was planned in advance, because you knew what your schedule for the day would be. Then, suddenly, a marvellous subject unexpectedly presents itself. Be flexible: try not to rule out the unexpected extra photo, just because you're following a particular daily rule. Later, that extra photo might acquire more significance than the other one taken on that day.

References

Berger, J. (1982) *Another Way of Telling*, London: Writers and Readers Publishing Cooperative Society.

Burgin, V. (1986) *The End of Art Theory: Criticism and Postmodernity*, Basingstoke: Macmillan.

Finnegan, R. (1997) '"Storying the self": personal narratives and identity', in H. Mackay (ed.) *Consumption and Everyday Life*, London: Sage, with the Open University.

Foucault, M. (1977) *Discipline and Punish*, London: Penguin Books.

Giles, T. *et al.* (1992) *Countervail*, Sheffield: Mappin Art Gallery.

Goffman, E (1979) *Gender Advertisements*, London and Basingstoke: Macmillan.

Kelly, M. (1983) *The Post Partum Document*, London: Routledge and Kegan Paul.

Kitson, L. (1982) *The Falklands War: a Visual Diary*, London: Mitchell Beazley International, in association with the Imperial War Museum.

Vaisey, D. (ed.) (1984) *The Diary of Thomas Turner 1754–1765*, Oxford: Oxford University Press.

Chapter 2

Ruth Holliday

REFLECTING THE SELF

THIS CHAPTER IS BASED ON ISSUES which arose from research
I conducted in 1998–9 using video-diaries to examine the performative nature
of queer identities. Any new research method raises practical problems as well as
new methodological issues, but it also inevitably leads us to revisit long-running
debates. This chapter describes the research method that I used and revisits some key
theoretical problems in the practice of methodology. I will begin by outlining the
research, and how I did it, focusing on the different methods of self-representation
which diarists employed in their videos. I will then examine some of the theoretical
issues associated with research methods that are currently contested. I hope to
conclude by providing a way of moving beyond the ethical and epistemological
impasses that dominate the study of methodology by presenting visual methods as
potentially a practice of *sharing* information between respondents and peers. The

camera lens is theorized as *reflecting* (or more accurately refracting) the lives, experiences and explanations of subjects through the lives, experiences and explanations of researchers where both borrow their discursive frameworks from their respective locations. I will argue that the taking of respondents' accounts and representations is not necessarily the appropriation of one self by another, but rather the prosthetic extension of selves which are never prior to supplementation. In this way the concept of reflexivity is replaced with the notion of *reflection*, which is always a process that takes place *outside* the researcher's (and the respondent's) self. First I will explain the logic for the video-diary method that I used.

Any thorough investigation of culture in western societies in the current period – a consumer society saturated with televisual imagery and replete with vast arrays of cultural and subcultural products – surely needs to examine both text and experience. But more important than either of these is the interplay of each with the other. How subjects, for example, construct and display identities is not just about experiences, or just about the products available to us through which we 'consume' our identities, but also about how those products come to inform and construct our identities and how these identities get mapped out through the products available to us as embodied subjects.

This is what I hoped to explore through the use of video-diaries, a method which captures not only the narratives of experience and lived cultural practices but also the visual nature of the construction and display of identities through the use of cultural products. The visual dimension of the research allows a glimpse of the configuration of these cultural products as they are mapped out on bodies, homes and other aspects of the habitus. In addition, the narrative enables an exploration of these configurations and importantly alludes to the meanings which products come to have, not just at the point of consumption, but as they subsequently become woven into narratives of self.

Reflecting video-diaries

The method I used involved giving respondents camcorders and asking them to make video-diaries. In the brief for these, respondents were asked to demonstrate visually and talk about the ways in which they managed or presented their identities in different settings in their everyday lives. The participants were asked to dress in the clothes they would wear in each situation, describing them in detail and explaining why they thought these self-presentation strategies were appropriate. This technique was designed to make sure that participants were as explicit as possible about the presentation of their identities in different spaces – at work, rest and play. Respondents kept the video cameras for up to three months and were at liberty to record, delete or rerecord their diaries as they liked.

I would like to emphasize the importance of the video-diaries in capturing the performativities of identity in ways that are qualitatively different from other sociological research methods. In one sense, the self-representation is more 'complete' than the audio-taped interview, which only provides aural data. Moreover, the visual dimension of the construction and display of identity is obviously more easily gleaned through this method. The use of video as a *process* in the research is equally important (compared with, say, the use of still photography), not only in allowing a representation of identities to show through, but also in running that alongside the narrativization of identity (through respondents' commentaries) and in reflecting the selection, editing and refining that constitute identity and performativity as process in all our lives (see Holliday 1999).

In theory (if not necessarily in practice) video-diaries afford respondents the potential for a greater degree of reflection than other methods, through the processes of watching, rerecording and editing their diaries before submission. Against other methods that focus on 'accuracy' or 'realism', then, this approach offers respondents more potential to *represent* themselves; making a video-diary can be an active, even empowering, process, since it offers the participant greater 'editorial control' over the material disclosed.

From the material submitted by respondents two important but fundamentally different styles of diary emerged. One style was primarily associated with those respondents who involved partners and friends in the filming process. These tended to be light-hearted pieces incorporating jokes and ironic statements. While concessions are made to the overall aims of the project, these diaries appear to be specifically designed to be 'entertaining'. So, for example, during the filming of one sequence, a friend of the diarist says: 'Why are you being so witty and funny today? You're only trying to make out that you're a more interesting person than you actually are!'

These diaries (or diary parts) are full of performances – dancing and singing, jokey telephone conversations, mock debates between soft toys, the baring of bottoms and much giggling. This seems to suggest a high level of self-consciousness on the part of the diarists. Of course, one would imagine that the diarists would be self-conscious in front of the camera; however, *alone* in front of the camera, these same diarists adopted a different style, as did those diarists who filmed themselves entirely without accomplices. The self-consciousness thus appears to be the result of performing in front of a *known* other. Alone, the diarists appear freer to disclose the most intimate details about themselves to the camera. The relative candour of the diarists when alone with the camera is, I would suggest, due not to the coercion that they feel to confess to it but rather to the desire not to be overly self-examining among friends. It also becomes more possible in the absence of potential contradiction.

Reflecting styles

The style used by these diarists is, in fact, highly reminiscent of the confessional, a notion made famous most notably by Foucault (1979) in his *History of Sexuality*. The confession is certainly a structure of enormous importance, given its prevalence in the (post)modern media, manifesting itself in many areas from biographical documentaries and celebrity talk-shows to the most sensationalist popular shows such as *Rikki Lake* and, most infamously, *Jerry Springer*. Michael Renov (1996) sees therapeutic discourse undergoing a transformation as it becomes mediatized. He argues that video is a particularly confessional medium:

> confessional discourse of the diaristic sort addresses itself to an absent, imaginary other. . . . In the case of video confessions, the virtual presence of a partner – the imagined other effectuated by the technology – turns out to be a more powerful facilitator of emotion than flesh-and-blood interlocutors. Camera operators, sound booms, cables, and clapperboards are hardly a boon to soul confession.
>
> (1996: 88–9)

Renov celebrates the immediacy of video as enabling greater freedom of expression: '[The video] monitor shows the subject only herself as she (re)produces herself. The screen-mirror also becomes a blank surface upon which an active projection of the self rather than a strictly receptive introjection reigns triumphant' (1996: 90).

Renov also sees confessional video as empowering in the sense that it is beyond conventional media control. It is frequently non-commercial and thus not susceptible to the whims of a viewing market. In some senses it redresses the media imbalance, turning 'passive' viewers into 'active' producers: video reclaims television as a two-way communication process. While Renov is perhaps a little over-optimistic, exaggerating the impact such video productions can make, there are two points in his argument which warrant further discussion. The first is the concept of the confessional which he employs in his analysis. As Foucault and many others have pointed out, the confessional is itself far from a one-way process. Confessing in psychoanalysis, for example, while always conducted within a network of power, is not enforced through domination. The confessional is rather a power game. The analyst cannot force the analysand to confess, but rather must coax a disclosure. The analysand may give a response willingly – with the aim of a catharsis or cure – but since these disclosures can be painful or embarrassing there may be resistance to such proclamations on the part of the analysand. The confessional is thus a game and the analysand may choose to withhold or disclose information if they feel potential benefits may arise from this. Benefits may arise simply out of the fact of having a particular space in which to confess, an audience intent on listening. The analysand may persuade the analyst that, after all, their disclosures are those of a 'normal' subject. They might even dismiss the analyst if the latter cannot be persuaded of their point of view, as Dora famously did to Freud. Thus, the psychoanalytic encounter may also afford the analysand power and space to speak which normal circumstances preclude. What the analysand risks, of course, is having that speech rendered into discourse. This paradox is one familiar to queer subjects whose worlds have frequently collided with those of the analyst.

In terms of the video-diaries, the power to present one's identity may override the risk of having that speech appropriated by others (for example, the media or, indeed, academics). Thus, the fullest confession opens up the greatest space to talk and affords the greatest power at that moment. If a distant authority subsequently appropriates that speech, then this is of little consequence to the diarists themselves. For example, in the research Gill says: 'Why am I telling you all these things about myself? Well, I think that if you asked me I'd tell you, but you're going to tell other people; um, because I think that it's important and I think I've got things to say.'

The second point to raise here is about Renov's analogy of the camera monitor as mirror. I feel that this is important because it inadvertently explains something about the perceived audience for the diary. Since we are accustomed to conceiving of ourselves as viewers of media productions rather than as creators of them, the mirror analogy seems appropriate since we are likely to imagine audiences of our productions through a strong process of identification: we imagine ourselves as audience for our own productions. It is often said that diarists and other confessors are narcissistic. In a sense the video-diary production is narcissistic, but not in the sense of self-love; rather in the sense of the imagined self for whom the diary is constructed (Freud 1914). The diarist thus engages in a form of confessional through a narcissistic identification with an imagined viewer. This further explains the candour with which the diaries are made, since one should not desire to have secrets from oneself.

Although these confessions are not made externally to relations of power, the explicit nature of the material is facilitated by the unique space which respondents are afforded in order to attempt to fix the meanings of what they say. Confessions are also facilitated by the narcissistic identification with imaginary viewers and possibly by an assumed sympathetic reading of the material from a similarly situated researcher. Finally, though the diaries do appear confessional in style, it must be remembered that for this project diarists were actually directed to talk around a number of specific foci. These were in effect fairly mundane (in terms of how identity is expressed, rather than arrived at) and thus they cannot be compared directly with, for instance, psychoanalytic encounters. Given this format, the frankness of the diarists' responses remains surprising. Yet one should not be overwhelmed into conceiving of this frankness as the truth itself. Rather, these accounts are *representations*.

A final point about the content of the diaries concerns their specifically visual nature and the possibilities they afford for actions and props. Most of us display our identities in visual ways through different arrangements of cultural products such as clothes and interior décor, and the kinds of books, records and CDs we choose to display. The diarists were keen to demonstrate aspects of their identities in such visual ways. The instructions for the project specified that diarists should dress in the clothes they usually wore in specific situations, but many of them went beyond this, going through their wardrobes and identifying trends in clothing or specific items with special meanings. They often used panoramic shots to show music and book collections, posters and prints, and also pointed out items imbued with personally important meanings.

The visual dimension of the diaries also enabled a certain amount of acting out of particular situations or activities. There were office shots of everyday work encounters, or much more personal activities such as the shaving of body hair or the taking of hormone tablets, accompanied by discussions about these rituals. Such performances were frequently made central to the diarists' identities, but were also sometimes discussed with a measure of ambivalence. Some of the diaries tended towards a more 'artistic' structure and included, for instance, recitals of poetry and background music. Video-diaries capture visual performances of identities and the fascinating ways in which identities are mapped onto the surfaces of bodies, homes and workspaces. Put together, the intertextuality (as well as the limitations) of identifications becomes apparent in the ways in which similar props, or cultural products, occur across different diaries. In fact, identities may also be expressed in the very structure of the diaries, which frequently borrow textual and visual codes from television programming and film. As James (1996: 125) explains:

> while video provides the arena in which an autobiographical self can be talked into being, the talking is realized only via video; the verbal is always mediated through its specific electronic visualization. Investigating

this mediation in successive tapes . . . the social relations that constitute [lives] are themselves similarly mediated through video as text and video as a social process, video as audiovisual electronic information and video as a network of social institutions and apparatuses in which this information comes into being.

Visualizing subjects

However, to suggest that the diaries are *only* confessional would be misleading. The idea that video-diaries represent a kind of auto-therapy may in part be true, especially in terms of style, but there are many other forms in which the diaries appear. For example, Simon Brett (Dinsmore 1996: 44) describes how the diary fulfils a variety of different roles:

> It can serve as a confessional or as apologia. It can be used to colour reality or to vent a spleen. It can be a bald record of facts or a Gothic monument of prose. It can chart the conquest of a libertine or the see-sawing emotions of a depressive, it can chronicle the aspirations of youth and the disillusionment of age.

Certainly all these elements appear in the video-diaries I collected, and the styles employed varied considerably across different diarists and within diaries.

The video-diary is a very particular method which generates specific concerns and opportunities in its visualization of respondents that other methods may not. However, more general issues about how to treat the ensuing 'data' are worth discussing too. I will now visit some central and largely unresolved methodological issues and though I will not attempt to solve them here, I hope at least to show their effects and the ways in which they serve to reinscribe the power relations of fieldwork.

Writing the self, writing others

A number of methodological techniques have been developed in order to address the issues of power in fieldwork and I will use two very different examples in the following sections to illustrate this. The concept of reflexivity is perhaps most notable, and has come to occupy a central position in methodological debates, especially in ethnographic and anthropological studies. A kind of self-awareness and self-scrutiny, reflexivity asks that researchers consider their own position in the research process, as well as investigating the positions of their respondents. It furthers the idea of research as a dialogic and transparent process between researcher and respondent, and aims to make clear the ways that the researcher's position shapes interaction in the field and subsequent interpretation. As a counter to the supposed objectivity and value-neutrality of traditional academic enquiry, reflexivity has a lot to commend it. Yet it is underpinned by ideas about the self that require critical scrutiny.

As an academic practice, reflexivity depends on two things. First, it relies on a stable sense of self (see Skeggs 2002); second, within that self, an internal process of self-examination should take place. However, poststructuralist conceptions dispense with both of these positions, locating the self externally at the intersection of discourses and within a performative logic. Moreover, reflexivity is often associated with reflection. Reflection again is colloquially thought of as something one might do in retreat, away from others, separate from outside influences, but there is a clue in the word which again hints at a poststructuralist agenda. While the word has been taken to mean an internal process of the self, it also incorporates another meaning: as in the mirror (or, as I will discuss later, the camera lens) the self is reflected back from an external location, so in discourse it is reflected in/constructed by identity categories. Reflections on the self and practices of reflexivity, then, can be regarded not as the internal processes of a stable subject, but rather as external positions, understandings and explanations.

What is clear from this conceptualization is that the potential self – and the potential for that self to be reflexive – is limited by one's access to discursive formations. Thus, while some academic selves might have access to theoretical, political, legal, journalistic, therapeutic, televisual and situated discourses, other selves may only be able to access the latter of these (and even then the televisual and situated discourses available to some are severely restricted). What emerges from this are selves that exist on a continuum. At one end are the 'discourse rich' – those with a high level of cultural and social capital, highly educated, with access to libraries, intellectual discussions with colleagues and friends, 'intelligent' television programmes, art and literary criticism, and counselling and therapy (all discourses that are highly valued). At the other end are the 'discourse poor' – the practically and vocationally educated (with access only to discourses that have little attributed value). That is not, however, to imbue 'the working class' with no possibility for resistance or ingenuity (situated discourses are often highly oppositional, as Stuart Hall (1980) and many others have pointed out).

This situation is made more complex in late modernity by the plethora of potential discursive positions available to the 'discourse rich'. In modernity, as a great many theorists have pointed out, conceptions of the self were confined to a set of strict codes, so that those selves that counted as selves were very limited (see

Shildrick 1997). This rendered academic authority as unproblematic, privileging the researcher's interpretation and disregarding respondents' positions as 'false consciousness'. However, the introduction and domestication of critical discourses in the academy presented the beginnings of the decentring of the academic self. Each potential self brought with it an array of new forms of cultural capital (situated knowledges) but simultaneously the anxiety of choice: is the new feminist self which brings with it a new explanatory potential the 'correct' self to be? This anxiety reached fever pitch as political correctness came to dominate the academy in the 1980s and 1990s with its ever-changing sets of terminologies which one could only know by being 'in the know'. As these discourses multiplied, each received its own validation in a culture that sought to undermine the authoritative voice of the centre, and explanations became increasingly temporary and contingent so that we must now spend more and more time pondering our selves in relation to these constantly shifting discourses. What appears to be an increasingly reflexive society (and academy), then, is really only one in which the number of potential (discursive) 'positions' is greatly multiplied.

One way of both acknowledging the subjective position of the researcher and overcoming the distance between respondents and researchers has been the practice of (auto)biography – writing the researcher's self and experience into the text. However, as Elspeth Probyn (1993) has pointed out, this can privilege the experiences of the researcher over those of her respondents. Furthermore, as Tim May (1998) explains, the problematization of social science methodology has ironically led in some quarters to a reprivileging of 'authorial authority', typically when it is based on the experience or identity of the researcher: identity comes to constitute a kind of moral and political high ground from which critical analysis is less important than 'experience'.

Feminist researchers, for example, have long been concerned to chart 'women's experiences of . . .', where *being* a woman is the signifier of primary importance in validating the research. For instance, Sarah Pink (2001) cites the project '"I didn't leave y'all on purpose": HIV-infected mothers' videotaped legacies for their children' (Barnes *et al.* 1997) as an example of good reflexive visual research. She explains that the researchers 'empowered' women dying of AIDS-related illnesses to make videoed 'letters' for their currently too-young-to-understand children to view in the future. Having 'empowered' the women, the researchers then viewed the videoed material to access the women's assumed 'private' thoughts, as opposed to the assumed 'public' ones they would ordinarily present to researchers. This, Pink explains, is good research because it is done not *about women*, but *for women*. This formulation hides a fundamental power inequality between the apparently homogeneous but actually highly differentiated 'women' of the equation and begs the question: *which* women is it for? Such equations have been subject to extensive criticism on the grounds of essentialism (see Harding (1986) and Haraway (1996) for a discussion). However, my point is that, according to the researchers involved, the women diarists here can't be trusted to tell 'the truth' about their condition and thus their accounts must be mediated by their equally disenfranchised children. Here is a clear example of *distinction* at work, whereby the researchers (in the know) distinguish themselves from the 'unknowing' 'ordinary women' by 'speaking for' them. In short, the formulation 'for women' is ruptured by the acknowledgement that 'women' occupy very different power locations in the research process.

Flattening the hierarchy by attempting to minimize the distinction between researcher and respondent has also been attempted through respondent validation – getting respondents to concur that the researcher's account reflects their view-points – and by more fully acknowledging respondents' inputs, for example by citing respondents as co-authors (Bell and Nelson 1989). This strategy, too, raises crucial questions of power, distinction and appropriation. White feminist academic Diane Bell, who co-authored her work with her aboriginal respondent Topsy Nelson, stands accused of appropriating Nelson's name and ethnicity in order to validate her own position – no matter how much Nelson protested the contrary (Bell 1993).

Sarah Ahmed (2000) argues that Bell and Nelson's friendship was strategic and only a technique of knowledge, drawing on Spivak's (1988) 'Can the subaltern speak' – but here Spivak is writing about *writing*. The subaltern is subaltern by virtue of its very exclusion from such resources. So it is not in writing that we need to look for subaltern voices. The subaltern is perhaps more adept at its own repre-sentation than we might like to think. Talk-shows like *Rikki Lake* or *Trisha* are regularly castigated for their vulgarity, yet it is through such shows that many of the subaltern make themselves heard (Gamson 1998). Of course, these testimonies are then interpreted within a moralistic frame, but 'guests' do not always acquiesce to the audience or the host. Maybe, then, we are simply looking in the wrong places. We need to be thinking precisely about *how* the subaltern *could* represent itself, not about how it has been represented. After all, Spivak's argument is less to do with speaking than with being heard, and this raises the broader questions of anthropo-logical and ethnographic writing and its potential appropriation of respondents.

Appropriated selves?

The major concern in this debate is the assumption that Bell used Nelson to validate her argument as truthful by virtue of Nelson's imagined claim to shared experience *as an* aboriginal woman: truth claims are here validated by experience as if experience is unmediated. Once we dispense with the idea that biology-produces-experience-produces-knowledge, however, what we have is simply a position or set of positions adopted variously by both researchers and interviewers. Thus we can see ethnographic interventions not as claims to truth but as temporary positions within an ongoing debate. The academy is no longer a homogenous bloc; people within it represent many different positions and theoretical traditions. Held in tension, knowledge becomes productive – once we have achieved a final 'correct' position we lose sight of the process of critical reflection in relation to new discursive structures. Equally, if debates continue to focus on the 'incorrect' ways of doing research we risk an increasingly introspective academy. What we must do to escape this impasse of ethical debates which operate in ever-decreasing circles is to *risk being wrong*, to 'learn from our *mistakes*'.

Furthermore, if we examine some of the assumptions that underpin the Bell debate, an even more problematic formulation of research relations appears. The idea that Topsy Nelson is exploited rests on the assumption that her only role is in providing *experiences* for the researcher. Diane Bell then provides the *interpretation*, thus 'producing' Nelson's experiences for her. If Nelson has an equal role in interpretation, then she has not been appropriated: she is simply a contributor. Thus, the assumption upon which Nelson's appropriation rests is *her inability to interpret her own world for herself and her 'false consciousness' in arguing against that assumption*. Furthermore, the fact that Bell is attributed the skill of interpretation rests on the premise that she has at her disposal theoretical techniques (feminist theory, for instance) which Nelson has not, *and cannot have*, even if Bell, through their 'friendship', explains them to her. Thus, Bell is positioned as being naturally capable of interpretative thought, while Nelson is positioned as being incapable of it. What this construction forgets is the technologies of the academy in producing academic subjects – that learning is a social process and not a naturally endowed capability. Is it any wonder, then, that the subaltern can't speak, or write, when academic subjects steadfastly refuse to give them voice or text, even in the name of their emancipation?

Appropriation or extension?

As researchers, we collect the stories of others and we reflect upon them in the light of the discourses 'we' have at our disposal and 'they' might not (initially, at least). However, do we always have to think about appropriation as a violence committed against respondents? The very point of appropriation is that the appropriator takes on part of the other.

In his 'consumption view of the self', Munro (1996) conceptualizes the self as extension, as prosthesis – an idea we can usefully apply to the research process. As researchers, we move through research settings consuming subjects and objects and supplementing our selves. Munro is careful to point out that there is no unsupplemented self at the core, no centred, inner self, but rather the whole self is prosthesis. We are nothing but the sum of appropriations we have made, and of course some of us have more potential for this than others by virtue of our 'movement' (i.e. contact with a range of 'others') but also by being 'discourse rich'. However, rather than reducing research subjects to disempowered objects, Munro mobilizes the metaphor of *sharing*. Thus (research) subjects share with us in an active way: 'Persons are active over making things present and making other things absent. Their explicit consumption of people, goods, and words, alongside any apparent non-consumption, instantiates their *belonging*' (Munro 1996: 256, original emphasis). While Munro uses this concept to refer to the sharing of culture within a community, we could also use it to talk about the sharing of culture by communities and individuals with researchers (as communities are not without their own power hierarchies).

All this agonizing over exploitation, appropriation and power seems simply to act to reinforce the subject–object relations of research, i.e. the independent selfhood of researchers. It is time that we too admitted to being products of discourses, albeit academic ones. A concern for the poor treatment of social science respondents in an era when researchers felt that that they had the right to exploit their subjects for the advancement of 'science' has been replaced by a neurotic concern to move to the 'correct' position. This has much more to do with the (symbolic) violence which academics mete out to each other than with any concern for the way in which we use respondents. As Probyn points out, it is in texts, not in practice, that we tend to find reflexivity:

> With the emergence of self-reflexivity in ethnography, epistemological and ontological questions about subjectivity come more immediately to the fore. In simple terms, we need to ask what exactly a self-reflexive self is reflecting upon. In addition, it needs to be clear where that self is positioned and whether it is a physical or a textual entity.
> (Probyn 1993: 62)

When reflexivity is confined to the researcher and representation confined to the text it is not surprising that respondents' selfhood is viewed as passive and subject to exploitation by the self-reflexive authors presented in conventional academic texts (of which this is one). However, in presenting the visual component of my study on sexuality through the video-diary material I collected, my reflexivity has been challenged a number of times by members of the audience who refer back to the diarists' statements. Thus, the diarists' selves and their reflections seem to be much more present within the authorial text which I have constructed through video than if I were simply reciting their accounts in my own words. As Caroline Knowles explains, 'It is precisely around the visual images (as well as the voices heard in the direct quotes) that the text opens up and lets the reader in' (2000: 18).

Sharing reflections

'The value of goods lies in their use by "members" to make their judgements on each other visible to each other. Thus the notion of visibility is central to understanding possibilities for sharing' (Munro 1996: 256).

Drawing on research by Douglas and Isherwood (1980), Munro relates the consumption view of the self to the visibility of culture as it is performed by bodies through the deployment of goods. Consumption 'uses goods to make firm and visible a particular set of judgements in the fluid processes of classifying persons and events' (Douglas and Isherwood, in Munro 1996: 56). It is this consumption of goods which makes our shared culture visible and thus binds the individual into the social – a set of shared cultural codes. Crucially for my research, then, the objects made visible by the diarists not only confirm their shared culture (and their relative positions within it) but also actively share their culture with the camera/researcher/ audience through *admission*. The visual, and thus visual methodologies, have a central part to play in the sharing of cultures.

Furthermore, there is something specifically visual about the nature of bearing witness to cultures. Shoshana Felman's (1992) essay on Claude Lanzmann's film *Shoah* – a film entirely devoted to the witness statements of Holocaust survivors – charts the importance of testimony and adopting the role of witness. Importantly, she stresses the role of the visual in the act of telling. 'Film would . . . seem to be the very medium which accommodates the simultaneous multiplicity of levels and directions, a medium that can visually [and aurally] *inscribe* – and cinematically bear witness to – *the very impossibility of writing*' (Felman 1992: 248, original emphasis).

While I would not like to equate the diaries which my respondents have made with the testimonies of Holocaust survivors, there is something in the process which would seem to have resonance. The video-diaries often seemed to capture testimonies of a kind, although these were less about the pain of being gay and more

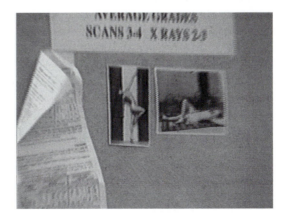

about trying to dispel the myth of pain represented in the characterization of the 'sad young man' (Dyer 1993). Diarists seemed strongly compelled to 'set the record straight'.

Thus, the conception of the victimized and passive respondent must be tempered (at the very least) by the opportunity to bear witness. The former depiction perhaps does more to reinforce the image of the autonomous researcher than it does to accurately portray the experience of diarists. In terms of the appropriation of respondents we must look at the medium of video as a way of recording a complex and multilayered text. It is a medium with which respondents have expertise – self-presentation, visiblizing culture, sharing culture, testifying. But it also, in presentation, prevents a total appropriation of the *meanings* of accounts, in that the meanings which respondents give to their experiences are also very much present. Thus, the reflexivity of the respondent and of the researcher are both *present* in the *present*ation, yet neither is a fully centred self outside discourse and separate from each other and the audience. Reflexivity should thus be replaced by the idea of *reflection*, not an internal process but a comparative one by which we look for explanations in the social world (be that in the academy or in other situated cultures) and compare them with our existing discursive repertoires and those of our respondents. This reflection, I would argue, is best undertaken through the lens of the camera where the reflection of selves is more fully present than in the text.

A final point concerns the 'consumption' of video texts by academic (and other) audiences. Far from 'the camera never lying', I would suggest that in an intensely media-literate age it is viewed with a healthy degree of scepticism, creating a critical distance between the text and the viewer. The visual text is rarely held up as 'truth' in the way that academic text so often is. At the very least visual texts produce a surprising array of interpretations. Thus, the camera lens, far from accurately 'reflecting' the social world it seeks to document, actually *refracts* it (as light through a prism), through the processes of selection (of the object to be filmed), editing (of the material to be presented), and the production of multiple 'reading positions'. The active creation of the text by the audience reflects as much about its differentiated and situated reading locations as it does about the author's.

To summarize then, I have argued that the idea of reflexivity is flawed in that it relies on the assumption of a stable and bounded sense of self. I suggest that this notion should be replaced by the concept of 'reflection' where external ideas and discourses come to shape self-understandings. Furthermore, this practice is not confined to (a privileged minority of) researchers but is something in which all subjects engage, although those who inhabit 'discourse rich' positions may be equipped with a greater range of explanations on which to draw than those who are 'discourse poor'. I have also shown how the 'problem' of appropriation can be reconceptualized as 'extension' (by rejecting a reification of the bounded and centred academic self), where all selves are, in effect, accumulative and 'shared'. Finally, I have employed the notion of 'refraction' facilitated by the camera lens to illustrate the multiple interpretative positions available to the audience for video-based research, thereby diminishing the centrality of the academic researcher in the production of social 'realities'.

References

Ahmed, Sara (2000) *Strange Encounters: Embodied Others in Post-Coloniality*, London: Routledge.

Barnes, D., Taylor-Brown, S. and Weiner, L. (1997) '"I didn't leave y'all on purpose": HIV-infected mothers' videotaped legacies for their children', in S.J. Gold (ed.) 'Visual methods in Sociological Analysis', special issue of *Qualitative Sociology* 20(1): 7–32.

Bell, Diane (1993) 'The context', in Diane Bell, Pat Caplan and Wazir Jahan Karim (eds) *Gendered Fields: Women, Men and Ethnography*, London: Routledge.

Bell, Diane and Nelson, Topsy (1989) 'Speaking about rape is everybody's business', *Women's Studies International Forum* 12(4): 403–47.

Brett, Simon (ed.) (1987) *The Faber Book of Diaries*, London: Faber and Faber.

Dinsmore, Sue (1996) 'Strategies for self-scrutiny: *video diaries 1990–1993*', in Colin McCabe and Duncan Petrie (eds) *New Scholarship From BFI Research*, London: BFI.

Douglas, Mary and Isherwood, Baron (1980) *The World of Goods: Towards an Anthropology of Consumption*, London: Routledge and Kegan Paul.

Dyer, Richard (1993) *The Matter of Images: Essays on Representation*, London: Routledge.

Felman, Shoshana (1992) 'The return of the voice: Claude Lanzmann's *Shoah*', in Shoshana Felman and Dori Laub (eds) *Testimony: Crises of Witnessing in Literature, Psychoanalysis and History*, New York: Routledge.

Foucault, Michel (1979) *The History of Sexuality*, vol. 1, Harmondsworth: Penguin.

Freud, Sigmund (1914) 'On narcissism: an introduction', in J. Strachey (ed. and trans.) *Standard Edition of the Complete Psychological Works of Sigmund Freud*, vol. 14, London: Hogarth Press.

Gamson, Joshua (1998) *Freaks Talk Back: Tabloid Talk Shows and Sexual Non-conformity*, Chicago: University of Chicago Press.

Hall, Stuart (1980) 'Encoding/decoding', in Stuart Hall, Dorothy Hobson, Andrew Lowe and Paul Willis (eds) *Culture, Media, Language*, London: Hutchinson.

Haraway, Donna (1996) 'Situated knowledges: the science question in feminism and the privilege of partial perspective', in Evelyn Fox Keller and Helen E. Longino, *Feminism and Science*, Oxford: Oxford University Press.

Harding, Sandra (1986) *From the Woman Question to the Science Question*, Milton Keynes: Open University Press.

Holliday, Ruth (1999) 'The comfort of identity', *Sexualities* 2(4): 475–91.

James, David E. (1996) 'Lynn Hershman: the subject of autobiography', in Michael Renov and Erika Suderburg (eds) *Resolutions: Contemporary Video Practices*, Minneapolis: University of Minnesota Press.

Knowles, Caroline (with photographs by Ludovic Dabert) (2000) *Bedlam on the Streets*, London: Routledge.

May, Tim (1998) 'Reflexivity in the age of reconstructive social science', *International Journal of Social Research Methodology: Theory and Practice* 1(1): 39–54.

Munro, Roland (1996) 'The consumption view of self', in Stephen Edgell, Kevin Hetherington and Alan Warde (eds) *Consumption Matters*, Oxford: Blackwell.

Pink, Sarah (2001) 'More visualising, more methodologies: on video, reflexivity and qualitative research', *Sociological Review* 49(4): 586–99.

Probyn, Elspeth (1993) *Sexing the Self*, London: Routledge.

Renov, Michael (1996) 'Video confessions', in Michael Renov and Erika Suderburg (eds) *Resolutions: Contemporary Video Practices*, Minneapolis: University of Minnesota Press.

Shildrick, Margrit (1997) *Leaky Bodies and Boundaries: Feminism Postmodernism and (Bio)Ethics*, London: Routledge.

Skeggs, Beverley (1997) *Formations of Class and Gender: Becoming Respectable*, London: Sage.

—— (2002) 'Techniques for telling the reflexive self', in Tim May, *Qualitative Research in Action*, London: Sage.

Spivak, Gayatri Chakravorty (1988) 'Can the subaltern speak?', in P. Williams and L. Chrisman (eds) (1993) *Colonial Discourse and Post-Colonial Theory*, Hemel Hempstead: Harvester Wheatsheaf.

Chapter 3

Sue Heath and Elizabeth Cleaver[1]

MAPPING THE SPATIAL IN SHARED HOUSEHOLD LIFE
A missed opportunity?

Picture this: two vignettes

The nurses, July 1998

AS WE ENTER THE NURSES' HOUSE – a large, run-down Victorian semi – we hear laughter and chatter coming from the living room. Six women in their early twenties are arranged expectantly around the room, two on beanbags, the remainder on an assortment of ageing settees and easy chairs: some supplied by the landlord, some hand-me-downs from parents. Seating ourselves on the floor – the only remaining space in a relatively small room – we are made to feel immediately welcome; we are plied with tea and invited to share with them a plate of doughnuts bought in our honour: 'We don't have visitors very often.'

Most of the housemates' spare time is spent in this room, and its décor reflects their efforts to create a homely atmosphere: a pair of curtains have been tie-dyed by Matty to match the newish blue carpet; the walls painted orange by Jane's boyfriend; the lightshade spray-painted purple and blue. In the corner, housing one of three TVs in the room in varying states of (dis)repair, we spy an oversized hostess trolley, and learn that it is appreciated rather more for its retro qualities than its questionable aesthetic appeal, but it nonetheless remains covered with a throw. It cost Matty and Lou fifty pence from the dump, 'a real bargain'. Likewise the VCR: a tenner between the six of them.

The more personalized touches make the deepest impression. On the wall above one of the settees is a collage of photographs from the housemates' recent holiday to Turkey. One of these snaps, showing all six of them together, has been framed and placed on a window ledge. A selection of holiday postcards graces the adjacent wall, fairy lights are strung around one of two windows in the room, and a poster of the singer Gary Barlow is pinned to the kitchen door. On the back of the living room door is a 'World Cup '98' wall chart, now just out of date. We are told that a poster of the camp TV presenter Dale Winton – drily described as 'the only classy bit of thing on our walls' – has recently been evicted from the lounge: 'Dale went, as did the blue walls'. Shelving on either side of the fireplace contains cookery books, rarely opened bottles of liqueurs brought back from overseas trips, a selection of glasses, and various videotapes, including an aerobics tape and popular British-made movies such as *Shallow Grave*, *Brassed Off* and *Trainspotting*.

The *pièce de résistance* is located on the mantelpiece over the fireplace: 'the tacky present shelf', a kitsch shrine to the 'tackiest, most disgusting souvenirs', recently augmented by a contribution each from the holiday to Turkey: 'we weren't allowed to show each other what tacky presents we'd bought till we got home'. Their friends have even started to contribute to the collection: 'everyone else jumped on the bandwagon, so anyone that goes away, we get lumbered with another'. Looking at the collection – Russian dolls, seashells adapted to perform various 'useful' functions, a fan-shaped letter holder, dolls in national dress – we can't help thinking that they don't really mind being 'lumbered' in this way. Not one bit.

Harriet and Andrew, November 1998

Harriet and Andrew greet us at the door with a polite handshake apiece. We accept Harriet's kind offer of a cup of tea, but find ourselves drinking alone: Harriet doesn't make one for herself, and the offer had clearly not been extended to Andrew. We had expected up to two other housemates to be present, but they have sent their apologies.

We are shown into an immaculately tidy living room: not difficult in its attainment, as it is virtually empty, except for two 1980s-style settees, a TV on a wooden chest, and a glass coffee table – with nothing on it – in the middle of the room. Shelving on one wall contains a handful of abandoned books and magazines. On the cream-painted walls are a number of framed prints: a Lowry, a Manet and a couple of rather bland paintings of the seaside, the sort one might expect to find in a dentist's waiting room, or a 'syndicate room' in a corporate hotel.

Andrew and Harriet perch on either end of the three-seater settee, Liz and I on the adjacent two-seater. 'Everything in here belongs to the house. Well, to the landlord, obviously,' Andrew explains. 'Nothing in the room at all is mine. Nothing.' 'Would you be allowed to put things up?' we ask. 'Oh yeah, I'm sure that will be fine. It's fine as it is, so . . .'. Anyway, they so rarely use this room, 'unless Ally McBeal's on, then everyone's in here'. Generally, his routine is to get up, go to work, come home, eat, ring friends, go to the pub, sleep: 'That's my sad existence.' And Harriet? 'The same really.'

As we drive away, we compare this interview with the ten that have gone before. There have been a lot of laughs in nearly all of these other households, but very few here. Liz puts her finger on it: 'They don't *know* each other.'

Exploring shared living in the 1990s

Unlike the other contributors to this book, we have relied on our fieldnotes and interview transcripts to generate our initial images, in this case images of domestic spaces within young people's shared households.[2] Our project did not anticipate the incorporation of photographic imagery in its original research design, yet part way through our fieldwork we decided to experiment with respondent-produced photographs. Given the small scale of this experiment – involving only two of the twenty-five households included in our research – we decided against using these images as a key source of data in our analysis. Nonetheless, we have learned some important lessons from this process about the limits of our text-based data, and the potential usefulness of photographic images in future research projects in this area.

Set against the broader backdrop of rapidly changing patterns of household formation among younger generations, our research sought to explore the experiences of 18- to 35-year-old non-students living in shared households. Following an initial exploration of the characteristics of sharers and their households at the national level using individual-level census data, the main strands of the project explored the routine operation of everyday life in shared households, and the routes by which sharers move into such accommodation. Consequently, we conducted semi-structured group-interviews with twenty-five shared households based in a southern English city. These interviews involved seventy-seven residents, and covered topics such as the organization of household space and time, divisions of labour, negotiations of privacy and intimacy, social interaction and mutual support, and processes of household formation, evolution and disintegration. We then conducted individual biographical interviews with sixty-three of these household members, allowing them to narrate their full housing histories on their own terms.

Our original research design included a visual element, as we had decided to appeal to our respondents' media literacy by structuring the household interviews around a series of video clips of representations of shared household living taken from the popular television shows *Friends* and *This Life* and the film *Shallow Grave*. Each section of the household interview was introduced with an appropriate clip, serving both as a useful ice-breaker and as an additional stimulus to discussion. We were amused and intrigued to note that many households had copies of these shows lined up on bookcases and video cabinets. Moreover, on several occasions the clips were greeted with obvious recognition, and punchlines anticipated with perfect timing and intonation. Indeed, as noted above, the watching of favourite TV shows was a popular ritual even in the least sociable of households, with *Friends* emerging as a strong contender for the title of overall favourite.

Most of our fieldwork was, however, characterized by a relatively straightforward interview-based research design. We had nonetheless anticipated that certain material and spatial aspects of home life might emerge as significant to shared living experiences. This anticipation, in part, stemmed from our knowledge of literature on 'the meaning of home'. In the last twenty-five years, 'house' and 'home' in western society have received a great deal of academic attention from a number of complementary disciplines. The importance of the architecture and aesthetic appeal of the buildings that comprise our homes, and the meaning and significance of the artefacts with which we personalize our domestic space, have been well documented and will not be repeated at length here (Desprès (1991) and Somerville (1997) provide two comprehensive literature reviews on this subject). However, it is worth reiterating that these aspects of home (among others) have been found to be a source, as well as an expression, of our identities and social and cultural values and tastes. As Brindley (1999: 39) states:

> The house, viewed from a sociological point of view, can be interpreted in terms of Western material culture where its fabric and the artefacts and objects it contains act as both material supports for a particular way of life and as symbols of social relations and social values.

In addition, the social groupings that form households, and the emotional and practical support that household members provide for one another, are fundamental to many individuals' sense of homeliness. Such social relationships are often reflected in, and supported by, the more physical and material aspects of home. Photographs of family and friendship groups, joint household purchases and shared decorating decisions can be viewed as evidence that 'home' is not simply a building or a collection of material objects, but also has a social dimension (Kenyon 1999; Sixsmith 1986).

Sure enough, and as our vignettes suggest, we found that various spatial and material aspects of shared living were closely intertwined with, and reflective of, the presence or absence of emotional closeness and social cohesion in shared households. In other words, emotional closeness or distance tended to have a spatial and material manifestation. We had decided from the outset that we would aim to produce diagrams and notes reflecting the layout and content of each of the household spaces in which we conducted group interviews – usually a shared lounge – so that we would subsequently be able to generate 'thick description' of these rooms. This we did throughout the project, taking notes while housemates completed two short questionnaires, and then pooling our observations afterwards. With hindsight, we should perhaps have considered asking permission to take photographs of these shared spaces, although, as we shall discuss later, this might have been greeted with some suspicion and might not have been regarded as a legitimate request.

Nonetheless, for each household we produced a rough sketch plan of the physical layout of the living spaces, and took notes on the finer points of décor: colour schemes; titles of videos, books and magazines lying around; details of prints, posters and photographs; the presence of board games; the contents of the alcohol shelf (see examples in Figure 1). In addition, we asked the household members to comment on the content and layout of their shared spaces during the group interview as part of a broader discussion of the use of shared and personal space. We asked about the ownership of particular objects within the shared space, whose tastes were reflected in the choice of décor, and how these objects and spaces were used at different points in time. These discussions were usually lively and illuminating. Each of our interview transcripts therefore provides us with a further reminder of the physical appearance of these rooms, as well as the practices of everyday life that underpin their use.

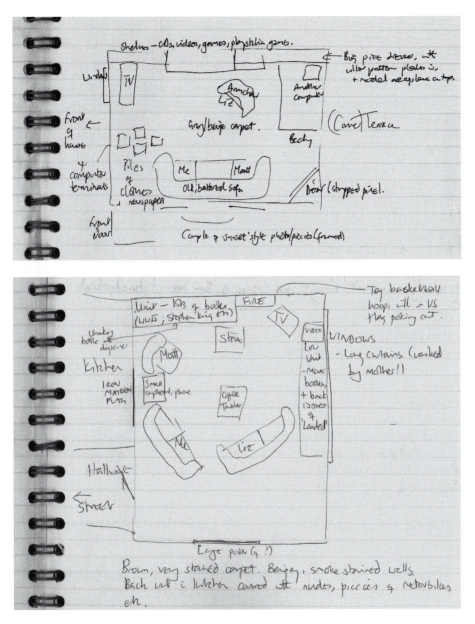

Figure 1 Sketches of shared living space.

After a few months of fieldwork, we toyed with the idea of providing a small number of households with disposable cameras so that they could provide us with their own visual account of the routine operation of shared living. From the evidence of framed photographs in several households, household events were a familiar subject for housemates' photographic endeavours, so we felt that this would be a readily accepted format. Our decision to use cameras was further influenced by our recognition of the prioritization of the visual over other human senses and the importance of the visual in contemporary culture (see Knowles and Sweetman, this volume). The recognition that people read messages from tangible aspects of our domestic lives – housing types, their external decorative order, the artefacts on display through windows and in gardens, the people who live there and the lifestyles they display and support (Kenyon 1997, 1998) – is key here. It is these tangible aspects of 'home' which are appropriated and adapted to create 'the public face' of the household that lives within (Munro and Leather 2000) and which, in turn, help to frame and support individuals' senses of identity and social and cultural status (Kenyon 2002). However, it is necessary to heed Hart's (1994) warning of the danger of assuming that individuals have complete autonomy over their homes and the concomitant identities and statuses they project; in reality such empowerment can be contingent upon economic and/or social status, the tenure of the property and its physical state prior to occupation. Indeed, this is reflected in the contrasting attitudes towards shared space revealed by our two opening vignettes.

Notwithstanding such potential pitfalls, it appeared appropriate and useful to compile some form of visual representation and interpretation of these material and social aspects of home, as we anticipated that they would bring a new (and perhaps more detailed) dimension to the 'word pictures' we were already able to produce through our sketches, notes and interview data. How, then, to do this? We decided to give a disposable camera to each member of four households, chosen to represent contrasting household composition. Instructions were handed over with each camera and read as follows:

> Using as many of the photos on the camera as you wish, we would like you to make a visual record of what to you are the significant and meaningful aspects of living in a shared house and a shared household. Your photos may be related to any or none of the topics we have previously discussed with you. It's your camera and your record. If you don't use all of the shots on the film that's fine – just rewind when you've taken the photos you require.

In the event, we only received back photographs from an amalgam of members of two of these households, amounting to only two twenty-four-exposure films. Both were households where the housemates all got on well together. One consisted of four graduate chemical engineers who had all met at university and, a year after graduating, were now all working for the same multinational company. The other consisted of James, a resident owner in his early thirties, and his three current tenants, one man and two women, ranging in age from their early twenties to their mid-thirties, and with periods of tenancy ranging from a couple of months up to six years.

Given the limited response, we felt that it would be difficult to justify a *post hoc* decision to use our finite resources on a method which in its piloting had proved to be only partly effective. As a consequence, we ended up sidelining this aspect of the research, concentrating our efforts on the elements that we had originally been funded to undertake. However, for the purposes of this book we have revisited these photographs in order to assess their value and usefulness within our broader research aims, focusing in particular on the extent to which the use of photographs across the project might have enhanced the 'word pictures' we were already able to produce through our sketches, notes and interview data. The initial focus of our discussion is very much on their potential use as a source of data *for our own analysis*, rather than on the use we might make of them in the public sphere. This is a crucial distinction, and a point we address in our conclusions.

Just a bunch of snaps?

It is fair to say that we had always viewed our decision to distribute disposable cameras as an interesting experiment rather than as an integral part of the overall project. Prior to the experiment we were not particularly conversant with the literature on using photographs in social research or with the results we could expect, or with what we might do with any photographs thus generated. While this was not our primary aim in handing out the cameras, we had nonetheless hoped that we might receive some photographs of the shared spaces in both households. In particular, we were keen to see whether respondents' own photographs would in any way enhance our fieldnotes and interview data, or even render them redundant. However, as we did not wish to place constraints on their choice of photograph, we had not explicitly requested such images and, in the event, each household produced just three images of its living room.

The living room images produced by the chemical engineers consist of a photograph of one housemate sitting in an armchair in his collar and tie, seemingly fast asleep; another, featuring the same person, this time lying (asleep?) on the settee in shorts and a football shirt with an empty wine glass and the remains of his dinner on the floor next to him, a children's table football game clearly visible in the corner of the room under a shelving unit groaning with bottles of alcohol; and a third photograph showing two housemates and four friends lying on the floor playing *Trivial Pursuit*. James's living room photographs show, first, a housemate sitting on the arm of an easy chair drinking a glass of wine; second, James's non-resident boyfriend sitting on the living room floor talking to one of James's housemates and his non-resident girlfriend (who appear to be sharing a bottle of wine); and third, James and his boyfriend sitting on the settee with cushions perched on their heads ('comic moment' is written on the back of this photograph).

In terms of the layout and content of these living rooms, it is gratifying to record that our sketches and notes correspond with the photographic images. In the case of the living room in James's household, for example, our notes read as follows:

> Red patterned carpet, 'Aztec'-style curtains, yellow walls, art deco up-
> lighters and chandelier, '30s-style tiled fireplace, 3 piece suite (reddish

velour), freestanding CD racks (lots!), hifi, TV & video, corner unit. Lots of knick-knacks around – 'Constable'-type paintings on 3 walls, lots of cards on mantelpiece/unit, B&W picture of Margaret Rutherford on telly, pottery reclining figure on speaker; lots of 'objets d'art' around the place – 2 blow-up figures on mantelpiece (one busty woman, one hairy-chested man!). Lots of art deco lamps.

We had later scribbled down the following comment: 'Felt like a Wallace and Gromett setting!' – which, we believe, was indeed more or less the desired effect! Our fieldnotes miss out surprisingly little by way of detail; indeed, as the photographs do not provide a 360-degree image of the room, our notes actually provide a *fuller* picture. And what do the photographs reveal about the use of this shared space? Again, nothing that we had not been told about in the interview. We had previously been told that the living room, while largely reflecting James's tastes, was freely used by all the housemates and their respective partners and friends as a place to unwind at the end of the day – not so much to watch television, but to sit and chat over a drink or two. Sure enough, this is reflected in each of the three photographs, with individuals in various states of relaxation, and with wine glasses, beer bottles, coffee mugs or drinks cans clearly visible in each.

These particular photographs certainly *underscore* the atmosphere in these two households which we had already picked up on from our own observations and from talking to household members as a group and as individuals. However, in terms of our own analysis they do not add very much to our word pictures or to our prior understanding of the relationship between emotional cohesion and support among household members and the use of household space and artefacts to frame and reflect this. That is certainly *not* to argue that such photographs are incapable of doing these things, just that *in these instances* they merely confirmed what we already knew. It is of course highly likely that, in the absence of any more clearly defined instructions as to what they should photograph, our households decided to record the sorts of events that we had earlier explored with them in interview, on the assumption that this would be what we were 'after'. In other words, they provided us with 'the film of the book'. Moreover, we are also aware that the limited analytical value of these particular photographs may have resulted from our initial subversion of the 'photo-elicitation interview' (Harper 1994: 410): we came to our analysis of the photographs of the living spaces in which we conducted our interviews and the activities that housemates shared within these settings with a certain amount of existing knowledge and first-hand observational data.

Photographs of shared spaces aside, the majority of the images we received were potentially rather more useful, and with hindsight we realize that production of these broader images across our twenty-five households would have been very useful. The remaining photographs tended to fall into one of three categories. First, many consisted of illustrations of the type of extra-household activities in which household members regularly engaged as a group or as sub-groups. These photographs variously portray a trip to a funfair and a day out at the seaside, housemates jogging in the park and playing golf, an evening outing to see one of the housemates perform in a local amateur operatic production, helping to move the set for this production in a van belonging to another housemate's employer, and the hosting by the four engineers at their employer's social club of a quiz night for new arrivals to the graduate training scheme. Once again, there were few surprises here, as most of these events had been discussed in earlier interviews. Nonetheless, they provided a useful confirmation and illustration of these events, and also showed the housemates *as a household* relating to broader groupings of friends and colleagues outside the private space of the home (a point which relates to our argument that shared household living produces an inner and an outer circle of friendship, and that many shared households have a very distinct collective identity which extends beyond the confines of the home).

Second, many of the photographs provided us with insights into other aspects of shared living as played out in the domestic space: food being prepared; meals being shared in the two households' respective dining rooms; washing up; a shared household takeaway arriving in a large cardboard box; the writing of a shopping list; putting out the rubbish; preparations for and, later, guests at a flamboyant fancy dress party on a theme of 'Space 1999'; a housemate sitting on the landing making a telephone call; another mowing the lawn (included, we were told, for the novelty value of the chore!). Again, these are activities of which we had some prior knowledge, but the added value lies in the provision of a window onto parts of the households' living spaces that we had only otherwise glimpsed in passing – kitchens, dining rooms and gardens. In many cases, we have interview data on the use of these spaces, but this is not generally backed up with a visual image of the space in question. It has therefore been interesting for us to reflect on the relationship between the text and the image in revisiting these photographs.

Third, both households produced several rather more abstract photographs (see Plates 1–4): close-ups of various artefacts and household spaces, devoid of housemates. These images are imaginative in composition and particularly thought-provoking, not least because some of them provide glimpses of more private spaces: bedrooms and bathrooms, and the interiors of cupboards, usually off-limits to anyone other than partners, close friends and other household members. These photographs include images of a cupboard containing several identical packets of breakfast cereal; eleven shirts hanging out to dry on the washing line; foam rubber lettering stuck on a bathroom mirror, spelling out 'dirty 'ole prancer'; a room in the early stages of being decorated; another row of shirts hanging up in a bedroom; an untidy bedroom directly off the living room in the engineers' house; a cork noticeboard covered with takeaway menus and bus and ferry timetables alongside a 'girlie' calendar from the magazine *FHM*; a sign in the back garden advertising a firework display – apparently stolen from the local park. In many ways, these are some of the more revealing photographs produced by the households, as they hint at important aspects of shared living that were not always discussed in either group or individual interviews. These, too, are much more 'off-script' than some of the other photographs, and perhaps hint at the sort of images we might have received if we had distributed cameras *before* we interviewed sharers.

With hindsight, we are aware that access to these more 'private' images was facilitated by our request that the respondents *themselves* took photos of their homes, and it would have been very difficult, if not impossible, for an outsider to gain permission to take most of these shots. Allan (1989) has highlighted the key indicators of the continuing 'outsider' status of strangers in the domestic space: for

Plate 1 'We do a lot of washing, and in the winter it's hard to dry it, so this place looks like a Chinese laundry a lot of the time.'

Plate 2 'This is the three boxes of cereals for the price of two bargain. Pete's the king of bargain shoppers! He'll scour the shelves of Tesco and come home with things we don't need, just because they're bargains.'

Plate 3 'This is a calendar from *FHM* magazine, which is by the telephone! Moving on, the other interesting thing is that we've got all the take-away menus up on the board! We've also got a Red Funnel ferry timetable, and bus time-table and train timetable and phone numbers, taxi numbers, all our mates' phone numbers.'

Plate 4 'This goes back a long time – Carole bought some children's letters for some-one's Christmas present, I think. It actually started as 'dirty pole dancer', then it turned, ended up as 'dirty 'ole prancer', and we just spend our time in the bath rearrang-ing the letters and doing a bit of anagram stuff, so it's just a way of leaving messages for each other.'

example, the offering of food or drink, the arranging of times of arrival and the public presentation of the tidy and harmonious home setting in 'reception' rooms. This notion of the stranger being 'out of place' within privatized home environments is of key relevance to researchers who enter respondents' homes. Researchers who do not wish to view a house from the stranger's perspective, but wish to tour or to photograph the 'private' spaces of respondents' homes, are therefore clearly stepping over a culturally created boundary (although two households did in fact give us a tour of the entire house). As Harper (1994: 406) states, 'because the camera intrudes and reveals, it must be used with the wants, needs and cultural perspectives of the subjects at the forefront of one's consciousness'. Our decision to let respondents control the images they presented through their photographs therefore overcame much of this dilemma, and produced some interesting results because of, rather than despite, the editing decisions that were taken by their producers, providing them with the opportunity to highlight the significance of items, people and events that might have escaped our attention.

Furthermore, while we had our own interpretations of the likely significance of the photographs, we nonetheless felt that it was important that we also solicited the housemates' interpretations in a form of photo-elicitation interview (Harper 1994: 410). Accordingly, we returned to each of the households and asked them to talk us through their photographs, inviting them to describe each image and to explain why it was of particular significance to them. This proved to be a useful exercise for clarifying the exact nature of some of the events that had been photographed, and it also served to challenge some of our assumptions. For example, the photograph of the multiple packets of breakfast cereal seemed to imply that housemates each had their own supply, suggestive of a high degree of individualized living within the household. However, the image was described thus: 'This is the "three boxes of cereal for the price of two" bargain. Pete's the king of bargain shoppers! He'll scour the shelves of Tesco and come back with things we don't need, just because they're bargains.' Further, the savings that were thus made were put towards, among other things, the cost of employing a regular cleaner!

Conclusion

The distribution of disposable cameras to households proved to be a useful experiment within our broader research strategy. We had decided to take sketches and notes of room content and layout, as well as to ask housemates to talk about their use of these spaces, to enable us to comment on the linkage between emotional cohesion and support among household members, and the use of household space and artefacts to frame and reflect this. The photographs produced specifically on this theme largely reinforced what we already knew and did not provide us with additional insights of any great substance. This was clearly due to our exploration of these issues and themes in household interviews prior to the cameras being distributed. Nonetheless, the photographs of spaces that we had not otherwise seen were particularly illuminating, as were the photographs of more abstract aspects of shared living. We can certainly see ourselves using respondent-produced photographs in the future to tap into otherwise off-limits themes and images. The beauty of these particular images lies in their spontaneity: we did not ask the housemates to photograph cupboards, noticeboards and shopping lists, and if we had they might have quite reasonably considered this to be an intrusive request.

Our discussion so far has focused exclusively on how we as researchers might have used these photographs as an additional source of data in our own analysis. However, one of the potential strengths of photographic data lies in their ability to allow others to interpret a scene first hand and 'to unlock the subjectivity of those who see the image differently from the researcher' (Harper 2000: 729). In contrast, our word pictures are obviously filtered through our own impressions and interpretations. There would, then, be some value in using the photographs we received as a way of allowing others to 'see' these households. We, after all, have a clear mental picture of these spaces in addition to our notes and interview data: the reader does not, and might find a photograph complements the picture that we can conjure up in words.

The use of photographs of this kind in the public domain would, however, raise an important question in relation to the protection of respondents' anonymity. Within the specific context of our research on shared households, we have been at pains to use pseudonyms when discussing our research, and on occasion have altered some of our respondents' details where we have felt that their anonymity might otherwise be compromised. However, most of the photographs that we were given by the two households included at least one clearly identifiable resident in shot at any one time. To use these photographs in our dissemination clearly invalidates our promise of anonymity. Both households have told us that they are happy for their images to be used, hence the reproduction of some of them in this chapter, but we remain slightly uneasy, given our broader strategies of protecting their anonymity, particularly in the light of warnings regarding the misinterpretation of visual images (Banks 2001: 113; Pink 2001: 95; MacDougall 1997: 276–95). While such issues are not insurmountable, we would nonetheless need to think this issue through with great care in any future research in which we might decide to use respondent-produced photographs.

Notes

1   Previous publications by this author were written under the name Elizabeth Kenyon.
2   The 'Young Adults and Shared Household Living' project was funded by the Economic and Social Research Council between 1998 and 2000 (award R000237033). See Heath and Kenyon (2001) and Kenyon and Heath (2001) for fuller discussions of some of the project's findings. We are indebted to all the young people who took part in the research. Their names have been changed to help protect their anonymity.

References

Allan, G. (1989) 'Insiders and outsiders: boundaries around the home', in G. Allan and G. Crow (1989) (eds) *Home and Family: Creating the Domestic Sphere*, London: Macmillan.
Banks, M. (2001) *Visual Methods in Social Research*, London: Sage.
Brindley, T. (1999) 'The modern house in England', in T. Chapman and J. Hockey (eds) *Ideal Homes? Social Change and Domestic Life*, London: Routledge.

Desprès, C. (1991) 'The meaning of home: literature review and direction for future research and theoretical development', *Journal of Architecture and Planning Research* 8(2): 96–114.

Harper, D. (1994) 'On the authority of the image', in N.K. Denzin and Y.S. Lincoln (eds) *Handbook of Qualitative Research*, London: Sage.

—— (2000) 'Reimagining visual methods: Galileo to Neuromancer', in N.K. Denzin and Y.S. Lincoln (eds) (2nd Edn) *Handbook of Qualitative Research*, London: Sage.

Hart, B. (1994) 'Meanings of a shared space', unpublished paper presented at the *Ideal Homes* Conference, University of Teeside, 6–8 September 1994.

Heath, S. and Kenyon, E. (2001) 'Single young professionals and shared household living', *Journal of Youth Studies* 4(1): 83–101.

Kenyon, E. (1997) 'Seasonal sub-communities: the impact of student households on residential communities', *British Journal of Sociology* 48(2).

—— (1998) 'A community within the community? An empirical exploration of the constitution and formation of "student areas"', unpublished Doctoral Thesis, University of Lancaster.

—— (1999) 'A home from home: students' transitional experience of home', in T. Chapman and J. Hockey (eds) *Ideal Homes? Social Change and Domestic Life*, London: Routledge.

—— (2002) 'Young adults' household formation: individualisation, identity and home', in G. Allan and G. Jones (eds) *Social Relations and the Life Course*, Basingstoke: Palgrave.

Kenyon, E. and Heath, S. (2001) 'Choosing *This Life*: narratives of choice amongst house sharers', *Housing Studies* 16(5): 619–35.

MacDougall, D. (1997) 'The visual in anthropology', in M. Banks and H. Murphy (eds) *Rethinking Visual Anthropology*, New Haven, Conn.: Yale University Press.

Munro, M. and Leather, P. (2000) 'Nest building or investing in the future? Owner-occupiers' home improvement behaviour', *Policy and Politics* 28(4): 511–26.

Pink, S. (2001) *Doing Visual Ethnography*, London: Sage.

Sixsmith, J. (1986) 'The meaning of home: an exploratory study of environmental experiences', *The Journal of Environmental Psychology* 6: 281–98.

Somerville, P. (1997) 'The social construction of home', *Journal of Architectural and Planning Research* 14(3): 226–45.

Chapter 4

Tony Whincup

IMAGING THE INTANGIBLE

Introduction

THE TITLE 'IMAGING THE INTANGIBLE' may appear to be a contradiction in terms as photographs are, for the most part, formed by light reflected from tangible things. The discussion in this chapter will centre on the extent to which concrete objectifications of experience can provide tangible forms for photography to visualize intangible dimensions of human activity.

The chapter is in two parts. The first part discusses the implications of considering the tangible as social construct, while the second explores the special case of the photograph as comprising these social constructs.

The ethnographic material that informs and illustrates the first part of the chapter is taken from a detailed study of object attachment in the site of the New Zealand domestic living room. Photographs in the second part are from ongoing research projects examining the role of ritual practices in contemporary society.

Objects as a social construct

Let us begin at the very beginning with memory, the importance of which it is impossible to overemphasize. Memory is no more than a trace of our experiences, a little-understood pulse across the synapses of the brain, upon which rests the whole constructed edifice of human social life. In this special function of being able to remember, to note consistencies and to recall them, lies the core of our survival, our humanity and our individual identity. As Butler (1989: 2) suggests,

Without memory, life would consist of momentary experiences that have little relation to each other. Without memory we could not communicate with one another – we would be incapable of remembering the thoughts we wished to express.

It is not surprising that the nature of memory is of vital concern to individual and group alike. Memory, a slippery and fragile thing, is constantly open to subtraction and addition. Inevitably, people have searched for strategies through which to restore the memory of those otherwise tenuous and transitory life events and socially agreed values.

The following photographs illustrate objects that have become significant to their owners because of the mnemonic values with which they have become imbued.

Referring to a teddy bear on the mantelpiece in this picture, the owner said, 'I had an old boyfriend and we used to have this thing about bears . . . together. We used to talk as mother bear and father bear; and he was like a panda bear, soft, lovely person.' The value of the bear is now directly related to the value of the memories to which it holds access.

Brent, the owner of this room and an aspiring 'rock' guitarist, admits 'I don't like the troll itself, but [I keep it] because it's a present from her and it's playing a guitar.' In the dilemma between 'taste' and the power of a gift's associations, the associations win. Close to the troll is a painting given to him by his young daughter. In the cupboard beside Brent's desk is an empty magnum of champagne, from his twenty-first birthday. The whole area around his desk is associated with memories of significant relationships.

In the struggle to maintain memories by charging objects with their safekeeping, the relationship between the owner and the object changes. Objects that are associated, even tenuously, at the time of the initial experience, can achieve immense importance. The personal mnemonic object becomes as priceless and unique as the memory to which it holds the key. There arises a levelling through 'pricelessness', whatever the original monetary value of the object. Driftwood, shells, a cheap teddy bear and so forth assume parity with gold wedding rings and antique clocks. In fact, monetarily valueless mnemonics displace goods such as expensive stereos and TVs in the hierarchy of personal possessions. No other 'teddy' will do, but any television set will provide the desired functional response. Similarly, a gift cannot be replaced by another similar object, as it would no longer be *the* carrier of the sentiments expressed by the original object. Witness the removal of plates and cups to a glass display cabinet, which not only protects the physical aspect of the objects but also denies their original functionality. Their meaning now depends upon the constructs which are brought to them.

By denying their original functionality and refusing to attribute any monetary value to them, objects are established as unchanging vehicles for memory. Although they remain inscrutable to the outsider, they are vital to the individual owner in the process of self-recognition. In reflecting important selected experiences, objects remind us of who we are and of our differences from and associations with others. As a group, mnemonic objects generally encapsulate the best of people's reflections about themselves. It is in these object attachments that a personal and 'advantageous' sense of self can be sustained. Objects as mnemonics are a complex business intertwined with edited past experiences, current constructions and orientations towards future aspirations. The direct relationship between object and memories of experience helps in understanding many aspects of the hierarchy of attachment to possessions.

Let us now shift our attention to the role played by groups of objects in revealing consistencies of experience. I suggest that an awareness of self is arrived at, retrospectively, by witnessing consistent patterns revealed and maintained in the concrete expressions of our experiences. Dilthey made a similar point when he wrote, 'Thus we learn to comprehend the mind-constructed world as a system of interactions or as an inter-relationship contained in its enduring creations' (in Rickman 1976: 196). In becoming attached to objects, people consciously or unconsciously, inevitably and unavoidably, map out their orientation towards their existence.

Individuals and groups appear to consistently work towards establishing personally coherent and satisfying combinations of objects, with the emphasis upon a particular sense of unity. Each object grouping is in some way personal and unique, and yet each is also a product of particular social influences of time and place. The recognition of consistencies to perceive existence is fundamental to this discussion. The clarity, vigilance and process by which consistencies of coherent groupings are arrived at and maintained will be seen to vary with individuals and groups. In this way a sense of a particular 'selfness' may be achieved. Dilthey (in Rickman 1976) suggests that understanding comes not from the straightforward route of gazing inwards upon ourselves but through the longer, more circuitous route of witnessing both our personal expressions and those of others. They provide a concrete manner

puts it, 'There are no "people" in the abstract, people are what they attend to, what they cherish and use' (1981: 16).

Although the meanings of objects are constituted by our actions towards them, objects also constitute the types of actions and experiences with which we become involved. Every aspect of our inevitable involvement in symbolic systems shapes the shaper. 'Each new object changes the way people organize and experience their lives' (Csikszentmihalyi and Rochberg-Halton 1981: 46)

Objects are vitally involved in both the experiences that are open to us and the way in which those experiences are expressed. A change in objective conditions and/or the socially attributed symbolism of these objects would immediately change the very nature of an individual or group. I can only conclude that the interdependence of subject and object is total – the constructor constructs but, equally, is constructed by the constructions.

> The relationship is clearly dialogical and dialectical, for experiences structure expressions, in that we understand other people and their expressions on the basis of our own experience and self understanding. But expression also structures experience.
>
> (Turner and Bruner 1986: 6)

From this close resonance of subject and object relationship, consistencies of expressions of experience are established and, in their dialectic interaction, produce a spiralling development. This dynamic interrelationship orientates a particular selection and organization of object attachments. Once started, it is logical that this interaction of a person and their object attachments will forever continue to influence their experiences and expressions.

Let us use an I-Kiribati navigator of Micronesia as an example. The navigator traces his position upon the apparently implacable vastness of the Pacific Ocean by observing often minute changes. A piece of driftwood, birds at sunset, a cloud with a turquoise underside lit by the reflection of a far-off lagoon, or the subtle feel of a cross swell reflected back from an atoll, will provide him not only with 'objects' of difference, but also signs to position the next low-lying atoll. I emphasize that recognizing difference does nothing more than signify change. What the new social or geographical space 'means' remains inscrutable, ambiguous and open to fictional constructions.

The navigator has learnt not only to see keenly, but to interpret what he sees appropriately for his context. The environment in which he operates changes only slowly and the 'maps' of the territory he uses have been gradually refined and handed down over the centuries. From generations past, our navigator has come to see his ocean through a particular set of interpretative patterns that have great value for him. As Dilthey observed, 'The world-views which further the understanding of life and lead to useful goals survive and replace lesser ones. A selection takes place between them. In the sequence of generations the world-views which are viable are constantly perfected' (in Rickman 1976: 139). The navigator's society has identified and taught him to see consistencies that combine to afford an interpretation of value. It is not hard to imagine that his ocean is very different from ours. Our experiences may be the same as his, the rise and fall of the canoe, the breeze on the cheek and so on, but we may be at a loss to interpret them so as to find the next atoll. We may not even know that we are experiencing something of value for the context.

These objects, in the context of the ocean, act as signs and are seen for their particular significations. In fact, their reality may exist only in their associated meaning as signs. The navigator is possibly not aware that his interpretation is a construction and that in fact other equally valid constructions of the same object may be made in other contexts. The reality of an object can be perceived as both the territory of initial experiences and as symbolic maps of those experiences. It would appear that objects are a part of a socially generated symbolic system within a particular context.

The object as a symbol serves not simply as a personal mnemonic, in a relationship from its particularity in the present to generalities of the past, but also as an agent of cultural construction. Objects within a social context have specific meanings for those with eyes to see them and a background to understand their relevant implications. The sociological construction is not static, however. It was born of experience and is reattended as a further experience in its own right. The symbol exemplifies both the past and the present. It is not a passive receptacle for attention. By its very existence, it exerts an influence upon further thoughts, memories and experiences. In the process, objects as symbols become a vital element in cultural construction and transmission. People cannot be a part of this structure without knowing how to read these objects. Conversely, the inability to recognize the value of these constructions places people in other social spaces. The logical development of this argument leads to the conclusion, which is the premise of most modern concepts of anthropology, that 'society' is a symbolic system.

Harker and McConnochie argue that, 'When we speak of a culture, then, we want to use the term to refer to the symbolic system which incorporates the rules that govern how an individual interprets his or her environment' (1985: 22). The differences in symbolic attributions provide boundaries of identification for differing cultures or units within a culture. The adoption and agreement upon a particular set of symbolic constructions leads to a unique view of reality and expression of values.

In much the same way as experiences of the ocean have gradually given rise to a system of interpretative patterns that enable the I-Kiribati to navigate from one diminutive coral atoll to another, so, too, have other societies formulated symbolic systems of interpretation to 'navigate' their social context. It is logical to believe that the more defined and unified the symbolic system, the more stable and cohesive will be the society or group, and even an individual's sense of self. A clearly defined symbolic system is likely to make the society or boundary of the territory clearly visible to approaching 'strangers', and 'strangers' clearly visible to those within.

What we see in the living room photographs is an expression of each experience of life through a particular symbolic cultural patterning. The personally structured coherence manifested through object attachments reflects three constituent parts of social expression. The first is the socializing agents of individual histories – the particular hegemony within which the existence is being enacted. As Bourdieu suggests, 'Between the child and the world the whole group intervenes . . . with the whole universe of ritual practices and also of discourses, sayings, proverbs'

(1977: 167). The second comprises objective conditions which include the physical nature of the environment and the products available. The third is the amount of individual choice that can be comprehended or attained. I propose that the vectors of objective conditions, social orientation and individual determination comprise the parameters within which coherent selections are developed and maintained.

Anything other than initial experiences must rely upon symbolic systems for their encapsulation, reflection and communication. It is the practice of symbolic systems, used in the expression of experiences, that demonstrates the unique relation of social context and the mediating properties of the individual. Every reflection and expression of experience is an interaction of a particular symbolic system, of the social group and the individual. Whatever the social context, object attachments are an expression of experiences in direct relation to it.

A sense of 'self', its protection and positioning, has perhaps never in history been such an individual and personal responsibility. 'In contemporary, particularly contemporary Western culture, individual identity is paramount so that the physiological concepts of self-identity and self-esteem are seen as linked and as a focal point in social, personality, developmental and clinical psychology' (Rapoport 1981: 11).

Object attachment is heavily implicated in the self-conscious projection, protection and reflection of 'self' in current consumer-orientated societies. On the one hand, objects are consciously associated with difference and implicated as vehicles for change and on the other hand are also charged with protecting memories in the attempt to provide a sense of continuity as stable social 'texts'.

It is not fanciful to consider that, as my objects have a reality through me, I am the voice of my objects. As I constitute my objects, so, too, do they constitute me. If these objects are considered to arise in part from the historical relationship of all other people and things, then I am as much a product of the world's history as it is of me. This returns me to the argument that although there exist internal and external forces, expressed in agency and structure, they are parts of a dynamic and interactive whole rather than separate entities. It can be argued that social relationships with objects are not so much dialogical as a form of holistic unity which is not always easily accommodated within contemporary western thought. 'Things' are then an essential part of social existence and images of 'things' become texts of symbolic significance.

The challenge for those who wish to use photography in sociological research is to transcend the readily available surface descriptions of the photographic image and, through the construction of compelling symbolic relationships, assert powerful readings of the intangible aspects of lived experience. To fully utilize the potential of photographs, a considered strategy for exploration, selection and communication needs to be established.

Photographic practice and the photographic image

The problem that faces the photo-ethnographer is to create a disciplined approach which does not filter out the experiential, intuitive and unavoidably interpretative but which, in fact seizes upon and validates the very excitement and depth of lived experience.

In practice, ethnographic understanding proceeds from a tentative assessment of context by reference to its constitutive parts. This in turn redefines the context and furthers understanding of the particular, gradually spiralling out towards the limits of interpretation. The principles of hermeneutics offer a framework that emphasizes the relationship between lived experience and social contextualization. Dilthey argues that 'understanding of the particular depends on knowledge of the general which, in turn, presupposes understanding of the whole' (in Rickman 1976: 196). In the construction of this hermeneutic spiral, three elements are of vital importance: the ethnographer's lived experiences, the objectifications and docu- mentations of others' lived experiences and the social context in which they both originate and are viewed. The photograph and photographic practice provide a powerful medium to engage with all three of these elements.

Historically, sociologists have leaned heavily upon the written text for image contextualization in order to reduce inherent ambiguities. Images were mainly treated as a visual resource or a particular form of contributory data within field- work. Ambiguity, though, exists on a number of levels for all forms of representation; between the experience of tangible things and their re-presentation in symbolic form, between the symbolic product and the viewer, and the influence of context upon interpretation. I suggest that, although there are essential differ- ences between symbolic sign systems, there are fundamental underpinning principles at work throughout and visual symbolism is no more or less learnt or problematic than others: 'all cultural codes must be learnt, including those that are visual. . . . To read an artwork, then, is to embark on a process as difficult and demanding as reading a written work' (Morgan 2002).

If the contents of photographic images are treated as signs, it must be recog- nized that signs are understood through socially accepted conventions. Photographic meaning, then, is to do with contextualization and the relationships of signs within the image. As signs are arbitrary and relational, photographic images do not simply 'tell' in a clear, unequivocal way. The connotations of an image arise from the constructions brought to it by the photographer and the viewer. Only through our past experiences and our current constructions can these richly factual records have a meaning.

To realize the aim of the chapter's title, that photography can 'image the intan- gible', we must examine how intangible connotations can be explicitly developed within the photographic trace of tangible surfaces. The following images demon- strate that by inter- or intra- sequencing and juxtaposing, relationships can be estab- lished that transcend surface facts and visually reproduce both the flow and emotion of lived experience. These relationships can be constructed either to emphasize the coherent and chronological, and work to reduce ambiguity, or to deliberately heighten this ambiguity through the 'surprise' juxtaposition of visual elements.

The following examples are from a photographic documentation of an ear- piercing ceremony on the island of Niue in the central Pacific.

The relationships of objects in this image tell a story in the simple chronology of a beginning, a middle and an end. The shining knife blade forms a clear transition from the live feral pig in the foreground and the body of the dead pig in the background. Both the chronological and the experiential are communicated in one image by the formation of significant symbolic relationships through careful framing.

In these two images, the thorns of the lime tree are juxtaposed beside a bloody and swollen ear. The inherent discontinuity of each image is emphasized and this ambiguity resolved through inter-contexualization.

Questions are posed by deliberately drawing upon the emotional empathy or synchronicity of the viewer's own lived experience. The emotional resonances that arise from these visual relationships are not so much of the particular activity, but result from the general human condition in which it originates. In the ear-piercing ceremony on Niue, I would suggest that it is from the particularity (the tangible) of lime thorns and the bleeding swollen ear that we come to identify with the generality (the intangible) of underpinning 'pain'. The connotations arise in the 'space' between denotations as social, mind-orientated constructions. I like to think a sense of revelation forms between the cracks in reality. What we feel, sense, empathize with and learn from comes from the constructive act that the photographer has initiated through a skill in image making. As viewers, our socially established backgrounds initiate individual readings in relation to the objects that comprise the image. These tangible objects extend mnemonically to emotions and associations that tap the intangible depth of a particular human existence.

Everything that is photographed has the potential for a particular symbolic attribution. It has been argued that the tangible objects that comprise the photograph are understood and have meaning as part of a constructed symbolic system. It is the relationship of these 'things' from which a visual text of intangible meaning is constructed. The skill, then, photographically, is to isolate and unite in the frame (or series of frames) symbolic relationships of appropriate coherence. The unique combination of relationships produces a holistic 'reading' greater than the parts.

To fully appreciate and develop such working strategies for visual communication, it is imperative that the social significance of 'objects', as a symbolic system, is understood and anticipated. Certainly the symbolic attributions have to be learnt, but that is an unavoidable part of belonging to a society that, by definition, is a learnt symbolic system. Objects as a symbolic sign system have a multivocality which provides for the potential of powerful communication in both particular and generic aspects of the social condition.

The following images are examples where I have used the photograph to establish particular relationships of tangible elements in the attempt to communicate intangible concepts. Through framing and juxtaposition, specific information of processual development, spatial orientation and personal relationships is formed and made explicit.

During this ceremony of a Greek Orthodox baptism, I was constantly reminded of its ancient qualities. The priest was clearly central in maintaining these traditions. I began to 'hunt' for visual relationships between the symbols of ancient and modern. At this point I became aware of the potential to align icons of the past and present. Through framing, the priest has been visually positioned as the guardian of unchanging practices and values between a centuries-old iconic church painting and the contemporary young mother mirroring its content.

Fortuitously, the church window echoes the halo of the icon around the young mother's head, continuing to reinforce the connection. The candles in the painting, apparently held by Christ's mother, are actually reflections of candles on the altar piece. An additional relationship of past and present is formed. The photograph references the significant but intangible aspect of the role of ritual process in intergenerational continuity.

While photographing the preparations for the celebration of the Greek Orthodox Easter, I was very conscious of the belief that the Son of God, made man, had been nailed to a cross and had endured all the agonizing suffering of human pain. I had been searching for a relationship between the life-like but symbolic two-dimensional wooden cut-out of Christ and the people around it. As the man behind the crucifix held out a candle I realized he was unconsciously echoing the posture of crucifixion. This image draws upon the ambiguous qualities of the 'real' arm and the symbolic representation of the crucifixion, while hands all around appear to reach out to him. The image becomes a reference for the intangible concept of the Son of God made man.

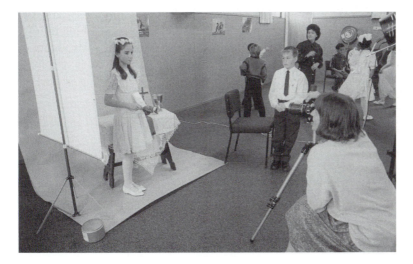

The intangible concepts of this image of a child's First Holy Communion in the Catholic Church deal with aspects of self-definition and self-recognition, which in this case appear particularly complex and layered. The church, the young girl and implicitly her parents all appear to be involved in the process of definition: the reconstructed altar, the young girl's participation, or at least acquiescence, the clothes which we could conjecture have been supplied by her parents and also the taking of the photograph, which will in its own symbolic way constitute evidence of the ritual, providing definition not only for the participants but vicariously for others. The image also provokes thoughts about contemporary technology and its integration/juxtaposition with historical practices.

Summary

This chapter has sought to establish that objects are implicated on a broad and funda-mental level of human social existence. The emphasis throughout has been upon the inevitable involvement of objects as a socializing agency in terms of self-definition and self-recognition.

I have argued that it is in the groupings of objects and in their relationships and specific 'coherence' that revealing insights for social research are manifest. Through symbolic cultural patterning, tangible objects constitute a significant and lasting medium of intangible social expression.

Photography has been cited as an ideal medium for exploration, recording and communicating the objectifications of human social experiences. As Berger and Mohr suggest, 'By its nature, revelation does not easily lend itself to verbalisation'

(1982: 118). The full potential of photographs as significant visual texts in socio-logical research can only be achieved by a sophisticated and sensitive appreciation of the complex role of objects in our existence. This awareness informs both the initial 'gaze' and also subsequent approaches to image making.

Objectifications of experience are myriad and whatever degree of isolation post-modern arguments impose, our empathy with expressions of common human conditions of love, hate, happiness, pain, sexual excitement, tiredness and so on can bring us closer to the meaning of the lived experience of another's social exist-ence. Through images and the emotional resonance they re-produce, both process and experience are united. Anchored and contextualized within the particularity of the photographs, we reach towards a revelation of our humanness in the lived experience of others. As Dilthey so elegantly puts it, 'Understanding is a redis-covery of the I in the Thou' (in Rickman 1976: 208).

References

Berger, J. and Mohr, J. (1982) *Another Way of Telling*, London: Writers and Readers Publishing Cooperative.

Bourdieu, P. (1977) *Outline of Theory and Practice*, trans. R. Nice, London: Cambridge University Press.

—— (1984) *Distinction: A Social Critique of the Judgement of Taste*, Cambridge, Mass.: Harvard University Press.

Butler, T. (ed.) (1989) *Memory: History, Culture and the Mind*, Oxford: Blackwell.

Csikszentmihalyi, M. and Rochberg-Halton, N. (1981) *The Meaning of Things: Domestic Symbols and the Self*, Cambridge: Cambridge University Press.

Harker, R. and McConnochie, K.R. (1985) *Education as a Cultural Artefact*, Palmerston North: Dunmore Press.

Harker, R., Mahar, C. and Wilkes C. (eds) (1990) *An Introduction to the Work of Pierre Bourdieu: The Practice of Theory*, Basingstoke: Macmillan.

Morgan, Sally (2002) 'The measure of yearning, of knowledge, of science and of art', unpublished paper.

Rapoport, A. (1981) *A Cross Cultural Perspective: Identity and Environment*, in J.S. Duncan (ed.) *Cross Cultural Perspectives: Housing and Identity*, London: Croom Helm.

Rickman, H.P. (ed.) (1976) *Dilthey: Selected Writings*, Oxford: Oxford University Press.

Turner, V.W. and Bruner, E.M. (eds) (1986) *The Anthropology of Experience*, Urbana and Champaign: University of Illinois Press.

Chapter 5

Douglas Harper

WEDNESDAY-NIGHT BOWLING
Reflections on cultures of a rural working class

T**HIS CHAPTER IS PREMISED** on the assumption that presenting social life photographically makes it more sociologically comprehensible. I offer photographs of a social scene – a bowling alley in northern New York, USA – to suggest a reading of working-class culture that is partly at odds with the received wisdom on the subject. The photographs are presented with an overview of the sociology of working-class life, and observations made during the many years I bowled in the lanes. I suggest that the three elements, visual images, sociological analysis and observations, build a composite portrait – a *Gestalt* – that offers more than the modes of analysis offer separately. At the same time, covering these elements in a brief chapter requires that they be treated rather briefly.

These assumptions regarding the usefulness of photography in social analysis derive from what is often called the empirical wing of visual sociology, which is closely related to documentary photography (Harper 1997). The assertion that photography may serve both visual sociology and documentary studies in a similar way does not, however, imply that the photographs are simple representations of social reality. Making a photograph is a complicated act that is influenced by gender, class, age and other sociological attributes of the photographer and subject; technological considerations in photography and the influences of the setting.[1] In other words, the photograph sees, but it sees the way it has been made to see. The best way of demonstrating this point is to present photographs in the context of how they were made and how they inform and contest other sociological knowledge. This is the strategy of this chapter.

The study

Between 1981 and 1990 I was a member of a bowling team that participated in a league every Wednesday, autumn, winter and spring. Conservatively speaking, this amounted to 250 evenings of bowling. The bowling lanes were in a small town in northern New York state, 25 miles from a town of 4,000, where I was a sociology professor. This was a decidedly rural environment, which my family participated in fully. A neighbour, Willie, invited me to join the league, and while my presence did not seem unusual at the beginning, I soon realized that I was the only member who was not from the working class or a farmer.

At the time I was teaching about the American working class in courses such as social movements and revolutionary change, social problems and community studies. As I was drawn into working-class culture I found myself at odds with the analyses I was reading and teaching. For several decades, roughly from the 1950s to the 1970s, studies of the working class were common and their conclusions were hotly debated. For reasons beyond the scope of this chapter, interest in the working class has since declined.[2] Thus my reflection on characterizations of the working class were generated in a different era, but have largely not been contested. First, I briefly review the sociological arguments concerning the working class, however dusty the books that tell that story.

Perhaps the most famous characterization of the working class was offered by Seymour Lipset, who in 1963 described it as authoritarian, rigid and intolerant. Shostak and Gomberg (1964) challenged this view in a collection of essays in which, for example, S.M. Miller and Frank Riessman wrote:

> It is now asserted that the working class . . . is incapable of deferring gratification and consequently unable to make major strides in improving their conditions. Frequently accompanying this view is the belief that this lower class is 'immoral', 'uncivilized', 'promiscuous', 'lazy', 'obscene', 'dirty', and 'loud'.
>
> (1964: 34)

Miller and Riessman identified middle-class sociologists' stereotypes of the working class: their lack of thrift, intellectual inferiority, habitual dirtiness and licentiousness.

Working-class men do not fare well in studies carried out by women. Mirra Komarovsky (1967) and Lillian Rubin (1976) focused on the inability of working-class men to communicate with their wives or play meaningful roles in their marriages. Rubin asserted:

> The problem lies in the fact that they do not have a language with which to communicate, with which to understand each other. They are products of a process that trains them to relate to only one side of themselves – she, to the passive, tender, nonverbal, unemotional side; he, to the active, tough, logical, nonverbal, unemotional one.
>
> (1976: 116)

Komarovsky stresses the isolation of married couples:

> The phrase 'trained incapacity to share' aims to convey a certain view about the men's inarticulateness. The ideal of masculinity into which they were socialized inhibits expressiveness both directly, with its emphasis on reserve, and indirectly, by identifying personal interchange with the feminine role.
>
> (1967: 156)

The text that most definitively portrays the working class as psychologically crippled is Sennett and Cobb's influential study on the 'hidden injuries of class' (1972). The well-known argument is that the working class has blamed itself for its failure to achieve social mobility, which led the class as a whole to develop a deep-seated insecurity and sense of defeatism. A rare working-class man who had achieved a degree of social mobility refuses to see it as evidence of his skill, intelligence or hard work:

> we found the declarations of self-satisfaction almost instantly giving way to a view of himself as a passive agent in his own life, a man who has been on the receiving end of events rather than their cause: 'I was just at the right place at the right time,' he says again and again.
>
> (1972: 20)

There are a small number of studies that emphasize how such cultural elements as the skill and danger of high steel construction work create a camaraderie that positively influences the social dimensions of working-class life (for example, Applebaum 1981). But these perspectives are most certainly rare in working-class studies.[3]

The contrasts I noted between the working-class culture in the bowling league and the sociological research on the topic may have been partly due to the effects of place and history. The literature on the American working class tends to treat it as a single phenomenon, although nearly all the classic studies are situated in cities or suburbs in the American north-east. Workers are either skilled tradespeople or factory assembly workers; most are of European ethnicity, and their communities and factories are generally multiracial. Most of the sociologists who studied the American working class during this earlier era were male East Coast urbanites (exceptions include David Halle, a British sociologist whose study of the East Coast urban working class was published in 1984, and Bennet Berger and Lillian Rubin, who studied the working class in California suburbs) whose political orientation was to the then New Left. Their studies of the working class focus on its failure to involve itself in politics that express more than its narrow self-interest, notably its failure to play a role in movements seeking radical social and political change. Indeed, most scholars pointed to the working class's reactionary politics, racism and even fascist leanings.

The era in which the studies were done also has an impact on their themes and assumptions. For example, LeMasters's portrait of tradesmen in a working-class tavern (1975) reflects American workers' rejection of the progressive politics (including the women's movement, student strikes against the university's complicity in the Vietnam war and anti-war protest in general) that resulted from the culture wars of the 1960s.

In any case, these studies tell a great deal about the preoccupations of sociology, especially in America, during the 1960s and its aftermath. They do not, however, tell a convincing story about the culture of the working class across time and place. My own position as a visitor to venues of the American working class offers a vantage point from which observations and photography may lend a different portrait of a working-class culture.

The setting and study population

My league mates were drawn from three distinct categories of the rural working class. The first comprised men who worked at an aluminium-processing plant 20 miles from the bowling lanes. They were well-paid workers in a low-income rural area. Most of these men drove a new pickup and lived in a well-kept house. Nearly all of them maintained informal jobs, invariably associated with machines such as backhoes, dumptrucks, bulldozers, flatbeds and tractors. They were able to do these second jobs because night shifts made the daytime available for additional work. Much of the bowling alley talk was about who could do what sorts of work for whom; what kinds of trading and exchanging might get a job done.

A second category comprised local dairy farmers who worked family farms that were not so busy that they could not take an occasional evening off. One team that bowled year after year consisted of a father and two sons, partners in the farm; a second team included a farmer, his son and a hired man. The dairy farmers often needed the skills, machines and labour offered by the other working-class men found at the lanes, and exchanges and other work arrangements were often part of the discussions.

The final category of workers were independently employed carpenters, mechanics and machine operators. Some were quite successful, with a garage of expensive machinery, while others lived at near subsistence level in homemade houses and a world of machines worn out several times. These workers also played an important part in the local working-class culture: they fixed machines needed by both groups; they offered labour and land for peripheral agriculture; and they often had particular skills that were otherwise unavailable.

The sociological characteristics of the group were influenced by the setting. Northern New York is cold, isolated and racially and ethnically homogeneous. While much of the work done by this class would be classified as unskilled, the men at the bowling alley were (nearly) all skilled at machine operation and repair, and many were creative inventors who would build such machines as stills for the illegal production of cedar oil, which was sold to pharmaceutical companies. Many were clever businessmen who managed a complicated social world of informally traded and occasionally sold time and materials. In this setting people were able to satisfy a large proportion of their own material needs: men built their own homes (often trading labour with others who had special skills or machines); families had large gardens and many raised animals for food; and the men hunted for food rather than sport.

National politics seemed to be played out on a far distant stage, and even state politics were centred in New York City, a nearly mystical place few had visited (or could imagine visiting), an eight-hour drive over a range of mountains. Thus the politics that most of the rural working class responded to was grounded in local issues such as control of wetlands, commodity pricing or other agricultural policies (such as the controversial programme of dairy buyout, where farmers were paid to sell their milkers for beef), and matters relating to zoning and school board issues. Several of the bowlers held positions on local political boards and many participated in local politics. The result was that the rural working class I studied and bowled with was quite different from the urban or suburban working class much studied by the sociological community.

Methods

After several years of observing the bowling lanes informally I began to systematize my observations in fieldnotes. I listened to what men talked about week after week and year after year, and I watched how the themes were borne out in their lives. I used a grounded theory strategy: I identified common topics of conversation and noted their development in subsequent conversations. I eventually came to know many of these men quite well and entered into the same work-based relationships outside the lanes as they did, so my view of their lives was also based on our shared experiences.

After living in the North Country for sixteen years I accepted a position several states distant. I had often thought about photographing the bowling culture, but the oddness of bringing a camera to the lanes, and the problems of photographing in the available light in the dim room with bright ceiling illumination, dissuaded me from trying. As I prepared to leave the area, I knew I had few chances left to make the images I had thought about for several years. So, with some trepidation, on the last night of my last season, I photographed the men and the lanes, producing many of the images for this chapter.

I had long realized that it would be difficult to illuminate the subject in a way that would replicate the light that existed in the lanes. The social ambience and social interaction were certainly affected by the environmental light, so this was an important consideration.

I decided to use a medium format camera – itself a large, conspicuous piece of equipment – and a strobe to counteract the odd and difficult lighting of the lanes. I decided to make the photograph call attention to itself. I made the portraits with the strobe and a second fill flash, but I took photos of men bowling with the available light, so as not to disturb their game. The effects of these lighting strategies are easily seen: the portraits are lit with clarity and evenness, and the photographs of bowlers in the act of bowling reflect the intense overhead light and otherwise muddy shadows.

The photos communicate the ambience and some of the norms of league culture which are described in photo captions. They show the clothes, postures and sense of comfort these men have with their bodies and with each other. My team member Willie photographed me bowling (with the strobe shot right into my eyes as I released the ball): this presents the bowler in the context of the social spaces of the lanes.

The photos are a glimpse into the world of working-class bowling. But they emerged from several years of routine interaction and they embody relationships built up over that period. Very different photographs would have been made by someone who was not a long-term member of the group. The bowlers accepted my photography as a part of our farewell.

I have presented these images at the end of the chapter alongside photographs that show the social worlds of the men's informal work. These are but two of at least four of the working-class culture's typical settings; family and formal work settings would complete the portrait.

Themes

I had extensive notes from at least fifty evenings of bowling. My content analysis of these fieldnotes identified three themes, which I will briefly present in the following comments. I note the difficulty of summarizing qualitative data in a short chapter, and include only a small number of representative stories in each case.

The first conversational theme addressed family life. Working-class men told stories of the successes of their children and the challenges they faced. They talked about children and teachers, grades, wives' jobs, family illnesses and the like. Sports were a popular topic and the men took great pleasure in watching and reporting on their sons' and daughters' participation, whether their teams were particularly successful or not. Some of these views are shown below.

The men were discussing one of their sons' experience of playing in the town hockey league. Gilbert Ray said: 'The coach is the best one I've seen. He lets every-body play; everybody is part of a line and each line gets equal time. If the kids do something wrong, he tells them, he doesn't yell at them; he doesn't jump up and down and holler.' His teammate adds: 'I can't stand that kind of coach – the ones that jump on the kids' ass. I wouldn't let my kid play because the coach was like that. They are supposed to go out there and have fun.' 'Yeah,' another bowler chimes in, 'Billy made a goal but they took it away from him. It went in and bounced out and they didn't see it. He got a little mad – he picked up a penalty for roughing – had to sit on the bench for a minute and a half!' It was common that the sons and sometimes the daughters worked with the bowlers on the jobs they did outside their regular employment. Murphy brought his son to build my chimney; van Patton brought his son (whose name was also listed on his business pickup truck) when he dug a trench for a new water line to my barn.

The men loved to do things for their children. One night I was talking about making some rather crude pine furniture for my son's bedroom. Ray Carlson, whom I had seldom spoken to, described a cherry bedroom set he was building for his daughter from wood he had harvested from his woodlot. The job had taken longer than he had imagined and his daughter, anxious for her new furniture, had become involved. 'She's becoming a fine carpenter', Ray said. 'She makes me wear my safety goggles; she's not afraid of the router. She likes to learn!'

When it became known that I was a college professor, the bowlers often sought my advice on teen troubles, college choices and other family matters. My own daughter was a high school athlete who played with several of the men's daughters in the three seasons of sports in the local high school. We often saw each other at the rural school where we cheered our kids and shared the tales of triumphs and disappointments on a weekly basis.

I also came to know several of these men's families. While I never interviewed women about their intimate family relationships, the family lives I came to know were characterized by shared projects: building houses, camps, house additions; holidays in local camping grounds or family cabins in the nearby Adirondak mountains. Women often had special women friends, and some 'ran the roads' together for evenings of bingo or other activities on the nights we bowled. Farm wives were fully integrated into the work of the small farms that depended on contributions from all family members. In the nine years I bowled I heard of only one divorce among the bowlers, and in this instance the wife had begun a clandestine relationship, via CB radio, with a truck driver, and had deserted her husband and young child to leave with him for Florida. In fact, a woman of loose morals was said to be 'running with the truckers'. The deserted bowler was nearly inconsolable for months and the sympathy of the others continued unabated.

I am sure that some family relationships resembled those described in the sociological literature on the working class but these were certainly not evident among the families I came to know through the bowling alleys. I noticed quite the opposite: affectionate and respectful relationships, family stability and a great deal of self-sacrifice for children and each other.

The second theme found in my bowling observations was the negotiation of male friendships, largely rooted in shared projects done outside regular jobs. These were a constant source of discussion. For example, Joe Morella bought a brush hog and small tractor, which he used to clean up a brush-filled field for Al Downey. Al repaid him by accompanying him on a 400-mile drive to buy an antique Ford Mustang for his daughter. Al described the great adventure, towing a flatbed on which the Mustang was transported, all the way to Pennsylvania and back:

> It was just beautiful, Doug. We left early in the morning. Stopped for coffee in Watertown. Picked up 81 South . . . I'd put new wheel bearings in the flatbed and it tracked behind my 3/4 ton pickup perfect. We'd stop now and then to check the bearings; have some more coffee. Got down to Pennsylvania late; got a motel for $29 dollars. Next morning we checked out the Mustang and Joe bought it on the spot. Loaded it up and made it back that night: four in the morning! We took turns all the way back. Both of us were at work on Monday.

The worlds inhabited by these men were rooted in their competence and experience with machines. But it was not only mechanical skills that tied the men together. George, for example, had a country and western band that performed for many events in and around family celebrations such as anniversary parties at the local firehall. George would be called upon to provide music, often exchanging the fee for work done on other projects.

Money would be exchanged for some but not all the projects, and there would be times when the exchanges were not easily sorted out. Small feuds would sometimes flare up. But when I had expected irreparable rifts I would be surprised to see new coalitions when it was practical for the parties to be friends again. Houses, garages, outbuildings, roads, dams, bridges, culverts and other projects were initiated in the bowling alley and completed by men working informally together. I hired (and sometimes traded labour with) men I met at the alleys to dig a foundation for a greenhouse with a backhoe; to tear down and rebuild a 40-foot chimney; to remove a tree fallen on my house; to fix a submergible pump; and to do a great deal of work on cars, trucks and other machines. In fact, the bowling alley was a constant source of problem solving: 'Who has a "picker" to get a damned tree off my roof?' 'Oh, that would be Delbert Henry. He's over there; you don't know him yet.' Very often it was a matter not of finding inexpensive workers, but rather finding people with expertise who would appear when they said they would and complete the work as described. Being part of the bowling lanes culture led me to durable relationships with a wide web of skilled rural artisans. In this way I was simply one of the many.

Certainly the work-based friendships, in a setting in which a great deal of self-sufficiency was required, were not only typical but rational. It was a way to overcome the generally low wages. For example, it would cost as much as $800 to buy heating oil for a long and cold winter, but with a small woodlot and modest equipment, a crew of two or three men would harvest wood for a season's heating in a long weekend. These shared projects led people to depend upon and value each other and they produced durable social relationships. These contrast with the social worlds that emerge from the collective experience of factory or other unskilled urban work.

The final common topic in the bowling alley was politics, local and personal. In these stories, as represented in Murphy's below, the working-class men described their interactions with people (and sometimes their institutions). Rather than victims, they saw themselves as negotiators with something to offer.

Murphy has been cutting wood. He has a good rig: a Bobcat on a flatbed, a truck to pull it and a small tractor to use in the woods. He's cut all of next year's wood and has cut a few cords to sell. He tells us:

> Eddie Berkeley wanted a cord. I gave him a good one; maybe a cord and a quarter. All nice and dry. He called me up; I told him twenty-five dollars. Took it up with my pickup; threw it off where he had some other wood. He drives up as I'm finishing: 'Are you going to stack it for twenty-five? – I'm a businessman; can't have that wood laying there like that.'

> I told him: 'if you want it stacked the price is thirty dollars.' 'No way,' he says, 'twenty-five. I'm a businessman; I can't stack that wood!' 'Fuck

you,' I says, 'I'm a businessman too and I ain't going to stack your wood!' I loaded up that whole load; he's standing there looking. When I'm leaving I says: 'You still got my phone number? Throw it away. If you need any more wood, don't call me!'

The antagonist was a well-off local businessman whom many people did not like. Murphy's tale was a common refrain of maintaining self-respect in dealings with those of higher social standing. Because most managed their world quite well, they were not, in general, mystified by a world of impersonal bureaucracies (of course, when the men did need public assistance for medical matters or other personal crises, they had to take on these bureaucracies). Generally the culture was assertive and even arrogant in its dealings with the outside world.

Conclusion

This chapter questions the sociological analysis of a segment of American culture which was once well studied in sociology. I hope to question some of the core assumptions that guided this research tradition, which itself has waned as interest in working-class life and politics has declined. In part, the contrast between my observations and those of other working-class studies derives from its rural and northern setting, and it part it derives from seeing the lives of the working class from a different vantage point. I observed the culture *in situ*, in work and play, while nearly all the previously published studies were generated with formal interviews.

Photographs play an interesting role in this process. They concretize the settings and interactions in the common social spaces. They also offer an empathic connection to strangers in an alien field setting. They are demonstrations of social relations between photographer and subject and thus they are data that speak to how people in this setting interact. In these ways they extend the understandings begun with words.

Histories of the season. The owner of the bowling lanes kept careful track of all games played. High scores were written by hand on posters that adorned the walls of the alley. These became a history of a season and the record of legendary feats: great nights when a bowler bowled a perfect game.

The owner kept fifty or more bowling balls of varying size, weight, finger hole placement and quality that were available for anyone's use. Many bowlers used the same borrowed ball for years.

The lanes were precomputerized. Teams kept score by longhand, which involved a reckoning of strikes; added points for spares (knocking all pins down in the second throw of two balls) and opens, where pins are left standing after the second ball is thrown.

A daughter of one of our team joined us each Wednesday to keep score. It was a chore that required constant attention and maths skills, and Julie enjoyed her important role on the team.

The non-computerized system allowed bowlers to warm up with as many practice balls as one could throw before the game began. The modern system has automated scoring and charges for each ball thrown, so it is impossible to warm up, and many bowlers do not even know how their score is actually reckoned. A Weberian sociologist would characterize the new system as rationalized through the use of technology that standardizes the experience and diminishes the human agency involved.

This photograph reflects the perspective from the half-circle seating that surrounds the score-keeping table. The bowler (left) has completed his throw and the bowler (right) prepares to step to his position. Several small rituals are completed in this process: bowlers wipe their hands on a communal towel that contains a drying substance such as talcum powder; position their feet in relationship to a mark on the floor; take two or three deep breaths; and then advance down the lane for three steps before releasing the ball. These rituals are understood as ways to focus concentration and they are respected by all players. I had to make these photos carefully (and without a flash), so as not to disturb the bowler's attention.

The bowler takes his turn. Norms dictate that no one will bowl in the lanes on either side of the bowler until he has delivered the ball. Bowlers spend a great deal of time arguing about the best posture, delivery style, and the amount and direction of spin to achieve maximum results. There is appreciation for skilful bowling, but bowlers with less skill are welcomed to participate. A handicapping system compensates less skilled bowlers in a complex algorithm that helps to even the playing field.

The captain of my team, Willie, who also worked at the bowling alley fixing the antiquated equipment and drilling balls to fit bowlers' hands, has crept down the alley and photographs me as I release the ball. This peculiar event has caught the attention of several spectators. Photograph by Willie Louie.

This team, intact for several years, was built around the farm of Charlie S. (pictured on the left). The two heavy-set men are his sons, who also work on the farm. Their farm, which at that time milked about eighty cows, was craft oriented. When I visited their farm I walked through the herd of seemingly identical black and white behemoths and listened to their animated discussion of breeding decisions several generations long. They knew the details of decisions and the results: 'Sara had great teats but bad feet; she is going to top out 16,000 pounds (of milk) this season!'

Jim, the thin member of a big bowling team (Jim used to say: 'I kinda get lost in the crowd!'), lived on the farm his father had built up in the 1950s. The farm had not modernized and Jim ran a business housing heifers for the large farms that surrounded his land. He also was a full-time maintenance worker at the local university. Jim was heavily involved with labour and equipment exchanges with many neighbouring farmers. Even though his primary income was from his janitorial job, his central identity was that of a farmer.

Charlie, who runs his farm with the help of his two sons, who are also members of his team, tends to his heifers.

Jim on his farm. In the background are dry cows he boards for a neighbouring farmer.

This team was also built around a family farm and the owner's long-term involvement with the National Farmers' Organization, a progressive agricultural movement. The team, from year to year, included hired men, sons, borrowed nephews, and friends. The team organizer and farm owner wore the NFO T-shirt faithfully and never missed an opportunity to discuss or lecture on farm policy and economics, but other members of the team wore normal street clothes. The farm fell on hard times and several members of the team pictured here are deceased. Conversations often addressed the changing rural scene: the disappearance of small farms and the neighbourhood relations that went with them. One day we were speaking about what had changed with the advent of larger and more industrialized farms. Loren, the farmer, said: 'It's not like they don't want to help, the neighbours. But they don't know anything about farming. They don't even know how to drive a cow!'

The workers in these photos were not in the bowling league, but were contacted through its informal network. They are typical machine-based entrepreneurs, like many of the bowlers.

In these photographs they are removing a tree that has fallen in a windstorm onto my house.

The second photograph documents digging a ditch with a backhoe for a waterline to a greenhouse. The backhoe is attached to the rear of a tractor; the job uses two people. Very often fathers worked with sons on jobs such as this.

My bowling team, 1990. I bowled on Willie's team (pictured on the right) for nine years. Each year the other members of the team were different. This year our partners included a rather dour farmer and a happy-go-lucky working-class man. Each year a particular form of friendship developed among the team; we worked hard to do well but never stressed terribly if we did not.

Woods work:
The week has been cold; ten below every night. Bill has been cutting wood for the next winter. The small tractor he uses can pull a log at a time. Other bowlers are telling him, with concern, to be careful not to tip the tractor back on itself, which would pin him on the ground. Bill scoffs at them: 'That tractor hasn't got enough power to pull itself over!' Willie: 'Remember Whiskers LaRouch? That's what he said! He was pinned underneath his for an hour and a half. Nearly froze.' Bill scoffs more: 'That tractor'll stall if it's pulling more than two logs. It's only twenty horse, skips like crazy. That ain't gong to pull me over.'

   Willie's daughter, who kept score for us most Wednesday nights, frolics as we cut wood. Julie accompanied Willie on many jobs he did for small farmers, often with his portable welder mounted on a tiny trailer. Willie also did a lot for Julie: I recall that the day after this photo was taken he cut and sewed a dress for her confirmation ceremonies.

'Did you hear the one about the city slicker who comes out to see the farmer? He wants to buy a pig. The farmer shows him his baby pigs and the city slicker says: "I like that one, the little black and white pig." The farmer hands him the pig. "How much does it weigh?" the city slicker asks. The farmer puts the tail of the pig in his mouth, swings the pig back and forth a few times (motions) and says: "Twenty-six pounds." "That's ridiculous," says the city slicker, "how did you know it weighs twenty-six pounds?" "Here, ask my son", the farmer says. The son comes in, puts the tail of the pig in his mouth, swings it back and forth a few times, and says: "Twenty-six pounds." The city slicker still doesn't believe him. The father says "We all weigh things that way in the family. Go get Ma," he says to the son, "she'll weigh the pig." "Can't," says the kid, "she's weighing the milkman."'

A member of the team pictured on the facing page who was absent the night the portrait was made owned a small front-end loader which he used to bury my chimney, broken when a tree fell on the house. He then rebuilt the chimney with the help of his 13-year-old son as Amish carpenters finished the roofing.

The choreography of bowling:

There is a complicated system of turn taking. The general rule is that when you step up to the lane, ball in hand, no bowler will step up to the lane on either side until you have thrown your ball.

One positions oneself precisely (depending on one's bowling style), holding the ball with two middle fingers inserted into holes that have been cut to match the bowler's hand. The bowler sights down the lane, fixes his or her eyesight on a mark on the floor, takes three steps in increasing speed towards the pins while swinging the 15-pound ball gracefully behind their back and then releasing it towards the pins. Most bowlers spin the ball sideways and aim for the pocket between the head pin and the second pin of the triangle. A spinning in the pocket has a good chance to strike, which means to knock all pins down on the first throw.

When a bowler makes a truly bad throw, for example one that misses all the pins and lands in the gutter, or misses remaining pins widely on the second throw, he turns to face his teammates and the few spectators with a 'body-language' apology or excuse. Perhaps the bowler will shake his fist, indicating that his fingers stuck in the hole of the ball. Or he will move his foot in a way to suggest that the damned soles of his bowling shoes are worn and thus he slipped just a bit when he was releasing the ball.

On the other hand, when a bowler gets a strike or picks up a particularly difficult spare (a spare is knocking all remaining pins down on the second ball) he faces his audience of peers and gestures in some kind of self-congratulatory way. The gesture might be the bowling hand in a fist raised triumphantly, as in upper right frame. During the World Series, which were televised each October in the lanes, bowlers used the 'strike' motion that baseball umpires make when indicating their own strikes. It was uncanny; happened every year.

Some teams touch flesh when they get a strike.

If three bowlers get strikes, the fourth has to get a strike (he's 'hanging') or buy a round of beers for the others. Even if the drinking game is not played, the bowler is referred to as 'hanging' if all preceding bowlers have successfully struck.

Notes

1   See Harper (2001) for a discussion of the social construction of photographic ethno-
     graphy in a visual ethnography.
2   One of the rare contemporary studies is Michele Lamont's (2000) study of working-
     class men in America and France. Lamont asserts that American working-class men
     have exclusionary attitudes towards other working-class and ethnic and racial groups,
     but that they have a fully developed critical take on professional and other classes of
     privilege.
3   Several community studies placed the working class into the contexts of work, family,
     ethnic groups, leisure and social networks (most recently Halle (1984); earlier notable
     studies include Berger (1968)). Other studies of politics, attitudes and working-class
     culture are Aronowitz (1973); Gallie (1978); Kornblum (1976); Rainwater (1959);
     Shostak (1969); Shostak and Gomberg (1964). What is fascinating about revisiting
     this extraordinary tradition of scholarship is the wealth of empirical research it
     reflects, and the consistent interest in working-class lives and culture. This is indeed,
     and sadly, no longer a growth industry in sociology.

References

Applebaum, Herbert (1981) *Royal Blue: the Culture of Construction Workers*, New York: Holt,
    Rinehart and Winston.
Aronowitz, Stanley (1973) *False Promises: the Shaping of American Working-Class Consciousness*,
    New York: McGraw-Hill.
Berger, Bennett (1968) *Working-Class Suburb: a Study of Auto Workers in Suburbia*, Berkeley:
    University of California Press.
Gallie, Duncan (1978) *In Search of the New Working Class*, Cambridge: Cambridge University
    Press.
Halle, David (1984) *America's Working Man*, Chicago: University of Chicago Press.
Harper, Douglas (1997) 'Visualizing structure: reading surfaces of social life,' *Qualitative
    Sociology* 20(1): 57–77.
——— (2001) *Changing Works: Visions of a Lost Agriculture*, Chicago: University of Chicago
    Press.
Komarovsky, Mirra (1967) *Blue-Collar Marriage*, New York: Vintage Books.
Kornblum, William (1976) *Blue-Collar Community*, Chicago: University of Chicago Press.
Lamont, Michele (2000) *The Dignity of Working Men: Morality and the Boundaries of Race, Class,
    and Imagination*, Cambridge, MA: Harvard University Press.
LeMasters, E.E. (1975) *Blue-Collar Aristocrats*, Madison: University of Wisconsin Press.
Lipset, Seymour Martin (1963) *Political Man*, New York: Doubleday.
Rainwater, Lee (1959) *Workingman's Wife*, New York: Oceana Publications.
Rubin, Lillian (1976) *Worlds of Pain: Life in the Working-Class Family*, New York: Basic Books.
Sennett, Richard and Cobb, Jonathan (1972) *The Hidden Injuries of Class*, New York: Random
    House.
Shostak, Arthur (1969) *Blue-Collar Life*, New York: Random House.
Shostak, A. and Gomberg, W. (eds) (1964) *Blue-Collar World*, Englewood Cliffs, NJ:
    Prentice-Hall.

PART TWO

Picturing the city, sociality and post-industrial change

Chapter 6

Alan Latham

RESEARCHING AND WRITING EVERYDAY ACCOUNTS OF THE CITY

An introduction to the diary-photo diary-interview method

Individuals' bonds to one another are the essence of society. Our day-to-day lives are preoccupied with people, with seeking approval, providing affection, exchanging gossip, falling in love, soliciting advice, giving opinions, soothing anger, teaching manners, providing aid, making impressions, keeping in touch – or worrying about why we are not doing these things. By doing all these things we create community.
(Fischer 1982: 2)

Cities, unlike villages and small towns, are plastic by nature. We mould them in our images: they, in their turn, shape us by the resistance they offer when we try and impose our own personal form on them.
(Raban 1974: 2)

We have dwelled so often on the dehumanization and the disenchantment with the modern world and the solitude it induces that we are no longer capable of seeing the networks of solidarity that exist within.
(Maffesoli 1996a: 72)

Introduction

I **WANT TO START THIS CHAPTER** by asking: What is sociality? This is a difficult question to answer in a few words. Yet it is a question that is central to understanding the need for the methodological discussion around which the core of this chapter is organized. At its most basic, sociality might simply be defined as all those interactions with others through which individuals navigate their day-to-day world. It consists of interactions with friends, neighbours, work mates and – at least to some degree – those everyday strangers met at the supermarket checkout, shopping mall, café or pub. And while sociality can in certain instances be understood as being structured by a desire for some kind of observable material or emotional gain, more often than not it is organized through strictly non-instrumental motivations. It is frequently playful in tone and serves no more obvious purpose than providing a pleasurable interlude from the more serious business of living. Indeed, in searching for a pithy summation of the essence of sociality, it is hard to improve on Simmel's (1950: 45) nearly century-old description of sociality as a form of social 'playfulness' having 'no objective purpose, no content, no extrinsic results . . . [i]ts aim is nothing but the success of the sociable moment and, at most, a memory of it.'

Perhaps it is because it is often playful and just plain banal that sociality has frequently been taken for granted or overlooked by mainstream social science. It has been left to inspired mavericks like Simmel (1950), Goffman (1956, 1961, 1963, 1971) and Garfinkel (1967) to study the patterns and dynamics of sociality. Nonetheless, an increasingly wide range of research by sociologists, anthropologists (who, to be fair, had always demonstrated more interest in sociality than researchers from other parts of the social sciences; see Hannerz 1980) and human geographers have come to recognize the importance of sociality in the structuring of social forms. In part this renewed interest reflects a resurgent theoretical concern for practice, a theoretical refocusing that is organized around a heightened appreciation of the significance of everyday interactions in the production and reproduction of wider social structures. In part, too, sociality is being recognized as central to under-standing new emergent patterns of social cohesion and community in contemporary societies. Ray Pahl (2000: 11), for example, talking about a key element of sociality – friendship – has suggested that 'informal solidarity . . . may well become more important by providing the necessary cement to hold the bricks of an increasingly fragmented social structure together.' Michel Maffesoli (1996a) goes further, arguing that spontaneous sociality has become *the* key organizing principle within contemporary societies, replacing more traditional axes of association and differen-tiation such as work, social class and kinship. As he writes, 'electronic mail, sexual networks, various solidarities including sporting and musical gatherings are so many signs of an ethos in gestation. Such trends are the framework of a new spirit of the times which we call sociality' (Maffesoli 1996a: 73).

Nonetheless, if the social scientific concern for sociality reflects something of the 'spirit of the times' as Maffesoli suggests, developing methodologies subtle and versatile enough to help lead us into this new social universe presents a challenge. This is not only because of the often commented upon ineffability of the everyday – an ineffability that finds its echo in the tendency of much research into sociality to somehow lose a sense of the essence of the relationships it is attempting to grasp (see De Certeau 1984; Maffesoli 1996a, 1996b). It is also due to the very complexity and subtlety of much sociality. Of course, complexity and subtlety are not attrib-utes unique to sociality. But studying sociality does present social researchers with (at least) three significant dilemmas. For simplicity's sake we can think of these three dilemmas as ones of context, mobility and production:

1   *Context*. Social interaction is profoundly bound up with the context in which
     it takes place (see Giddens 1984; Pred 1986; Goffman 1956). This is so
     obvious as to appear almost trivial. Nonetheless, if we recognize this simple
     fact, then it is clear that there is a need to examine the contexts within which
     the sociality we are studying takes place. Methodologies like participant obser-
     vation and Garfinkel's breaching experiments offer some well-established
     routes into the problem of context, but they are not without their weaknesses.
     For one, we still have to engage with the question of what elements of context
     matter: talk? body language? particular objects? The answer is far from self-
     evident. More prosaically, the demand for the presence of the researcher
     within a context of social interaction often cannot be met, whether for ethical
     or practical reasons. Does this mean these areas must remain *terra incognita*?
     Or is it possible to employ proxies and other strategies to gain some kind of
     entrance into these otherwise misplaced instances?

2   *Mobility*. Context is not only bound up with a particular place. It is also defined
     by the sequencing of what Torsten Hägerstrand (1975) called time-space
     paths. The sequence within which people and materials pass through and
     inhabit particular locales, as well as the frequency and intensity with which
     they do so, is a fundamental element of the contextuality referred to above
     (see Giddens 1984; Pred 1986; May and Thrift 2001). The question here is
     one of mobility – both personal and collective. Now, as John Urry (2000) has
     argued, while the social sciences have been interested in various aspects of
     mobility over the past century, they have rarely placed it at the centre of their
     thinking, preferring to focus on more static and definable relations. But if –
     as Urry also argues – we acknowledge the centrality of mobility in structuring
     many social relations we gain a rather different view of what such phenomena
     are about (see also Eade 1997; Appadurai 1996; Thrift 1996; Serres 1995).
     Conceptually this is challenging enough. Practically it presents the social
     researcher with a set of basic questions of how (and when and for how long)
     to follow things around as they pass from locale to locale, and how to draw
     out the relations (or non-relations) between different locales and the material
     passing through them.

3   *Production*. Reading many of the classic works on sociality, particularly those
     of Goffman and symbolic interactionists like Garfinkel, as well as more recent
     theorists who draw heavily upon them (see Giddens 1984; Pred 1986, 1990),
     can leave one with a view that sociality is essentially mechanical and repeti-
     tive. These writers stress the importance to individuals of adjusting their
     personal deportment to fit the social contexts they find themselves in. But
     social actors do not simply 'manage' (Goffman 1956) these contexts within a
     pre-established framework of readily available conventions and norms. The
     form and style of people's day-to-day interactions are also part of what Ulf
     Hannerz (1980: 229) has called a 'world building activity' (see also Ingold
     2000). In everyday interaction individuals are involved in the practical bringing
     together and maintenance of networks of relationships between friends, rela-
     tives and work colleagues, as well of a range of other more transient
     relationships. The shape of these networks involves a significant element of
     choice, both in who becomes bound up within the network (and who does

not) and with what kind of intensity. It also involves a kind of practical ethics in as much as the style in which different people are addressed is expressive of the individual's stance towards the world (Spinosa *et al.* 1997; Maffesoli 1991; Thrift 2002). Acknowledging this 'world building' capacity means we must also recognize that sociality has a productivist edge – it is bound up with the generation of forms of self-hood, subjectivity and collectivity (see Maffesoli 1996a, 1996b; Amin and Thrift 2002; Urry 2000; Hetherington 1998).

In the following pages I want to offer a guide through a set of methodological tools with which I sought to work through these three 'dilemmas' in a recent research project. In particular I want to focus on the usefulness of a number of visual techniques, both as paths into the life-worlds of individuals and as ways of exploring individual practices of world making within the city. The project itself focused on three streets in Auckland, New Zealand, each of which was a centre for a particular style of urban public culture. This public culture is defined by its focus on cafés, bars and restaurants, its urbanness and an apparently free-form, casual, pattern of sociality. There is a particular New Zealand inflection to this story inasmuch as New Zealand had – and to a certain degree retains – a dominant popular culture that is virulently anti-urban, seeing the city as fundamentally corrupt and emasculating (see Phillips 1987; Fairburn 1989). Nonetheless, the basic aim of the project, to trace out the forms of community and patterns of sociality through which this emergent public culture was made, shares a close affinity with a growing body of literature on elective communities (see Maffesoli 1996a, 1996b; Urry 2000; Hetherington 1998; Adams and Allan 1998; Pahl 2000). And the methodological challenges it presented were also in many respects common to any project on contemporary sociality: How should a research site as dispersed as a city street be approached? How can we can gain a sense of how individuals weave particular locales into their daily life paths? How should we understand the forms of association that are enacted within them? How can a sense of the productiveness of individual and collective action be incorporated into the core of the project?

Brenda

Tuesday 1 June 'Another day at the office and another morning tea at Robert Harris. At the first opportunity Tim and I are off for breakfast – although we go most days our times vary considerably due to work commitments. Today we made it about 10.45 – a late breakfast! The service was not so snappy today – we compare it from day to day – today they were very busy and with the new staff there was much fiddling around. The coffee is normally really good here but today the blend of coffee to milk was not quite right. Life goes on.'

Wednesday 2 June 'The day was coming to a close and the phone rang with an invitation to a favourite Japanese restaurant on Queen St. Of course I was keen so I stayed on at work with some extra paperwork to fill the time until the 6.30 appointment. Of course I drove – too far to walk! Shochiku was its usual popular self. I wanted to be home to watch a particular programme at 7.30.

Fried tofu and chicken teriyaki, one beer and I was there long enough for a good catch-up, a good meal and no drama.'

Sunday 6 June 'Unexpectedly a spontaneous trip to Masala Indian restaurant happened. It wasn't a long trip – we left (me and 2 friends) from my house about 7 for the 5 minute walk to its place on Ponsonby Road. The restaurant filled up a lot while we were there. It's hard to describe the other diners except perhaps that they appeared to be like-minded people.'

Brenda is a 27-year-old computer layout operator who works for a major news-paper publisher. In many ways Brenda is typical of university-educated, middle-class New Zealanders. From a comfortably prosperous middle-class family in a moder-ately affluent provincial city, after finishing university she spent a number of years working and travelling around Europe. Two years ago she returned to New Zealand with the aim of establishing herself in a proper, serious, career. Originally she had intended to move to Wellington where she had an established network of relatives and friends, but work opportunities took her to Auckland. She enjoys Auckland, both for the work it offers and the lifestyle.

Brenda is the writer of the three diary excerpts on pp. 120–1, and from reading them we can also see that she likes chicken teriyaki, eating out and weekday break-fasts at cafés. We can also see that she is quite sociable, and that her weekly activities are widely dispersed: she lives in a shared house in inner-city Freeman's Bay, works in downtown Auckland (some 3 or more kilometres from her home), meets friends downtown or in Ponsonby Road (which is five minutes' walk from home). Now, not only is Brenda's personal biography in many ways typical of a certain kind of professional, mid-twenties urban dweller, so too is her use of the cafés, restaurants and bars, which play an important role in her social life.

The social sciences offer two obvious ways to approach studying Brenda's use of cafés, bars, and restaurants. The first is that of the in-depth interview. In-depth inter-views have a long and established place in social research. They also have many positive attributes. They are inexpensive and relatively easy to carry out, and their format generally makes intuitive sense to those being studied. Similarly, the second method, participant observation, offers an approach that is intuitively sensible to lay people. Through observing and participating in events and interactions, the researcher attempts to build up an interpretation of events from both his or her own and the other participants' points of view. Unfortunately for us, both these methods have serious limitations in cases like that of Brenda where the social interaction under study is both spatially dispersed and involves a significant level of routine.

Let us start with participant observation. Participant observation works well when one is dealing with either a single, reasonably contained, group, or activities that take place within tightly defined spatial and temporal boundaries. This is not the case with Brenda. On work days her daily breakfasts at Robert Harris are frequent and predictable. But much of her out-of-work socializing is less predictable, if hardly unstructured. She has a series of favourite bars and restaurants which she often meets friends in – Shochiku in central Auckland and Masala on Ponsonby Road are two mentioned in the diary quotes above, but there also others. Yet she is hardly what could be called a 'regular' in any of these places. If we focused our partici-pant observation on one or more specific leisure spaces we might have the good fortune to bump into Brenda. But this would leave us with little sense of the context of her visit, the people she was with, what she had done before, or how often she might come to that particular place. Similarly, attempting to follow Brenda around for a week while she went about her day-to-day business would be extremely time consuming, as well as unacceptably invasive.

If participant observation presents logistical difficulties, the problems with in-depth interviews are more to do with the usefulness of the accounts produced. If it is unrealistic to follow people around all day, then why not simply ask them what they got up to? Well, of course we could. But remember we are interested in context – when and where things took place, in what order, who was involved, how an event came to take place. These are details that are rarely readily to hand. Try writing down everything you did last week. Recalling the basic routine of the week is usually easy. Recalling more detail, especially chance events and one-off meetings, is much harder. What is more, the kind of details that are interesting to a project on everyday sociability, interaction with work colleagues, chance encounters with friends, chats with storekeepers, to name just a few possibilities, are both trivial (even if such encounters are often valued for precisely this reason) and taken for granted by most people. It follows that, while people may be capable of talking about friendship and everyday sociality, without a certain amount of information about their everyday patterns and routines the usefulness of these accounts is limited.

The problem here is not so much that people cannot talk about what they are doing and have no insight into their own patterns of sociability (although obviously these abilities do vary greatly from individual to individual). The problem is that a single interview does not provide respondents with a robust enough set of narrative resources that they can productively work through and recount the detailed patterns of their everyday life-worlds. But this is a problem that can be worked through. If we think about what makes interviews work – that is, the simple fact that they are essentially built around normal conversational skills, and people's abilities to build accounts of their actions – then it becomes possible to consider extending the basic premise of an interview into a more extended relationship, and using other media in addition to conversation. This was the idea behind asking Brenda to write the diary and take the photographs illustrated at the start of this section. In essence, through her diary Brenda leads me through her week. Simultaneously in writing the diary she has to reflect upon her relationships with others. This technique, which, following Zimmerman and Wieder (1977), I have called the diary-photo diary-interview method (DPDIM), was the central methodology employed in my research in Auckland. I want in the following two sections to explain: (1) the basic method – and particularly the place of photography within it; and (2) the ways in which the accounts gained through it can be used.

Diaries and life paths

The use of diaries has a long, if far from prominent, history in social research, perhaps most obviously by social historians who have long utilized personal diaries to gain insights into the everyday life-worlds of past periods (see McDonald 1990; Simpson 1997). Social scientists have also experimented with diaries as a research tool. The British Mass Observation Project, for example, which ran from 1937 to 1965, asked volunteers to write research-directed diaries on a range of themes, such as 'pace of life' or 'doing a job' (Holloway and Latham 2002; Sheridan 1993). In a similar way, a number of anthropological and sociological studies have asked respondents to keep daily or weekly journals (Hammersley and Atkinson 1995; Coxon 1988; Robinson 1971; Ball 1981). As a methodological approach this usage of diaries was perhaps most carefully elaborated by Zimmerman and Wieder (1977) in their study of countercultural lifestyles in the United States. Worried about their (in)ability to infiltrate the countercultural scene, and the difficulties of keeping track of a culture which by its very nature was highly dispersed and casual, Zimmerman and Wieder recruited a number of informants to keep one-week diaries of their activities within this milieu. The idea was that the diarists would act as proxies for the absent anthropologists. For thoroughness and to check the integrity of the diarists' accounts, the writing of the diary was followed by an in-depth interview. Zimmerman and Wieder christened their approach the diary diary-interview method.

Diaries (or time-space budgets) were also an integral research tool within time-geography. A distinctive school of human geographic thought that emerged from Sweden in the 1960s and 1970s, time-geography sought to develop a set of conceptual and empirical tools through which to understand society as a kind of 'situational ecology' (Hägerstrand 1976). While many of the above-mentioned diary-oriented methods placed a stress on the experiential dimensions of the diary, time-geography's time-space budgets focused almost exclusively on the collection of quantitative data. Through a detailed mapping of the structuring of individual and institutional projects in time-space, time-geography hoped to gain a carefully contextualized understanding of the processes through which societies maintain and reproduce themselves. To this end, Hägerstrand and his colleagues devoted themselves to developing a notational language through which just such a mapping of this 'choreography' (Pred 1977: 207) of movement and interaction could be undertaken (see Figures 1a and 1b).

It was these mappings that first sparked my interest in diaries. They suggested a way of thinking about the context of people's routine inhabitations of the urban environment. Thus, using this notational language from time-geography a mapping of Brenda's movement through Auckland would look like Figure 1c. This simple time-space diagram provides a useful introduction to the spatial-temporal rhythm of Brenda's week. It tells us where she goes in the course of a particular day, what she does, and how she got there. Clearly it has limitations. Such a tracing provides little more than a ghosting of the individual's path through an environment. Nonetheless, as Hägerstrand himself wrote,

> the fact that a human path in the time-geographic notation seems to represent nothing more than a point on the move should not lead us to forget that at its tip – as it were – in the persistent present stands a living body-subject endowed with memories, feelings, knowledge, imagination and goals.
>
> (Hägerstrand 1982: 323–4;
> see also Gregory 1994; Pred 1986)

Hägerstrand doubted the possibility of developing tools for representing these more sensual and perceptual/cognitive dimensions within a time-geographic framework. And it is precisely this gap that many critics of time-geography have focused upon, arguing that time-geography presents us with a mechanical, lifeless, picture of society (see Rose 1993: 29–31).

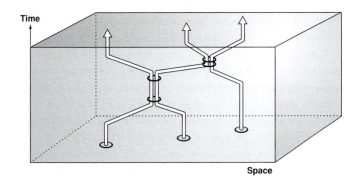

Figure 1a Time–space 'aquarium'. The basic dimensions of time-geography. The arrows are of individuals' daily paths through time-space (after Thrift 1977: 8).

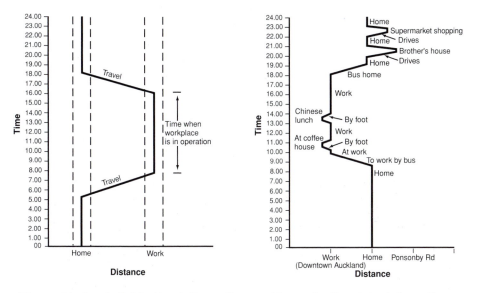

Figure 1b An individual's daily path through time and space.

Figure 1c Brenda's daily path – a Monday in May.

In fact, to dismiss time-geography in such a fashion is to overlook its considerable potential. That earlier versions of time-geography appeared lifeless merely suggests the need to develop techniques that properly acknowledge the productivist element of the body-subject's everyday practices. So, following the lead of Zimmerman and Wieder (1977), for my project on urban sociality in Auckland regular users of cafés, restaurants and bars – like Brenda – were recruited to write a diary of one week out and about in Auckland. Diarists were asked to provide a log of their movements around the city – where they went, at what time, to what purpose, who they went with and who they met. This provided a basic time-space path of their movement through Auckland. Diarists, however, were also asked to describe, in as much detail as time and talent allowed, impressions and reactions to the events of the day. To aid them in this work of description diarists were also provided with a disposable camera with which they were asked to photograph things that interested them.

Unlike with Zimmerman and Wieder, the purpose of the descriptive element of the process was not for the diarist to stand in for the absent researcher. Rather, the diary and accompanying photographs are an extension of the conversation that started between the researcher and the research participant when the two first met and carried on in the interview process that follows the production of the written and photographic diaries. Not only do the diary and photo-diary provide a neat summary of the respondent's week, they also offer a narrative structure around which the subsequent interview can be organized. Thus, as I suggested on p. 123, through the diary (written and photographic) the diarists lead the researcher through their week, a process that is repeated in more detail in the diary-interview. What is more, this leading through is organized around the respondents' own narrative abilities – the aim is not to train the diarists to see like an ethnographer, but rather to offer them the resources so that they can tell a narrative about themselves that retains a strong sense of social and personal context (see also Latham 2003a; Kindon and Latham 2002). The process of writing the diary is intended to offer respondents a technique through which they can focus upon their week and the routines and interactions that give it structure. In a similar way the use of the disposable camera offers a (further) way of capturing a sense of the context and texture of the respondents' inhabitation of the city. Photographs offer a simple and easily intelligible medium through which diarists can present a kind of introduction to the places that are of importance to them, a kind of 'scene setting'. Photographs can also be used to 'capture a moment'. That is, photographs often present a sense of the mood and ambience – of the colour and energy – of a particular moment in the diarist's week in a way that is difficult to capture with pure text (Harper 1998). (For an example of such 'scene setting', see the photograph on p. 120 accompanying Brenda's diary excerpt from Tuesday 1 June; for an attempt at 'catching a moment' see the photograph on p. 121 from Sunday 6 June)

This bricolage of text, talk and photography opens up a wide range of possibilities for narrating people's life paths that simultaneously convey a sense of people's movement through time-space and something of the sensation, style *and* *productiveness* of that movement. It is on these narrative possibilities that the final section will focus.

Photographs and diagrams

What then is to be made of the bricolage of 'texts' produced through the diaries, photo-diaries and interviews? Before this question can be properly addressed it is necessary to define a little more closely just what kinds of accounts we are hoping to construct. Frequently, multitechnique methods – particularly those using explicitly visual techniques such as participant photography – are justified by the triangulation they allow the researcher (Kindon 2003; Young and Barrett 2001). They offer the opportunity to compare and weigh up the overall veracity of the respondents' accounts. However, in developing the diary-photo diary-interview method to study the texture and rhythms of urban public sociality, the idea was not that, taken together, the diary, photographs and interview provide a more complete picture of an individual. Rather, in a way similar to that described by the anthropologist Tim Ingold (2000), each of the different elements of the method is designed to lead us into the world of the diarist in different and broadly complementary ways, while not claiming to fully capture or exhaust the meaning of that world.

Take the photographic diary, for example. Despite the apparent realism of photography as a medium, the photo-diary is not designed to provide a uniquely authentic account of the places visited by the diarists – although, as has already been mentioned, photographs *do* provide a very straightforward way of framing particular places and moments. The diarist's photographs were often of poor quality and poorly executed (see for example the photographs on pp. 120–1). Nonetheless, the usefulness of the photo-diary can lie as much in what the individual photographs fail to capture as in what they do. By providing a concrete, apparently independent and dispassionate point of view, the photographs offer the diarist and the interviewer a starting point to discuss the place or situation photographed: what the photograph is about and how successfully or otherwise it catches what the diarist was trying to portray. And once it comes to writing up the diaries, the photographs offer a wealth of illustrative detail that leads back to the materiality of the world being described.

Which brings us back again to what kinds of narratives can be fashioned from the diary, photographs and interview texts. Any strategy for analysing and re-presenting the narratives from the diaries and interviews needs to retain a sense of the openness that is central to the diary-photo diary-interview method. Indeed, just as the raw material from the method has an obvious bricolage-like character, it is – I think – productive to view the kinds of final accounts produced from the raw material in a similar way. It is perhaps best to illustrate this by coming back to Brenda. From Brenda's diary and her subsequent interview it is possible to draw up fairly conventional ethnographic accounts of her experiences in Auckland. But along with such established techniques it is also productive to employ less conventional strategies. We have already discussed (p. 124) how, through her diary, it is possible to trace out Brenda's daily path through Auckland using time-geography diagrams (see Figure 1c). This conveys something of the structure and rhythm of Brenda's day. But it is devoid of the sensual and experiential elements through which Brenda's day is lived, and it tells us little about the kind of sociality that is bound up within Brenda's particular inhabitation of Auckland. By overlaying details from Brenda's diary, photo-diary and interview (along with the researcher's own observations) onto the basic daily path diagram, however, it is possible to produce diagrams that convey a much greater sense of the sensual and affective elements of Brenda's movement through Auckland. Such diagrams can also give a much richer sense of the topological complexity of the spatial-temporal foldings through which Brenda's inhabitation of Auckland is organized than is possible in a conventional time-space diagram (Latham 2002).

Given the limitations of space I will discuss just one diagrammatical possibility. Figure 2 shows a day in the life of Brenda. In its basic structure it is much like Figure 1c. The time of day is on the vertical axis and distance is on the horizontal axis. As such, the diagram remains oriented around clock time and Euclidean space. This is

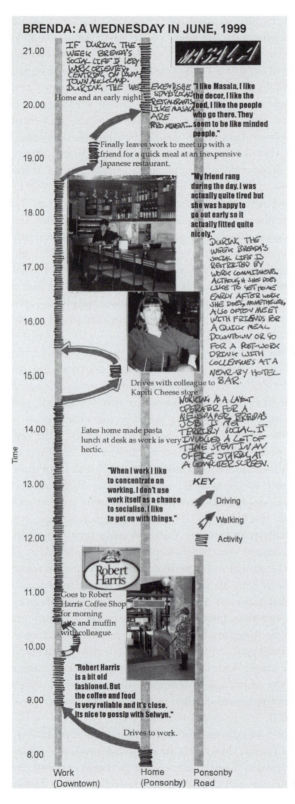

BRENDA: A WEDNESDAY IN JUNE, 1999

IF DURING THE WEEK BRENDA'S SOCIAL LIFE IS VERY WORK ORIENTED, CENTRING ON DOWN-TOWN AUCKLAND. DURING THE WEEKENDS SHE STAYS LOCAL, RESTAURANTS LIKE MASALA ARE 'PRO MOMENT'...

Home and an early night!

"I like Masala, I like the decor, I like the food, I like the people who go there. They seem to be like minded people."

Finally leaves work to meet up with a friend for a quick meal at an inexpensive Japanese restaurant.

"My friend rang during the day. I was actually quite tired but she was happy to go out early so it actually fitted quite nicely."

DURING THE WEEK BRENDA'S SOCIAL LIFE IS RESTRICTED BY WORK COMMITMENTS. ALTHOUGH SHE DOES LIKE TO GET HOME EARLY AFTER WORK SHE DOES, NONETHELESS, ALSO OFTEN MEET WITH FRIENDS FOR A QUICK MEAL DOWNTOWN OR GO FOR A POST-WORK DRINK WITH COLLEAGUES AT A NEAR-BY HOTEL BAR.

Drives with colleague to Kapiti Cheese store

WORKING AS A LAYOUT OPERATOR FOR A NEWSPAPER BRENDA'S JOB IS NOT TERRIBLY SOCIAL. IT INVOLVES A LOT OF TIME SPENT IN AN OFFICE STARING AT A COMPUTER SCREEN.

Eates home made pasta lunch at desk as work is very hectic.

"When I work I like to concentrate on working. I don't use work itself as a chance to socialise. I like to get on with things."

KEY

➤ Driving

🚀 Walking

≡ Activity

Robert Harris

Goes to Robert Harris Coffee Shop for morning latte and muffin with colleague.

"Robert Harris is a bit old fashioned. But the coffee and food is very reliable and it's close. Its nice to gossip with Selwyn."

Drives to work.

Work (Downtown) — Home (Ponsonby) — Ponsonby Road

Time: 8.00, 9.00, 10.00, 11.00, 12.00, 13.00, 14.00, 15.00, 16.00, 17.00, 18.00, 19.00, 20.00, 21.00

Figure 2 Brenda: a Wednesday in June, 1999.

important, as it still conveys a sense of the routines that are central in structuring Brenda's day (and these routines are very much clock based): for eight hours or so of every work day she is largely stuck in her office in downtown Auckland; the time and location of her work dictate to a significant degree when, where and for how long she meets with friends to socialize. However, quotes and comments from Brenda's diary (both in typed fonts), along with accompanying commentary from the researcher (handwritten), are now included in order to explain and comment on what she is doing, why, how typical this activity is for her, and so forth. Here the use of photographs is particularly productive as they can convey a sense of the feel and texture of a place or moment with a succinctness that words can rarely achieve. For all of photography's much discussed representational limitations (see Rose 2001; Harper 1998), photographic imagery points the reader to the materiality of the world with a concreteness that is difficult to match. In addition, the photographs and the commentary work to disrupt the smoothness of clock time and the Euclidean geometry of the figure's basic grid. They help locate Brenda's daily movement within a more complex spatial-temporal topology, providing a context for her actions, a sense of Brenda's biography, and also a sense that not all moments in her day feel the same, nor do they all occupy the same sense of time. Lastly, the commentary and figures – along with the simple use of hand-sketched arrows to describe Brenda's daily path – convey at least something of Brenda's engagement with the world around her, and the strategies and tactics she employs to help make it habitable.

Conclusion

Diagrams like Figure 2 are not designed to replace more conventional accounts – ethnographic or otherwise. The strength of such diagrams – much like the diary-photo diary-interview method on which they are based – is that they offer a range of new narrative resources and possibilities through which social scientists can attempt to think out empirical questions. They offer novel ways of thinking through and engaging with 'the empirical' that explicitly acknowledge (even if only partially) the complex weavings of time-space through which body-subjects make their place in the world. Such diagrams are also organized through a recognition that this world making takes place – and is structured – through all sorts of spatial and temporal routines and structures over which the individual has varying control. In short, they offer a series of tools for dealing with the three questions of context, mobility and production with which this discussion began.

Of course there are all sorts of limitations and difficulties with the methodological style upon which the diary-photo diary-interview method is based. It requires a high degree of commitment and effort from the research respondent and researcher. Some people might also object to the apparent methodological and empirical naïveté that characterizes aspects of the method presented in this chapter. In particular, the relatively undirected participant photography used by DPDIM and the naïve realism it is based on perhaps beg a number of questions about just how such data should be treated. Certainly, there is a need to think further about the status of such photographic sources (see Rose 2001; Harper 1998). But there is an equal need, perhaps an even more important one – see Knowles and Sweetman's Introduction, this volume – for empirically oriented social scientists to more actively acknowledge and engage with the central place visual technologies and practices have in contemporary society. Using visually based techniques like photographic diaries in combination with more conventional approaches like written diaries and interviews not only can help us to develop the scope and utility of these established approaches, but also pushes us to engage with this everyday visuality.

References

Adams, R. and Allan, G. (eds) (1998) *Placing Friendship in Context*, Cambridge: Cambridge University Press.

Amin, A. and Thrift, N. (2002) *Cities: Reimagining the Urban*, Cambridge: Polity.

Appadurai, A. (1996) *Modernity at Large: Cultural Dimensions of Globalization*, Minneapolis: University of Minnesota Press.

Ball, S. (1981) *Beachside Comprehensive*, Cambridge: Cambridge University Press.

Coxon, A. (1988) 'Something sensational . . .: the sexual diary as a tool for mapping detailed sexual behaviour', *Sociological Review* 36(2): 353–67.

De Certeau, M. (1984) *The Practice of Everyday Life*, Berkeley: University of California Press.

Eade, J. (ed.) (1997) *Living the Global City: Globalization as a Local Process*, London: Routledge.

Fairburn, M. (1989) *The Ideal Society and Its Enemies: the Foundations of Modern New Zealand Society, 1850–1900*, Auckland: University of Auckland Press.

Fischer, C. (1982) *To Dwell Among Friends: Personal Networks in Town and City*, Chicago: University of Chicago Press.

Garfinkel, H. (1967) *Studies in Ethnomethodology*, Englewood Cliffs, NJ: Prentice-Hall.

Giddens, A. (1984) *The Constitution of Society: Outline of the Theory of Structuration*, Berkeley: University of California Press.

Goffman, E. (1956) *The Presentation of Self in Everyday Life*, Harmondsworth: Penguin.

—— (1961) *Encounters*, Harmondsworth: Penguin.

—— (1963) *Behaviour in Public Places*, New York: Free Press.

—— (1971) *Relations in Public*, New York: Basic Books.

Gregory, D. (1994) *Geographical Imaginations*, Oxford: Blackwell.

Hägerstrand, T. (1975) 'Space, time and human conditions', in A. Karlqvist, L. Lundquist and F. Snickars (eds) *Dynamic Allocation of Urban Space*, Westmead: Saxon House.

—— (1976) 'Geography and the study of interaction between nature and society', *Geoforum* 7: 329–34.

—— (1982) 'Diagram, path and project', *Tijdschift voor Economic en Social Geographie* 73(6): 323–39.

Hammersley, M. and Atkinson, P. (1995) *Ethnography: Principles in Practice*, 2nd edn, London: Routledge.

Hannerz, U. (1980) *Exploring the City: Inquiries Towards an Urban Anthropology*, New York: Columbia University Press.

Harper, D. (1998) 'On the authority of the image: Visual methods at the crossroads', in N. Denzin and Y. Lincoln (eds) *Collecting and Interpreting Qualitative Materials*, London: Sage.

Hetherington, K. (1998) *Expressions of Identity: Space, Performance, Politics*, London: Sage.

Holloway, J. and Latham, A. (2002) 'Using the diary diary-interview method in human geography', manuscript available from the author.

Ingold, T. (2000) *The Perception of the Environment: Essays in Livelihood, Dwelling and Skill*, London: Routledge.

Kindon, S. (2003) 'Participatory video in geographic research, a feminist practice of looking?', *Area* 58(1): 14–22.

Kindon, S. and Latham, A. (2002) 'From mitigation to negotiation: ethics and the geographic imagination in Aotearoa New Zealand', *New Zealand Geographer* 58(1): 10–18.

Latham, A. (2002) 'Re-theorizing the scale of globalization: topologies, actor-networks, and cosmopolitanism', in A. Herod and M. Wright (eds) *Geographies of Power: Placing Scale*, Oxford: Blackwell.

—— (2003a) 'Research, performance, and doing human geography: some reflections on the diary-photo diary-interview method', *Environment and Planning A* 35: 1993–2007.

—— (2003b) 'The possibilities of performance', *Environment and Planning A* 35: 1901–6.

McDonald, C. (1990) *Women of Good Character*, Auckland: University of Auckland Press.

Maffesoli, M. (1991) 'The ethics of aesthetics', *Theory, Culture and Society* 8: 7–20.

—— (1996a) *The Time of the Tribes: the Decline of Individualism in Mass Society*, London: Sage.

—— (1996b) *Ordinary Knowledge*, New York: University of Columbia Press.

May, J. and Thrift, N. (1996) 'Introduction', in J. May and N. Thrift (eds) *Time-Space*, London: Routledge.

—— (2001) *Timespace: Geographics of Temporality*, London: Routledge.

Pahl, R. (2000) *Friendship*, Cambridge: Polity.

Phillips, J. (1987) *A Man's Country? The Image of the Pakeha Male: a History*, Auckland: Penguin.

Pred, A. (1977) 'The choreography of existence: comments on Hägerstrand's time-geography and its usefulness', *Economic Geography* 53: 207–21.

—— (1986) *Place, Practice and Structure: Social and Spatial Transformation in Southern Sweden, 1750–1850*, Cambridge: Polity.

—— (1990) *Lost Words and Lost Worlds: Modernity and the Language of Everyday Life in Late Nineteenth-Century Stockholm*, Cambridge: Cambridge University Press.

Raban, J. (1974) *Soft City*, London: Collins Harvill.

Robinson, D. (1971) *The Process of Becoming Ill*, London: Routledge and Kegan Paul.

Rose, G. (1993) *Feminism and Geography*, Cambridge: Polity.

—— (2001) *Visual Methodologies: an Introduction to the Interpretation of Visual Methods*, London: Sage.

Serres, M. (1995) *Angels: A Modern Myth*, Paris: Flammarion.

Sheridan, D. (1993) 'Writing to the archive: mass observation as autobiography', *Sociology* 27(1): 27–40.

Simmel, G. (1950) *The Sociology of Georg Simmel*, ed. K. Wolff, New York: The Free Press.

Simpson, T. (1997) *The Immigrants: the Great Migration from Britain to New Zealand, 1830–1890*, Auckland: Godwit Publishing.

Spinosa, C., Flores, F. and Dreyfus, H. (1997) *Disclosing New Worlds*, Cambridge, MA: MIT Press.

Thrift, N. (1977) *An Introduction to Time Geography*, Norwich: Geoabstracts.

—— (1996) *Spatial Formations*, London: Sage.

—— (2002) 'Summoning life', manuscript available from the author.

Urry, J. (2000) *Sociology Beyond Society*, London: Routledge.

Young, L. and Barrett, H. (2001) 'Adapting visual methods: action research with Kampala street children', *Area* 33(2): 141–52.

Zimmerman, D. and Wieder, D. (1977) 'The diary: diary interview method', *Urban Life* 5(4): 479–98.

Chapter 7

Les Back

With photographs by Nicola Evans, Antonio Genco and Gerard Mitchell

LISTENING WITH OUR EYES
Portraiture as urban encounter

*A*RE PHOTOGRAPHS GIVEN OR TAKEN? *When we listen to people, do they give us their stories or do we steal them?*

Picturing the social landscape involves facing these questions because at the heart of all social investigation is a dialectical tension between theft and gratuity, appropriation and exchange. The balance between these forces is more complex than it seems on first sight. What follows is an account of the use of street photography as a means to open up a space of exchange and engender a form of reciprocity between research subjects and observers. It centres on the *About the Streets Project* facilitated by photographer, filmmaker and cultural sociologist Paul Halliday in February 2001. He invited his students at Croydon College, South London, to try to produce a visual story reflecting the ebb and flow of metropolitan cultural life. The setting was Brick Lane in East London, a place that Paul had photographed many times over a period of twenty years. This part of East London harbours the trace of many migrants who have made it their home, from the French Huguenots to European Jewry and, most recently, Bengali communities. Brick Lane is also a magnet for weekend migrations from other parts of the capital. On Sunday morning people converge on its markets from the suburbs, often crossing the river to buy everything from leather goods and the fruits of the 'rag trade' to cheap cigarettes. Paul took his students to Brick Lane and set up large format cameras in the street. On successive Sunday mornings, with the market in full swing, they invited people, often laden with shopping, to give their portraits.

My initial involvement with the project was to prime the students with ideas drawn from urban cultural theory, and particularly the work of Walter Benjamin. It must have been a bizarre spectacle on that first Sunday morning in 2001: the 'pavement tutorial' took place just outside the Bagel Bake at the northern end of

Brick Lane. I offered the students a potted summary of Walter Benjamin's classic essay 'Thesis on the philosophy of history'[1] while my son sat on my shoulders eating a jam doughnut and sprinkling sugar in my hair. The photographers set off down the busy thoroughfare holding light meters up to the sky as if tuning into extra-terrestrial messages.

After that initial session three of the photographers embraced the idea and made it their own. Each added a unique contribution to the group effort. Nicola Evans was the coordinating force and calming presence, Antonio Genco the technical alchemist and Gerard Mitchell the urban collector calling people to the lens. Gerry reflected that:

> No one person was in charge. It took away the preciousness of the photographer because we all contributed to the images. It was just a fluke who pressed the shutter and to my mind all these images are ours. It's like an art school punk band – instead of the electric guitars and drums we had a camera.[2]

Over a period of two years the group returned most Sundays with their large ancient-looking equipment to Brick Lane and literally set up in the street. Beneath the cloak of the camera the world was literally turned upside down, *camera obscura*. The Victorian camera drew the attention of everyone who saw it. On one occasion tourists asked if they could buy it. People were drawn to the camera's ancient aura. Sometimes queues of people would line the street, waiting their turn to go before the lens. This chapter is an attempt to right the 'inverted images' and discuss the quality of what they brought back. The large 5/4 film holders were prepared before each shoot as if polishing cultural mirrors to reflect and hold still the life of the city.

A handful of sand . . .

The brilliantly melancholic writer Theodor Adorno once commented that truth is like a handful of water. I think Adorno chose the right analogy but his chemistry is wrong. Truth might better be viewed as analogous to a handful of sand. Most of the grains slip through our fingers but some stick and can be held in the palm. In a desperate attempt to hold onto these pure grains – and in the intense heat produced by the desire to know and understand – a lens is forged. It is made up equally of the grains of truth that form its elements and the hand that fashions it.

I think the metaphor is appropriate to the way the work has been conducted here because the images all share a commitment to connect with the world, to enter into dialogue with it. This commitment produces an intense presence that is evident in all the portraits. In Plate 1, Reverend Paul W. Bowton is pictured in front of Christchurch, Spitalfields. He looks back at us silently through the lens. Set against the wooden backdrop of his church there is stillness in the image. The photographers asked all their subjects to hold still because of the necessity of using a slow shutter speed that was between 1/4 and 1/8 of a second. In that moment a presence, or a likeness, is communicated. As John Berger has commented a 'presence is not for sale. . . . A presence has to be given, not bought.'[3] The stillness needs to be set against the reality of dynamic and sometimes anarchic urbanity. This part of London has undergone remarkable physical transformation in the last ten years. Smoked-glass cathedrals of commerce sprout from the concrete on an almost monthly basis. Between 2000 and 2002 over 40 per cent of all commercial development in London took place in this district. The stillness contained in the portrait is precious evidence of a human presence in the midst of this tumult, where the high-speed circulation of capital fashions the cityscape in its image. But equally, these photographs are not views from nowhere; they are made from a vantage point and they are guided – if not completely controlled – by the photographers' hands.

How much can we know about the people who offer their presence to the lens? This is a complicated question that cannot be fully answered here – what can be said for sure is that we cannot know everything. Indeed, one of the appealing things

Plate 1.

about the project was the fleeting nature of some of the encounters that produced these portraits. It was this passing quality that drew Nicola Evans to the method: 'It fits in with my whole obsession with everyday life – just that split second, the face that you recognize, the person that you meet and never see again.'[4] This reminds us of the partial nature of what is drawn in the portrait. The size of the Victorian cameras also reminded those who went before them that they were being pictured. The technology itself militated against subterfuge. Nicola accounted for this in the following way: 'They have to come to the camera, it is not sly – it is really honest. It is really straight up. "Can we take a photograph, yes or no? OK stand in front of the lens."'[5]

The human presence that is evident in these portraits is not necessarily narrated. I think this is one of the great advantages of photography in that photographs need – in one sense – simply to be shown rather than explicated. The quality of the images operates outside language and the conventions of The Word. Yet, at the same time, there is something to be listened to in these silent portraits. Part of what is compelling about them is that they contain voices that are present yet inaudible. We have to listen for them with our eyes.

Speaking into the lens

Much has been written about the way cameras operate to survey and govern the definition of what is 'real'.[6] Filmmaker Anastassios Kavassos has commented that cameras are like weapons. When Anastassios is filming he doesn't look through the lens. He points the camera and has developed a blind feel for its eye.[7] Others have pointed to the reluctance of vulnerable communities to having the camera trained on them. The photographers involved in this project found it difficult to approach Bengali subjects, particularly young women. This was in part a result of the sensitivities of the photographers, who were reluctant to invite young Bengali Londoners to the lens for fear that it might seem like an imposition. At the same time public space is not open to Bengali women in the same way as it is for the rest of the people who live here. Monica Ali captures this sense of gendered confinement in her novel *Brick Lane*, that tells the story of a young Bangladeshi woman. For the protagonist of the novel, the journey from the house to the street is longer than the migration from Bangladesh to London.[8]

This is not to say that young Muslim women are not present in the public world of the street. The story is always more complex than can be apprehended in general principles. Plate 2 shows two young Muslim women – Zarina and Shireen – pictured close to Petticoat Lane Market, laden with shopping. On this particular morning they had crossed the river from Norbury, South London – where they live – to buy clothes. Of all the images in this project this is the most furtive. It is a beautiful image: the glow of the vibrant pink and blue suits they are wearing somehow transposes to the monochrome photograph – it seems literally to shine. But contained in it is a nervousness that is not present in the other images. Antonio explained:

> We saw these two girls and they were with their father and a younger daughter. We showed them our book of previous photographs and asked them if we could take their picture. We took a family portrait first and

Plate 2.

then we took an image of the two girls. In a way the first picture was
just a kind of family snapshot. But we really wanted to get the two girls.
We said: 'Your outfits are really nice could we take a picture of the two
of you together?' The first one was a kind of classic family portrait, the
second one seems more engaged in a way.[9]

Perhaps they sensed the ruse, which would account for the tentativeness of the image.
    Part of what I want to argue is that lenses are not always about the control and
fixing of subjects. To see photography as merely a governing technology misses the
instability and complexity of the drama that unfolds on either side of the lens. In a
recent interview Brazilian photographer Sebastio Salgado commented: 'Sometimes
people call you to give the pictures. People come to you, to your lens, as if they

Plate 3.

were coming to speak into a microphone.'[10] It is a mistake, I think, to see the lens as only looking one way. The figures in these portraits look back. They stare back at us. Cameras in this context are like windows that look out onto the street, and through which the street looks in. Perhaps windows are a little like lenses. While we may pass by each other in cities and refuse eye contact, these portraits announce a kind of eye-to-eye recognition, even though the subject looks into the dark void beyond the aperture as if looking into the retina of the eye itself.

What the *About the Streets Project* also offered was recognition to those who are usually not recognized. Barry's portrait, shown here in Plate 3, is a good example. Barry has lived with his mother all his life, in Middlesex Street, close to Petticoat Lane Market. They are part of an East London Jewish community that is diminishing as people move on and out of the area. Gerry explains:

If [Barry] saw, say, a fashion shoot set up in the street, Barry would just walk by and go back to see his mother – it wouldn't be for him. But he saw me and we got chatting because of the way we were doing it, and the 5/4 camera and all. Barry was drawn into the whole atmosphere of what we were doing. He does his shopping at eleven o'clock every Sunday. It meant a lot to him that we were there.[11]

This kind of acknowledgement or 'taking notice', through inviting people to the lens, might easily be dismissed. The value of respectful listening, be it through making photographic images or collecting people's stories, is easy to miss. It is rare, in some ways unique, for people like Barry to be listened to or noticed. Equally, what is true of this image is that the photograph does not try to make its subject into a heroic figure.

On 12 November 2002 an exhibition of the photography entitled *E2 Portraits* (after the postal district) took place at the Spitz Gallery in the Old Spitalfields Market. Many of the 'subjects' were there to see themselves in the show. It was a unique event – I could not imagine a similar equivalent in the context of sociological or anthropological proceedings. It is rare that research participants are present at sociology conferences where their lives are being discussed. Somehow the presence of 'the subjects' made it impossible for their representations to be cast in caricature. The people and the images were allowed to be prosaic compounds of vice and virtue, they were allowed to be annoyingly human. There was something precious about this, yet at the same time people like Barry felt that they had been acknowledged and taken seriously, perhaps for the first time. Gerry remembered:

When he came on the night of the show in Spitalfield Gallery there were tears in Barry's eyes when he saw himself in that show. It's made a difference to his life that he was in that show. It made me feel better about it.[12]

The portraits capture a moment in someone's life that is gone in a fraction of a second, that 1/4 or 1/8 of a second in which the aperture is exposed. It is often said that photographs are 'taken'. It is interesting to me that Salgado in the above quotation speaks of pictures being 'given'. There are at least two senses in which these pictures are given. The first is in the sense of the verb, to give. Those who look back give them; their look is a gift that is received. The second is in the sense of the adjective, something that is assumed as a premise. This is a description of a condition that outlines a sense of being that isn't fully articulated.

Epitaphs to the living

These photographs are a gift in which existence is performed and presented to the camera's lens. This does not mean such 'impression management' is inauthentic, for all social relations are like this. In a way part of the conceit of the 'whole truth' version of social analysis is that it claims to know it all.[13] It is an advance to say that these social selves are incomplete and partial as they are presented and dramatized.

We cannot claim to know it all but it does not follow that we grasp no likeness at all. The portrait of Jackie in Plate 4 could not be more staged. She addresses the camera and she takes her spot and strikes her pose. Nicola remembered:

> She was just larger than life. It was like 'How do you want me?' She was ready to go. She just posed where she was and there was no staging of the image. She was that kind of person. She called everyone 'Honey!'.[14]

Jackie comes to Brick Lane each Sunday from her home in Peckham to buy cheap cigarettes. For all her confidence and poise, there is something else that is opaque

Plate 4.

beneath the veneer of brashness, perhaps hidden injuries or confidential frailties. Roland Barthes once wrote: 'In front of the lens, I am at the same time: the one I think I am, the one I want others to think I am, the one the photographer thinks I am, and the one he makes use of to exhibit his art.'[15] What is being played out on the surface of the image is the inside and outside of identity and existence. But it is also an existence that has passed.

The Peruvian poet César Vallejo once asked in a poem: 'Must we die every second?'[16] Of course, the life that is outlined in these images is a phantom life passed in living. The merit in recording a life passed in living might be easily dismissed or scoffed at. Actually, I think this is exactly where the ethical value of projects such as this one is to be found. The photographs are like epitaphs to the living – unlike their flesh they will not age. Donna's unusual portrait (Plate 5) reminds us too that

Plate 5.

our skin can serve as a canvas for remembrance. She shows the tattoos inscribed on the inside of her upper arms, tattoos that are usually obscured by her arms, although not completely hidden. The music we have to listen to through looking is the melody of Stevie Wonder's 'Isn't she lovely'. Donna lives in West Norwood, South London, and she had the tattoos done to commemorate her goddaughter, Lyric, who died of brain cancer at Christmas in 1997. Donna kept a vigil beside Lyric's bed along with the baby's parents. 'Isn't she lovely' was a lullaby they had sung to Lyric before her illness, but they also comforted her with it in hospital. Donna chose to have the tattoos on the inside of her arms because that is where she held Lyric before she died. 'I guess I hug my tattoos', she said. In the portrait she turns the notes and melody outward and shows them to us. The tattooist's needle perforated inside and out, and the price of these indelible lines was a physical pain that is fitting, given the grief and loss that inspired them. Donna's look contains a strong presence – it is both frail and inviolable.

Nicola, Antonio and Gerry took the idea of the photograph literally as a gift. All those who gave their presence to their camera were given a print in return. There was, however, one exception. Bill is pictured in Plate 6, close to the Bagel Bake. At the time Bill was homeless, or more accurately he was sleeping rough. But this is not a picture of destitution; in fact Bill had made a world for himself in front of the bagel shop. From the beginning of the project he was fascinated by the mechanics of the camera and was insistent about being included. Nicola remembered, 'Bill just followed us down the street and said "Could you take my photograph?" He kept saying to us "What's that? What's that?"'[17]

Bill became one of the regular cast of Sunday morning characters. As time passed he seemed to be fashioning a place for himself. A sense of 'home' can exist without a postal address, it is the 'centre of the world – not in a geographical, but in an ontological sense'.[18] In this way Bill was 'at home' in front of the Bagel Bake. He would set up a stall of trinkets, mostly rubbish, and became a kind of trader in what others had discarded. He hardly sold anything. Gerry reflected:

> You wouldn't think that was a man who was living on the street – there
> is a life in it, he hadn't given up on life. The bagel shop was the centre
> of his universe in a way – he was still enjoying himself. In a way he'd
> found his patch, his place in life.[19]

It is important to say that the Bagel Bake is a place of encounter. It is a twenty-four-hour place. On any given night all stripes of London life come through its door – clubbers, policemen, vagrants, cabbies, newspaper delivery men, all come to pick up bagels, onion platzels, chollahs, lox and salt beef sandwiches laced with pungent English mustard. It is the oldest of its kind and an Israeli who wears a big gold 'Chai' symbol around his neck, which literally means 'life', owns it.

One of Bill's close associates is Nobby, shown here in Plate 7. Nobby is one of the Jewish 'Old Boys' who turn up each Sunday in Brick Lane to work their trade. Originally from Bow, in his youth Nobby was a featherweight boxer, and knew the infamous East London gangsters the Kray twins. He has his dog Snoopy with him, part as companion, part protector. Around his neck are gold chains and rings that are 'for sale'. Nobby is one of the key sources of local knowledge – he knew

Plate 6.

everyone in the area and Antonio developed a special rapport with him. In the lead-up to the show at the Spitz Gallery, the photographers tried to contact all the participants. Antonio remembered:

> Bill didn't have an address – we wanted people at the opening – we went looking for him, we couldn't find him. I had a print of his picture and then a few days before the exhibition I spoke to Nobby. He told me that two and a half weeks before, Bill was killed on the streets – a car hit him, smacked his head and that was it. He looked so alive in the photograph I'd been carrying around with me and then he was gone.[20]

Plate 7.

Bill's photograph takes on poignancy now, like a gift from the dead to the living that can never be reciprocated.

Cities of time

The E2 portraits are about the city and its citizens. Paradoxically it is through these intimate portraits that we learn about a place or landscape that we usually hardly see. I think at its core the project is also about time – the shutter time, the long exposure. In the two years that the photographers worked in Brick Lane they took a total of 200 negatives. Taken as a whole, the shutter on their ancient camera was exposed for less than a minute. 'We were collecting things from time,' commented Gerry:

> We were scraping against the fabric of time and then you would be normal for the rest of the week and you'd think about it and then you would worry the fabric of time again. When you are taking a photograph you are really aware of time.[21]

The photographs are also about engagement and about spending time. But the rhythm of each session couldn't be controlled and the photographs couldn't be staged. Some days the photographers would go looking for particular people and settings but would never find them. They would have to respond to the rhythm of the street. These portraits are cast against the commercial panoramas evident in the publicity material and websites produced by the corporations of the New London. The panorama itself is a form that attempted to represent the 'whole truth' about the natural order, these portraits tell a different story and they won't be cheapened in the same way.[22]

Marshall Berman has written:

> I think it's an occupational hazard for intellectuals, regardless of their politics, to lose touch with the stuff and flow of everyday life. But this is a special problem for intellectuals on the left, because we, among all political movements, take a special pride in noticing people, respecting them, listening to their voices, caring about their needs, bringing them together, fighting for their freedom and happiness. . . . Unless we know how to recognise people, as they look and feel and experience the world, we'll never be able to help them recognise themselves or change the world. Reading *Capital* won't help us if we don't also know how to read the signs in the street.[23]

What's refreshing about Berman is how much his work on urban culture contrasts with the jaded cynicism produced under the influence of anti-humanism and its various companions. Berman is acutely aware of this:

> The bad news is how sour and bitter most left-wing writing on culture has become. Sometimes it sounds as if culture were just one more Department of Exploitation and Oppression, containing nothing luminous or valuable in itself. . . . Read, or try to read, a few articles on 'hegemonic/counter-hegemonic discourse'. The way these guys write, it's as if the world has passed them by.[24]

Berman challenges us to try and read the signs in the street. This is something that the work here has already anticipated. It avoids the kind of heroic immersion that has also been part of the left's legacy in its writing on culture from George Orwell to Bea Campbell. At the same time it is driven by a desire to engage with people in their ordinary circumstances of life.

As James Clifford once warned, in order to return to naturalism we first have to leave it.[25] These photographs are not 'unproblematically realist' images; they are produced by many hands. What is compelling about them is precisely the attention to dialogue, their way of reaching out and trying to read the signs, but always from a particular point of view. The city is ground anew in this lens. It may be labouring the point but the reason why there are no quotations from Bill, Jackie or Shireen here is that they communicate with us through their photographs. They come to the camera like a telephone box, with a direct line to eternity. Paraphrasing Walter Benjamin's famous phrase, it is not what they *say*, it is what they *show* that is important.[26] This is another way to think about the place of photography in accessing and investigating social life. Here images are not 'eye candy' but contain the essence of the message. The photographs also invite a reading that transcends purely visual terms of reference within wider ranges of senses. Of course, photography is a mute form; there is no sound, no smell or touch. But I think there is also an invitation being issued in these photographs. To hear the still voices of the citizens who inhabit these pictures we have to listen as we look at them. We need to project ourselves into them in order to hear the spectral chatter of those who address us directly with their look.

Notes

1   Walter Benjamin, 'Thesis on the philosophy of history', in *Illuminations* (London: Fontana, 1992).

2   Interview, 15 April 2003.

3   John Berger, *The Shape of a Pocket* (London: Bloomsbury, 2001), p. 248.

4   Interview, 9 April 2003.

5   Interview, 9 April 2003.

6   See particularly John Tagg, *The Burden of Representation* (Basingstoke: Macmillan, 1987).

7   Anastassios Kavassos, plenary contribution to the *Street Signs Conference*, Parfitt Gallery, Croydon College, Croydon, 20 November 2001.

8   Monica Ali, *Brick Lane* (London: Doubleday, 2003).

9   Interview, 9 April 2003.

10   Quoted from 'Salgado: the Spectre of Hope', *Arena*, BBC2, 30 May 2001.

11   Interview, 15 April 2003.

12   Interview, 15 April 2003.

13   Erving Goffman, *The Presentation of Self in Everyday Life* (London: Allen Lane, 1969).

14   Interview, 9 April 2003.

15   Roland Barthes, *Camera Lucida* (London: Verso, 2000), p. 13.

16   César Vallejo, *The Complete Posthumous Poetry*, translated by Clayton Eshleman and José Rubia Barcia (Berkeley: University of California Press, 1978), p. 219.

17   Interview, 9 April 2003.

18   John Berger, *And Our Faces, My Heart, Brief as Photos* (New York: Vintage International, 1991), p. 55.

19   Interview, 15 April 2003.

20   Interview, 9 April 2003.

21   Interview, 15 April 2003.

22   See Walter Benjamin, *The Arcades Project* (Cambridge, Mass. and London: Belknap Press, 1999), p. 6.

23 Marshall Berman, *Adventures in Marxism* (London: Verso, 1999), pp. 168–9.
24 ibid., p. 260.
25 James Clifford 'Introduction: part truths', in James Clifford and George Marcus, *Writing Culture: the Poetics and Politics of Ethnography* (Berkeley, Los Angeles and London: University of California Press, 1986), p. 25.
26 Benjamin commented of his own work and his use of montage in particular that: 'I have nothing to say, only to show.' Quoted in Susan Buck-Morss, *The Dialectic of Seeing: Walter Benjamin and the Arcades Project* (Cambridge, Mass.: MIT Press, 1991), p. 73.

Chapter 8

Charles Suchar

AMSTERDAM AND CHICAGO
Seeing the macro-characteristics of gentrification

S INCE 1985 THIS AUTHOR HAS examined the transformation of Lincoln Park, an urban neighbourhood in Chicago, Illinois; also, more recently, the Jordaan and the Western Harbour area, adjacent neighbourhoods in Amsterdam, the Netherlands. Lincoln Park is a former working-class community originally settled by German, Irish and Italian immigrants before the turn of the twentieth century. The research in Lincoln Park, combining photographic documentation and ethnographic fieldwork, has culminated in the publication of a series of articles examining the meaning of community, home and identity to a variety of residents (see for example Suchar 1988, 1992). The Jordaan, a neighbourhood sharing a working-class heritage, has, like Lincoln Park, also experienced significant gentrification and community change during the past quarter century. The communities have other similarities that made them candidates for comparative examination (Suchar 1993).

Lincoln Park and gentrification: a micro-analysis

Lincoln Park was one of the very first central city neighbourhoods in Chicago to experience an extensive transformation process that has, over the years, come to influence community redevelopment in many other, contiguous as well as more distant, neighbourhoods within the city. It has been recognized by other scholars on gentrification and community development as a leading example of trends towards gentrification occurring within industrial countries and elsewhere.[1]

My early photographic examination of Lincoln Park focused on the social and cultural meanings of gentrification and the physical transformation of the neighbourhood to three distinct groups of residents: '*older residents*' who had lived in the neighbourhood for twenty-five years or more and had known it prior to the major changes in the community leading to gentrification; '*urban pioneers*' who had moved to the neighbourhood a dozen or more years before and had helped to change it to its current status; and finally, '*recently arrived*' residents, young, single and/or married professionals for whom the neighbourhood was particularly attractive as a well-developed community with a distinctive lifestyle, socio-economic status and identity.

Through my photography of the minute physical transformations to property, and interviews with residents based on these documents, I was able to discover some social and cultural themes underlying the redevelopment of the neighbourhood. In addition to a vast photographic survey of structures and the physical transformation of the neighbourhood, I photographed fifty families – approximately seventy-five residents – and, using the method of *photo-elicitation interviewing*, I was able to unravel some of the social meanings attributed to the material cultural artefacts and the physical and material cultural changes perceived by members of the community to be taking place within the neighbourhood. The photography of the physical structures and community residents and their private belongings, apartments and homes functioned as an entrance point to the micro-world of attitudes, values, beliefs and personal perceptions (Suchar 1992; Suchar and Rotenberg 1994). For example, I was able to discern attitude sets like '*urban romanticism*' which were an amalgam of beliefs and values that favoured 'Victorian-style' houses, embellishments and ornamentations, as well as a host of other specific predilections, and I was able to link these to attitudes about the community and fellow residents (Suchar 1997).

The Jordaan and comparative analysis: the need for a macro-approach

In the mid-1970s (before the research and documentary photography of Lincoln Park), I had the good fortune to receive a National Science Foundation/NATO post-doctorate at the Sociological Institute of the University of Amsterdam. My wife and I lived in central Amsterdam for over a year, within walking distance of a neighbourhood, the Jordaan, that even then reminded me very much of Lincoln Park, the neighbourhood which also happened to be the primary campus location of DePaul University, where I had begun my university and academic career in 1971. These neighbourhoods, in fact, apparently shared many similar characteristics both in terms of the social-class profiles and demographics of their respective post-Second World War populations, and the trajectory of devolution and neighbourhood revitalization that appears to have been initiated for each during the early to mid-1970s.

The return to Amsterdam and the Jordaan in the late 1980s and through the early to mid-1990s confirmed for me the fact that both neighbourhoods had, indeed, undergone many similar but also some distinctly different transformations. My more detailed research on Lincoln Park, by this time, made me acutely aware of and sensitive to social and cultural characteristics associated with gentrified communities, and seeing and photographing these same features in the Jordaan, particularly in the summer of 1992, on an extended documentary photographic field trip, laid the groundwork for a comparative visual documentation of community change and gentrification in Amsterdam and Chicago (Suchar 1993).

By the mid-1990s, however, my sociological and photographic interests had shifted methodologically to the ability of documentary photography to reflect issues of gentrification that were more 'macro' and structural in nature. This raised a number of structural-theoretical as well as empirical questions. In neighbourhoods that have gone through extensive gentrification, what occurs in the end-play of the process, particularly in post-industrial corridors and areas that are often contiguous to housing development? How is gentrification in these neighbourhoods related to changes and redevelopment taking place in each of the cities involved? How has the urban transformation in these neighbourhoods, which largely began in the 1960s and 1970s, influenced transformations in the 1980s and 1990s and thus the trajectory of gentrification as a social process? What do they portend for changes that will impact on these cities in the first decade of the new millennium?

Of equal interest to these theoretical and substantive urban sociological issues was the corresponding set of methodological issues related to how documentary photography might help provide answers to such vexing questions. I was particularly drawn to the methodological issue of the different ways in which photography might be used to document structural aspects and characteristics of gentrification beyond the personal, home environments and private, meaning-laden worlds of residents. I had explored methodologies such as photo-elicitation interviewing, and had already utilized a grounded-theory approach in tandem with shooting scripts as a basic method to unite field strategies commonly used by photo-journalists, documentary photographers and field ethnographers.[2] I have, more recently, written about these visual methods and the characteristics that influence their potency and effectiveness (Suchar 1997). The opportunity to explore these new structural, urban sociological issues held the promise of testing and applying still other visual methods. The current project extends this methodological exploration as it hopefully also provides answers to the substantive questions regarding gentrification and comparative urban development under examination.

The research issue

Many gentrified neighbourhoods are in close proximity to downtown industrial corridors and areas that have, for decades, experienced sharp economic declines and physical deterioration – the post-industrial 'rust belt' or 'brown fields' to be found in cities like Chicago and Amsterdam. As factories shut down and industry moved outside the city limits in the post-Second World War period (or moved to different cities, as the case may be), many of these central-city industrial/manufacturing zones became no man's lands and very undesirable areas. What patterns of change and transformation are to be found in such areas in different cities? Are there differences between the American and European experiences? These basic questions and those mentioned above formed the basis of a wide-ranging and general shooting script that structured the photographic examination of these neighbourhoods that I initiated in 1997 and concluded in 2001.[3]

These former industrial areas, of which both Lincoln Park's Clybourne Corridor and the Western Harbour area adjacent to the Jordaan are examples, are generally the very last portions of neighbourhoods to be transformed in the process of gentrification and redevelopment. There are many reasons for this, not least of which is the fact that these former industrial parcels are usually the least attractive, but the largest and thus generally most expensive, land parcels available. As property in central-city areas is revalued or 're-valorized' (Smith 1986; Hannigan 1995; Wittenberg 1992), these particular parcels are held onto the longest by owners and municipal and other government authorities who may have conflicting and complicated claims on the deteriorating structures and land (e.g. in American cities, through such means as tax-delinquency and court-ordered property transfers, land held in complicated ownership trusts, etc.). This makes it difficult, or at least economically risky, for redevelopment to occur. The fact that, in some places, the very low value of the land adjacent to these former industrial zones was cause for government authorities in the United States to erect public housing (also now in marked deterioration) made it a potential minefield of politically controversial issues. This pitted private development forces against the interests of local populations, with local citizens' and resident groups and government authorities as participants in often fractious dialogue and debate.

The focus on the macro-issues in these two neighbourhoods in Chicago and Amsterdam allowed me to see new patterns of urban development and structural influence. In fact, the photographic images of each community, seen as a comparative set, I believe, demonstrate the *polarity* of revalorization that can take place in previously devalorized or devalued areas of the central city.

The photographic method and documentary framework

In an essay on uniting a grounded-theory approach to sociological fieldwork with documentary photography, I defined the meaning of documentary, utilizing what I called the 'interrogatory principle':

> A photograph is documentary to the extent to which information within it can be argued as putative facts that are answers to particular questions. . . . This process of asking and answering questions – based on field observations or archival research, and engaging in a discovery process – is an essential characteristic of the meaning of documentary.
>
> (Suchar 1997: 34)

Documentary work can thus be seen as a *process* of engaging photographic images as either answers to particular questions or a basis upon which to ask questions about a particular reality. Photo-elicitation interviewing – the use of photographs as interview probes – represents the latter operational application of the interrogatory principle. The use of shooting scripts (lists of conceptually grounded or theoretically grounded questions about a particular subject to which the photographs will provide potential answers) represents the former.

For this current project, I needed to decide how best to use photography's documentary potential to respond to the theoretical questions being addressed. How to match the theoretical questions to the proper documentary procedure? I chose to utilize a rather modified form of a documentary technique suggested by Collier and Collier in their by now classic book *Visual Anthropology: Photography as a Research Method* (1986): the photographic inventory. I conducted a systematic photographic inventory of representative physical structures located in the comparable former industrial areas adjacent to waterways in both Lincoln Park and the Western Harbour area directly neighbouring the Jordaan.

The field research strategy, essentially, was to systematically photograph these former industrial areas, block by block, sampling/inventorying physical structures of the community in the hope of discerning comparable patterns of use, function and transformation. The sampling procedure I utilized reflects what has been called 'theoretical sampling'. This is a process whereby observations (and photography) sample on the basis of evolving coding categories (Suchar 1997). The photographs produced through this process generally respond to the working query: 'What's to be photographed here that best represents dominant or representative structures and features of these neighbourhood blocks and areas?' A shooting script was constructed that provided a framework for the daily photographic fieldwork in both areas. Shooting scripts were revised on the basis of reviews of the content of these forays and the descriptive/cataloguing and coding work accomplished. The exact procedure for this method of working has been outlined previously (Suchar 1997). The resulting collection of photographs, made and collected as part of this comparative inventory, would be examined for patterns of social, political, economic and cultural meaning.

The photography for this project was accomplished with a minimum of equipment. In contrast to the interior photography of material culture in Lincoln Park during the 1980s, where I employed tripod-mounted medium and large format cameras and umbrella strobes on stands in order to capture as much fine detail and corresponding resolution as possible in the environmental portraits, the present photographs were shot with one 35mm camera and one lens (28mm). The portability and mobility afforded by such a working outfit allowed for a much larger number of photographs to be made in a relatively short period of time. Searching a block for representative images to respond to the shooting script questions driving the field photography was thus greatly facilitated.

The Clybourne Corridor and the Western Harbour: a visual comparison

An initial look at several photographs is instructive: many similarities and differences exist between these two areas in these geographically distant cities and neighbourhoods. Both areas are contiguous to waterways that formed the industrial arteries of the respective communities. Both areas are reasonably close to the former central business districts of the respective cities. Lincoln Park's Clybourne Corridor, due to its positioning relative to the north branch of the Chicago River, influenced the development of the steel industry in the nineteenth century and other industries

dependent on the river both as a means of transportation of raw materials and products and as an integral energy source and processing aid: an example is a
leather-tanning industry visible in a few vestigial, remaining structures (see Plates
1 and 2). From Amsterdam's earlier history to the beginning of the twentieth
century, the Western Harbour area near the Prince's Island was dedicated to ship
repair and ship building, and, was a functioning fishing and commercial harbour
area. The street names clearly reflect this history (e.g. Zeilmakerstraat – Sailmaker
Street, Drieharingen Brug – Three Herring Bridge, Blokmakerstraat – Nautical
Pulley Street, etc.). A few vestigial structures and establishments still remain,
largely servicing a private yachting and boating clientele (see Plates 3 and 4).

The Western 'Dok' or Harbour area: samples from the photographic inventory

After a review of the photographic inventory of structures and areas in this post-
industrial, former harbour district of Amsterdam (375–400 photographs of
representative structures and areas), particular themes and underlying patterns
began to emerge that, collectively, began to characterize the Western Harbour.
Space limitations in this chapter allow for only a very small number of representative images to be considered, but the major patterns can be summarized.

An important point to note is that urban development in Amsterdam is largely
government controlled. Amsterdam, and the Netherlands in general, demonstrate
a pattern of urban development where government plays a significant role in the
redesign of urban areas, including much of Amsterdam and the neighbourhood
under examination.[4] The city has had a very aggressive 'social housing' policy that
has provided subsidies for housing and other physical development affecting the
entire city of Amsterdam including the Jordaan and adjoining Western Harbour
area. More recent government policies have targeted a growing free market sector,
virtually reversing the 70/30 ratio of social to open or free market housing in this
section of the city.[5] Despite this, many of the visible, current transformations in
this area of the city evidence a more specific patterning to the revalorization of the
area in the last quarter of the twentieth century. Social planning and controlled
development reveal a central-city community intended for an economically diverse,
mixed-use, family-based population, the markers or indicators of which were readily
apparent, upon examination, in the documentary inventory.

Housing

My first impression in reviewing the hundreds of photographs of this delimited area
of the city was the extensive amount of new construction as well as renovation and
conversion work on the large structures in the harbour area, most of which are
former warehouses converted to loft apartments (see Plate 5). New developments
almost always include multi-unit apartment buildings and renovated/converted
units redesigned for a multi-tenant/mixed-income clientele, in accordance with
government policies aimed at enhancing the diversity of the local area – even in
building rehabilitations on a rather large scale. An example can be see in Plate 6,

Plate 1 Webster Street and the Chicago River, the Gutmann Tanning Company. One of the few remaining leather-tanning companies located along this section of the river. At one time, leather tanning, one of the industries influenced by Chicago's significant stature as an animal and meat-processing centre, was a significant part of the neighbourhood's local economy. Photographed in spring 2000.

Plate 2 2000 block of Kingsbury Street, the A. Finkl and Sons Company. One of the few remaining steel production and manufacturing plants in the neighbourhood. In the first decades of the twentieth century the neighbourhood supported tens of thousands of jobs in related metal-work industries. Finkl and Sons has played a major role in erecting physical reminders, such as this gateway, of the historical significance of the industry to the community. Spring 2000.

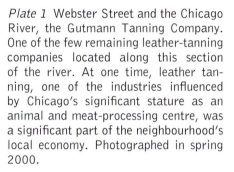

Plate 3 Near the confluence of the Bickersgracht canal and the Realengracht canal. A boat repair facility by and large servicing pleasure craft. My photographic fieldwork in 2000 and 2001 revealed a number of such remaining shipworks' garages and repair structures converted to housing all along the Bickersgracht. December 1999.

Plate 4 Ships' small motor repair facility along the Bickersgracht. The owner informed me that this was the last of such facilities still located in the Westerdok area. On my last return to the neighbourhood in December 2001, the shop had closed and it appeared to have been sold and was being converted to a housing unit. December 1999.

which shows the redevelopment of an enormous former grain silo into housing and office space. The sign announces that portions of the project are to be reserved for 'social housing' as well as 'free sector' or market housing. The conversion of former industrial space to multi-tenant apartment housing as well as the building of new multi-tenant and mixed-income apartment blocks was most evident. During the five years in which I photographed this neighbourhood I observed many industrial structures such as boat storage and repair facilities converted to apartments and numerous new apartment buildings built on land formerly occupied by dilapidated and 'rusting' boat repair facilities that had been 'torn down' to make way for the new structures and their attendant housing functions.

Recreation across the age range

The photographic inventory, in addition to revealing a predominance of housing units either built or renovated from former commercial and industrial structures, also revealed a second leading category of newly built structures: numerous

Plate 5 Housing units along the Zout-keetsgracht on Barentsz Island. The new structures as well as the converted ware-houses visible in the photograph contain both social and market housing units. An increasing number of units of late have been earmarked for market rate housing in this sector of the city. December 1999.

Plate 6 The huge former grain silo undergoing conversion to a massive housing and office building complex. As the sign indicates, the development offers both social housing and market rate housing units. The development is the combined effort of neighbourhood housing corporations, the City of Amsterdam, the social housing department and private sector funding. December 1999.

examples of carefully planned recreational facilities, public and private, intended for residents of mixed ages, most particularly for children, but also for the diversified interests of adults. The large number of playlots of various kinds in an area not even as large as one square mile was notable and impressive. My photographic inventory included more than two dozen different playlots, basketball courts, a soccer field, a skateboard park, a small-animal zoo for children, and so forth (see, for example, Plates 7 and 8). Clearly, the development of this former industrial area had been planned for a population that included children and adolescents, as a family-based social environment. The presence of several primary schools in the small area, built relatively recently, further attested to this. In addition to facilities for children and adolescents, a squash club, live theatres/playhouses and a small number of 'ethnic' restaurants and bars also dotted this small area of the Western Harbour neighbourhood (see, for example, Plate 9).[6] The five-year photographic inventory revealed a neighbourhood that was rapidly being converted from its former mixed-use housing/commercial/industrial character to one with a more densely populated, family-based, mixed-income community with apartment housing units and developments dominating the physical landscape. The revalorization or revaluing of land that had become quite marginal and devalorized following the demise of the immediate shipyard-related services and harbour function of the area was being accomplished through a decidedly socially conscious agenda. (A much expanded and modernized harbour facility has been built due west of this area, while much of the shipping industry has actually been transferred south to Rotterdam, the largest port city and harbour facility not only in the Netherlands but in the world.)

Lincoln Park, the Chicago River and the Clybourne Corridor: samples from the photographic inventory

The photographic inventory of Lincoln Park, the western portion of the community adjacent to the Chicago River and what has come to be called the 'Clybourne Corridor', reveals a very different process and pattern of redevelopment and

Plate 7 Playlot and rollerblade park along the Realengracht canal. December 1998.

Plate 8 Playground/playlot located in the central area of the Westerdok neighbourhood. December 1998.

Plate 9 'Squash City' – A squash and racquetball athletic/social club located on Hollandsetuin Street at one of the entrance ways (pedestrian-bikepath) into the Westerdok area – approached by going under the railroad bridge to the west of the Central Station area. The neighbourhood, during the five-year period of observation, added a number of social and recreational facilities catering to the growing residential population. December 1999.

revalorization. Over the five years in which the inventory was conducted, this area has witnessed transformations and changes that reveal a different set of priorities and a different set of political, economic and social functions and forces at play in this, one of the most intensely gentrified neighbourhoods of Chicago. It should be noted that the city had declared portions of this area an 'industrial preservation zone' or, officially, 'Chicago Industrial Corridor'. A few large industrial concerns, most notably the Finkl and Sons Steel Company, General Iron, and Lakin Industries remain in what was, at the turn of the last century, an industrial area employing over 40,000 workers. The area, however, has succumbed to both the pressures of the gentrified surrounding community and the designs of developers, and has assumed a most interesting set of roles and functions for the community.

Housing

Like Jordaan's Western Harbour extension area, the former industrial area along the Chicago River and the western portion of Lincoln Park has undergone some redevelopment for housing purposes. The type and form of housing, and the proportion of housing units to other structures, for whom it has been developed and built, and what it reflects politically, socially and economically, are all decidedly different, however. The free or open market economy that has largely dictated the redevelopment of this area has produced a social and physical landscape loaded with visual and visible contrasts and anachronisms.

Like the Jordaan's Western Harbour, the area had, at one time, some very small, cottage-like working-family structures that are still present (see Plate 10). Where new housing has been created, the contrasts in scale between old and new are often considerable (see Plate 11). The new housing is quite large, with a heavy emphasis on single-family, privately owned structures. Many houses would not be out of place in an upscale, suburban setting, but when situated and seen in a post-industrial environment, they offer some unusual juxtapositions and views (see Plate 12).

Housing, however, is only a very minor element of the built environment of the Clybourne Corridor area. Relative to commercial development, it was not prominent in the redevelopment planning or, therefore, in the character of this western portion of the neighbourhood. As we shall see, commercial development and recreation were, by far, the dominant defining and characterizing markers of this redeveloped portion of the community.

Commercial development: the shopping mall strips

The photographic inventory of the Clybourne Corridor area of Lincoln Park clearly revealed the dominant pattern of development in the area. Through the confluence of zoning practices, concentrated private development, the focused financial backing of loan institutions, and the necessary political decision making to enable this to happen, the area had become one vast commercial zone – what has elsewhere been called a 'zone of consumption'.[7] The photographic inventory revealed a very large number of 'strip malls' that are highly reminiscent of innumerable similar developments in suburban areas throughout the country (see Plates 13 and 14). Block after block of strip commercial malls – literally as far as the eye (and camera) could see – from the (by now) stereotypical Starbucks coffee shops (Plate 15) to every conceivable chain store outlet and 'box store' commercial developments of many kinds (Plate 16) were to be found in this area and were the most dominant form of built structure documented in the photographic inventory.

The shape and form of the street-paralleling, commercial strip mall (with its off-street car parking offering convenience of access not easily available elsewhere in the community) gave the area a look of uniformity that was in stark contrast both with the rest of the community and with the industrial environment it had replaced. Clearly, the emergence of this area, the sheer concentration of commercial development, its location in the community, and its positioning relative to other neighbourhoods in the city, were neither accidental nor incidental. As in the Western Harbour region of Amsterdam, a design, conception or vision of planning was clearly at work here, but one that departed dramatically from its Dutch counterpart.

The Clybourne Corridor strip mall stores, when inspected for the variety of commercial enterprises represented, revealed a predominance of material goods being sold, with clothing and furniture establishments the most common. There were also a significant number of 'lifestyle' stores selling speciality items of a highly specific variety: e.g. a beer- and wine-making paraphernalia store, a travel book and travel item store, antique stores, art galleries, an organic and imported food store, a house renovation store specializing in brassware, etc. The principal service establishments that were documented in the inventory comprised a surprising variety of recreational and entertainment establishments, including a mix of restaurants and bars (see Plate 17).

Plate 10 1700 N. block of Clybourne Avenue. A nineteenth-century workingman's cottage. During the period between 1997 and 2001, dozens upon dozens of these small cottages were torn down and replaced by new homes, condominiums and apartment buildings but also commercial shopping facilities in the Sheffield/ Clybourne and North Avenue section of Lincoln Park. Spring 2000.

Plate 11 900 W. block of Concord Place. A typical collection of older cottages and the new construction/housing units that have replaced the torn-down structures. Spring 2001.

Plate 12 2000 block of N. Magnolia Street (Magnolia and Clybourne Streets). The siting of new construction so close to the former industrial area's collection of former factories and warehouses produces some startling visual contrasts. Houses approaching the million-dollar value fronting on industrial lots, buildings and commercial developments. Spring 2000.

Discussion: issues of gentrification

The photographic inventory of the Clybourne Corridor region in Chicago's Lincoln Park and the Western Harbour area adjacent to Amsterdam's Jordaan neighbourhood revealed several clear patterns of development. Despite the significant age and 'vintage' differences between these areas, their transformation from their former industrial identity to their present character roughly parallels one another chronologically. The patterning and nature of the redevelopments, however, were noticeably different.

The Western Harbour area of Amsterdam represents a pattern of *social revalorization* and redevelopment. The principal power brokers and decision makers here are the state and the urban and municipal planning agencies that influence social policy and political decision making in Amsterdam on urban redevelopment. In general, local and regional government authorities and housing associations address social housing requirements through mixed-income, mixed-development planning policies and conscious decisions about the family and the need for diversity, to accommodate what is perceived as a more balanced demographic profile in the emerging inner city. The photographic inventory of representative structures and physical transformations revealed a dense pattern of apartment development with a distinct set of patterns favouring families with children and an economically diverse set of housing options.

The Clybourne Corridor area of Chicago's Lincoln Park represents a process of more purely capitalist *economic revalorization* – based on open or free market economic redevelopment where the interests of private developers and financial institutions, and the needs and wants of the highest bidders for their urban 'products', rule the future direction of the urban organization of the central city. The photographic inventory revealed a significant patterning favouring commercial development. This despite the designation of the Clybourne Corridor area as one of Chicago's 'Planned Manufacturing Districts' with the avowed purpose of protecting industrial real estate and, ostensibly, balancing housing, commercial and industrial development within the area. The density and extensiveness of this

Plate 13 Shopping mall, 2000 block of Clybourne – west side. Spring 2000.

Plate 14 Shopping mall at the corner of Sheffield and North Avenue. Spring 2000.

commercial development were significant and when plotted on a map and seen in juxtaposition to and in context with the surrounding cityscape, offered numerous suggestions for understanding macro-developmental patterns.

Particularly interesting here are the implicit strategies taken for enabling the mega-development of multiple-nuclei gentrifying areas. Here, developers seek to consolidate the economic transformation of the central city as a '*consumption zone*' for the upper-middle and upper class, much as described by Sharon Zukin (1991). To say the least, the Clybourne Corridor and Western Harbour areas represent two very different solutions to the social, economic and cultural organization of the inner city of the twenty-first century. The comparative photographic inventories and subsequent analyses revealed a few additional characteristics of community transformation and gentrification as well.

In particular, at the macro-level of neighbourhood regional redevelopment where 'spill-over' gentrification now extends between many different neighbourhoods in Amsterdam and Chicago, the process takes on a 'macro-development' pattern, utilizing 'interstitial' or 'connective structures' or 'zones' as unifying or integrating features to extend this process of urban redevelopment. In the form of economic 'revalorization' exemplified by the Clybourne Corridor, 'zones of consumption' are established as the 'connective tissue' or 'bridges' between communities. These specifically include strip shopping malls and 'entertainment zones' that draw the commerce and 'tourism' that have always stimulated the development of gentrified neighbourhoods.

Plate 15 Starbucks Coffee store. Webster and Clybourne Avenue, north-west corner. Spring 2000.

Plate 16 'Webster Place' shopping centre and the Barnes & Noble Bookstore. Webster and Clybourne Avenue, south-west corner. Spring 2000.

In Amsterdam's Western Harbour area, the regional government has supported the redevelopment of housing by the rehabilitation of old structures and the clearing of former industrial sites to make way for new apartment blocks. It has also, lately, taken the policy position of encouraging some privatization in response to private market forces that see the area as a very attractive alternative and addition to the increasingly expensive market of the canal-belted Centrum. The latter trend evidences clear signs of encroaching gentrification and an increasing tension between the policies of social revalorization and purely economic revalorization impacting on Dutch cities and urban areas – the Randstad – in the area bounded by Amsterdam, Utrecht, The Hague and Rotterdam. This tension between forces leaning towards increasing privatization and state-supported and subsidized social housing policy also has a broader-based relation to larger social, political and cultural forces impacting on the Netherlands and other EU nations grappling with issues of globalization and their respective 'places' in the 'new Europe'.[8]

In Chicago, the creation of 'interstitial' commercial shopping and entertainment zones provides the urban connective tissue to unite gentrified community development in neighbourhoods previously divided by physical, social and cultural barriers. Where at one time the interstate highway system, the Chicago River, the no man's land of the industrial rust belt and ethnic enclaves divided neighbourhoods such as Wicker Park, Bucktown and Logan Square from Lincoln Park and changing neighbourhoods to the east (along a roughly east–west corridor), these new strip shopping malls serve to 'bridge' geography and contiguous neighbourhood development. The shopping malls function as a buffer between up-scale housing development and the remaining, vestigial industrial businesses in the area, serving the needs of both.

Plate 17 The 'Crazy Horse Too' – A Gentlemen's Club 1500 N. block of Kingsbury Street. A very diverse collection of entertainment establishments are located in this southern section of the Clybourne Corridor area – bars, nightclubs, restaurants, young singles athletic/social clubs, off-track betting facilities, as well as a handful of remaining industrial/manufacturing facilities and structures. Spring 1999.

They also serve to unite other axes of neighbourhood development, including the newest south to north 'spill-over' or expansion of central city redevelopment: e.g. development in the South Loop and areas to the south, including Chinatown. All of this has made for a vastly new and changing central city.

Discussion: the photographic documentation of urban patterns

The photographic inventory that provides a visual survey and documentation of the structures, landscape and topography of a region is a method used by a variety of disciplines and professions including geographers, cartographers, city planners and the like. This particular project has confirmed, for me at least, the significant potential that resides in a visual/photographic survey of the cityscape to reveal social, political, economic and cultural patterns and characteristics that mark changing cities. The patterns thus revealed can be linked to structural realities and macro-processes that help establish a more textured understanding of urban social transformation. The photography, when combined with a grounded-theory approach to discern conceptual and theoretical patterns emerging from the intensive sifting and comparison of inventory content, produces a significant empirical documentation, rich in detail and social and cultural meaning. As a basis for a sociological and comparative analysis of urban change, photographic documentation, systematically conducted, provides an excellent basis upon which to see larger patterns of structural transformation that form the 'bigger picture', a macro-perspective on what is happening to urban life at the dawn of the twenty-first century.

More specifically, the photographic documents in this study pointed to very specific physical and social patterning in the two community areas under study. The photographs of Amsterdam's Western Harbour area gave a detailed visual documentation of the patterning of housing development and structural redevelopment, of specific transformations of structures and spaces from commercial and industrial to other functions and purposes, of the social composition of resident groups and the consequences of municipal and regional housing policies. Taken as a whole, at the macro-level, the photographs attested to a pattern of inner-city redevelopment that 'extended' what was already taking place in adjacent sectors of the city (the Jordaan). These documentary photographs allowed for a conceptual clarification of the concept of 'revalorization' to note its distinctive valence and quality as decidedly more 'social' than 'economic' in substance and character.

The photographic inventory of Lincoln Park's Clybourne Corridor revealed a patterning that confirmed theoretical understandings of the function of 'zones of consumption' and gave significant detail to the manifestation of these zones as market-driven or 'economic' solutions and outcomes of the revalorization process. Details in the photographic images regarding the specific sitings and spatial positions of structures and redevelopment helped form a macro-perspective on neighbourhood transformation. The specific features and characteristics of commercial establishments, and the goods and services sold, added significant visual detail to the emerging portrait of community social distinctions and 'material cultural' characteristics which would have been difficult to achieve by any other method. In

fact, I would argue that photography, by virtue of its ability to present a perma-
nent picture of physical and material reality, is the method of choice to document
such subject matter.

The photographic documentation by photographer-sociologists such as Camilo
Jose Vergara in his *The New American Ghetto* (1995) and Jon Rieger's work documenting social, economic and cultural changes in the Upper Michigan town of
Ontonagon (1996) reveal a particularly useful strategy. Utilizing a photographic
inventory including *re-photography* over several decades to reveal changes to city and
townscapes can contribute more than any other methodology to achieving a detailed
understanding of emerging patterns and specific examples of social/urban change.
The photographic inventory work of Peter Menzel in *Material World: A Global Family
Portrait* (1994) also comes to mind as an example of the rich, textured documentation of material culture and the comparative analysis of social class and stratification
characteristics that is possible.

Much has been written about the potential of photography and sociology to
jointly investigate the social world.[9] It might be added that both share a common
interest in the depiction of urban issues and patterns of urban change. The documentary photographic tradition has recorded urban life for almost two centuries –
for much of its entire history – and its record of accomplishment is an impressive
one.[10] It is therefore somewhat surprising that not much urban sociological research
has utilized a documentary photographic strategy to investigate patterns and
processes of urban change and transformation and 'urbanism as a way of life'. It is
my hope that this can be corrected and changed, and that sociologists will be encour-
aged and stimulated by the many possibilities this methodology offers for
understanding changes taking place in our world cities.

Acknowledgements

A brief note of thanks is due to several individuals for their support and assistance
in this project: Jennifer Hoover for her instruction allowing me to further my own
knowledge of digitalizing these photographic images; to Fassil Demissie for his
continuing collegiality and support in our jointly taught study abroad course every
December in Amsterdam; Michael Mezey for his collegiality and understanding,
allowing me take leave of my associate dean's responsibilities during the month of
December, for many years, to engage in our university's study abroad programme
and in this research; and last but not least, my wife Edie, for her generous support,
guidance and counsel in all matters. Needless to say, despite the help and support,
the responsibility for this project is entirely my own.

Notes

1   See for example Fidel (1992) and Hannigan (1995).
2   See Suchar (1997) for a discussion of shooting scripts and a grounded-theory approach
     to documentary photography.
3   The photography and research in Amsterdam was aided by my involvement in my
     university's study abroad programme: a colleague and I developed a three-week study

abroad programme based in Amsterdam, where I would spend three weeks of each year (during our December break) teaching a course on comparative urban develop-ment to a group of university students. I also used the occasion to conduct the photographic fieldwork. This programme is now in its seventh straight year – 1997–2002. The photography in Amsterdam was conducted during the period 1997–2001. The corresponding photography of Lincoln Park was accomplished each subsequent spring during this time frame.

4   For a concise history of Amsterdam's physical and urban planning an invaluable resource is published in English by their Planning Department: *A City in Progress: Physical Planning in Amsterdam* (Amsterdam: Dienst Ruimtelijke Ordening, 1994). This book reviews the various development plans, housing policies and local and regional government policies and programmes affecting the city's growth and transformation, including the Western and East Dock/harbour areas.

5   Personal communication/information from Professor Leon Deben of the University of Amsterdam's Sociological Institute and Amsterdam Study Centre for the Metropolitan Environment (Centrum voor Grootstedelijk Onderzoek) or AME. See also Deben *et al.* (2000).

6   It is important to note that this neighbourhood is within a ten-minute walk or two- to three-minute bike ride of central Amsterdam, with its cafés, coffee houses, restaurants, shops, bars and the tourist 'themepark' attractions that have made Amsterdam particularly attractive to the millions who flock to it year round.

7   See, for example, Zukin (1991), especially pp. 267–70, for a discussion of the meaning of such zones or spaces of consumption in gentrified communities.

8   See, for example, Manuel Castells, 'European cities, the informational society, and the global economy', Paul Claval's 'The cultural dimension in restructuring metrop-olises: the Amsterdam example', Edward Soja's 'The stimulus of a little confusion: a contemporary comparison of Amsterdam and Los Angeles' and Ulf Hannerz's 'Cities as windows on the world', all in Deben *et al.* (2000), *Understanding Amsterdam: Essays on Economic Vitality, City Life and Urban Form*.

9   See, for example, Becker (1986) and Harper (1988).

10   See, for example, Bales (1984).

References

Bales, Peter Bacon (1984) *Silver Cities: the Photography of American Urbanization 1839–1915*, Philadelphia: Temple University Press.

Becker, Howard S. (1986) 'Photography and Sociology', in Howard Becker, *Doing Things Together: Selected Papers*, Evanston, Ill.: Northwestern University Press.

Collier, John and Collier, Malcolm (1986) *Visual Anthropology: Photography as a Research Method*, Albuquerque: University of New Mexico Press.

Deben, Leon, Heinemeijer, Willem and van der Vaart, Dick (2000) *Understanding Amsterdam: Essays on Economic Vitality, City Life and Urban Form*, 2nd rev. edn, Amsterdam: Het Spinhuis.

Fidel, Kenneth (1992) 'End of diversity: the long-term effects of gentrification in Lincoln Park', in Ray Hutchison (ed.) *Research In Urban Sociology: Gentrification and Urban Change*, Vol. 2, Greenwich, CT: JAI Press.

Hannigan John A. (1995) 'The post-modern city: a new urbanization?', *Current Sociology* 43(1): 152–214.

Harper, Douglas (1988) 'Visual sociology: expanding sociological vision', *The American Sociologist* 19(1): 54–70.

Menzel, Peter (1994) *Material World: a Global Family Portrait*, San Francisco: Sierra Club Books.

Planning Department, City of Amsterdam (1994) *A City in Progress: Physical Planning in Amsterdam*, Amsterdam: Dienst Ruimtelijke Ordening.

Rieger, Jon H. (1996) 'Photographing social change', *Visual Sociology* 11(1): 5–49.

Smith, N. (1986) 'Gentrification, the frontier and the restructuring of urban space', in N. Smith and P. Williams (eds) *Gentrification of the City*, Boston: Allen and Unwin.

Suchar, Charles S. (1988) 'Photographing the changing material culture of gentrified community', *Visual Sociology Review* 3(2): 17–21.

—— (1992) 'Icons and images of gentrification: the changed material culture of an urban community', in Ray Hutchison (ed.) *Gentrification and Urban Change. Research in Urban Sociology*, Vol. 2, Greenwich, Conn.: JAI Press.

—— (1993) 'The Jordaan: community change and gentrification in Amsterdam', *Visual Sociology* 8(1): 41–51.

—— (1997) 'Grounding visual sociology research in shooting scripts', *Qualitative Sociology* 20(1): 33–55.

Suchar, Charles S. and Rotenberg, Robert (1994) 'Judging the adequacy of shelter: a case from Lincoln Park', *Journal of Architectural and Planning Research* 11(2): 149–65.

Vergara, Camilo Jose (1995) *The New American Ghetto*, New Brunswick, NJ: Rutgers University Press.

Wittenberg, Patricia (1992) 'Perspectives on gentrification: a comparative review of the literature', in Ray Hutchison (ed.) *Research In Urban Sociology: Gentrification and Urban Change*, Vol. 2, Greenwich, Conn.: JAI Press.

Zukin, Sharon (1991) *Landscape of Power: From Detroit to Disneyworld*, Berkeley: University of California Press.

Chapter 9

David Byrne and Aidan Doyle

THE VISUAL AND THE VERBAL

The interaction of images and discussion in exploring cultural change

Introduction

THE PROJECT DESCRIBED IN THIS chapter began when the authors noted something dramatic happening in the landscape of County Durham. In 1993 almost immediately subsequent to the closure of the last remaining collieries – the very big deep coastal collieries which worked reserves under the North Sea – the structures of coal mining, which had shaped the whole landscape of the area, were rapidly physically eliminated. The elimination was itself dramatic for those who observed it but the longer-lasting impact for many people was a sense of absence in the landscape. Thus David Byrne was driving from his home in Gateshead to his mother's house in South Shields, a routine Sunday trip, and at the half-way point noticed something was missing. The Crown Tower (Plates 1 and 2) was gone from the skyline. It had been demolished the previous week and the whole landscape had changed. The programme of 'elimination' of mining progressed very rapidly. In mining parts of South Tyneside, an area which until the 1970s had four large modern collieries and where coal mining had been historically the largest single source of employment for men, there is actually more visual evidence of the Roman occupation, which ended in the fourth century AD and has no historical connection to any contemporary experience, than of an industry which at its peak in the 1920s directly employed more than 12,000 men as miners, indirectly employed as many again as railway workers, dockers and collier seamen, and still employed more than 2,000 when it ended in 1993.

We wanted to find out how people felt about this profound change – from an industrial economy and culture founded on carboniferous capitalism to something else. We thought that we might be able to use images as a way of getting at those structures of feeling. Images of change – images of how things had been and how they are now – could be used to elicit people's response to those changes.

There are representations of mining as heritage, for example in Beamish Museum in Durham, but such representations periodize mining working life in a distant 'historicized' past, far removed from personal experience. Said questions the authenticity of such cultural representations because the 'new middle class . . . who work in the cultural industries . . . are most well disposed to experiment with the reconstruction of locality' (Said 1993: 97). Jenkins (1992) expresses concerns about the sanitizing process through which innocuous stereotyped images of communities are presented. Representations of mining communities are simplified to ease their consumption, but do not necessarily concur with the 'reality' of lived experience. This seems to be part of the process of understanding the present through a post-modern frame of reference. Historylessness and depthlessness are constitutive features of the postmodern: whole histories are homogenized into a fungible mass. Kaye notes that

> post-modernists not only portray contemporary experience as discontinuous with the past but contend that 'a permanent change has taken place' in Western and world culture and history. In essence they, too, assert that the present, our contemporary experience, represents an *ending* or, actually, an *afterwards*.
>
> (1991: 147)

We thought that we were not dealing with a fixed time of 'afterwards' but rather with the actual lived experience of change, with a process of becoming something else. In the sense in which the word was used by Thompson we were dealing with a period of 'experience'.

> Experience arises spontaneously within social being, but it does not arise without thought; it arises because men and women (and not only philosophers) are rational and they think about what is happening to themselves and their world . . . changes take place within social being, which give rise to changed *experience*: and this experience is *determining*, in the sense that it exerts pressures upon existent social consciousness, proposes new questions, and affords much of the material which the more elaborated intellectual exercises are about. Experience, one supposes, constitutes some part of the raw material which is offered up to the procedures of scientific discourse of the proof. Indeed, some intellectual practitioners have suffered experiences themselves.
>
> (Thompson 1978: 200)

We thought that we could construct a narrative of change by the use of images which showed what had been, and then see what this visual narrative elicited in terms of the way people talked about their lived experience. The use of images to elicit understanding was founded in the simple principle that people talk about what they know. At exhibitions where images of mining have been displayed people come forward and explain their understanding of what has been presented. Visual images were selected for exhibition representing different facets of collieries and mining working life. Much of the landscape of mining available to the outside world is concerned with heapstead buildings and detritus. Mines appear on the surface in terms of the entrance to the underground and the rubbish left after coal has been extracted from below – as pit heads and spoil heaps. As buildings are removed after the industry ends, all that remains is the blighted landscape and even that is now disappearing through major programmes of land reclamation. The actual activity of mining was carried on unseen – below ground – out of sight – hidden.

Availability of images of mining

Examining the significance of photographs and what they communicate raises questions about the reasons for their existence. How and why were they taken? By whom? For what purpose? Beamish Museum archive incorporates at least 200,000 images, of which more than 40,000 are concerned with mining and mining communities (Doyle 2001). The photographs in the collection can be grouped into generic types indicating how mining is photographically depicted. These include topographical views which locate industrial activity in a geographical context, showing heapstead buildings in their relation to towns. Some of these are family photographs and incidentally or accidentally include the coal mine in the background. Photographs of social events depicting mining communities include those of evictions and strikes. Somewhat ironically, the most true to life photographs of groups of miners working were taken during strikes, depicting people on spoil heaps scratching for discarded coal. Photographs documenting collieries at the time of closure present empty and lifeless pictures.

Photographs of people include individual portraits of working people; photographs of groups of workers, such as blacksmiths or sinkers; groups of workmen or individuals at work; commemorative photographs, such as face teams engaged in record productivity for newspaper use; and photographs of specific events. No photograph can give a sense of the vastness of underground undertakings. The other event-type photographs depicting mining communities are journalistic pictures taken at the time of disasters. These often present groups of people waiting at the pithead for news – of what is happening away from view. Mining work is never available for visual recording without some form of deliberate intervention.

The photographs nearest to the 'reality' of underground working life in the Beamish collection were taken by a miner named Tulip in the 1930s. The work areas were illuminated by burning strips of magnesium ribbon which were hung from the roof or roof supports by bits of clay. They are pictures of his 'marras', or co-workers, at work and clearly exhibit old methods of working. Other underground photographs include 'how to' photographs for the training of boys, photographs of machinery and of the construction and erection of plant for trade circulation. These are staged and represent the view the mining machinery manufacturer or the colliery company wishes to present. A photograph may depict objects out of place, or in a dangerous condition which, whilst accurate, is not something that the commissioner of the photograph wishes to portray.

The problem with mining photography is that the industry is carried on in very dark places, the lighting of which, even for everyday working purposes, is problematic. Photography, by definition, requires light to activate its processes. In order to create sufficient light to take photographs in a coal mine, various expedients are employed. Flash photography is forbidden in all flame-lamp protected coal mines because of the potential danger of an electric impulse making a spark in an explosive atmosphere. Specially designed underground flash units, with intrinsically safe housings for batteries, are needed; and the batteries may not be accessed underground. Safe cameras must also be used, with all-mechanical shuttering. Before the flash can be fired gas testing must be carried out. Alternatively, long exposures of exceptionally fast black and white film stock, pushed to the limits of its capabilities in the developing process, capture the essence of ambient light. When this technique is used the directional light from a cap lamp can burn the photograph out, but the result is closer to actual visual experience. Flash photography, on the other hand, flooding the workings with light, would show everything that is there, but would make visible an entire picture which would never actually be witnessed underground.

We used a series of sets of images drawn from those available since the early nineteenth century. As far as possible we tried to use sequences of images – images made at different times of the same scene. Thus we had a set for the St Hilda Colliery in the middle of South Shields which included an engraving by Hair of 1841, a photograph of the pithead in 1900, and an image of the same pithead as a preserved memorial in 1993. We also had sets of images taken underground using flash-light photography which 'revealed' the hidden scene in a way in which it would never normally be seen by those who work there. The flash light illuminated the whole scene which normally would only have been lit by the focused light of a miner's lamp.

The method

In this project we wanted to try out the use of visual images as stimuli for focus groups. That is, we wanted to show groups of people paintings, photographs and simple graphical representations and get them to talk about what these things conveyed to them in relation to a particular theme. We retained the use of a researcher as 'moderator', but the approach was less directive than in most sociological research using group discussions. It resembled the approach of the 'unstructured' interview where a researcher interviewing one individual simply specifies the topic and engages in a discussion about it which is driven forward by the interests of the person being interviewed. This can be contrasted with the 'semi-structured interview' where the interviewer has a set of topics to work through. The images set a context. The content of the discussions emerged from people's response to that context. This technique has been described as 'photo-elicitation' and Harper (1998: 35) describes it thus:

> A shocking thing happens in this interview format; the photographer,
> who knows his or her photograph as its maker (often having slaved over

its creation in the darkroom) suddenly confronts the realization that she or he knows little or nothing about the cultural information contained in the image. As the individual pictured (or the individual from the pictured world) interprets the image, a dialogue is created in which the typical research roles are reversed. The researcher becomes a listener and one who encourages the dialogue to continue.

It is quite conventional for commercial researchers to use images in 'focus group' research, but their use is fundamentally different from ours. Commercial researchers are concerned with the effects images used in advertising have on people's actions. They want to determine what images will lead people to do. We were interested in exploring not what people might do but what they felt about something, in establishing meanings rather than causes. The 'gold standard' method for the establishment of meaning is participant observation. This approach has very considerable value and was employed in literary work (Hudson 1994) which deals with the same substantive topic as our research. However, we wanted to get beyond the reach of simple observation.

The tradition in ethnographic work privileges the observer. The record is the observer's, and so too is the interpretation which results. Moreover, despite the clear contemporary recognition of the far from timeless nature of the social processes which the observer explores, the general character of ethnographic work emphasizes the routine, general and ongoing character of social action. We were concerned not with something which was ongoing but with the social and cultural consequence of a profound social change, with the ending of a history of 900 years. We were interested, not in the routine, but rather in the breaking of the routine, with the lived experience of a point of bifurcation. The images were of what had been, in contrast with what is now. We wanted a response precisely to that break, that discontinuity.

The social construction of meaning engages with processes of immense complexity. Bourdieu's concept of 'habitus' provides a theoretical framework which accounts for culturally mediated, embodied schemes on which established social structures, as well as personal and interpersonal behaviour, thoughts, feelings and judgements are patterned. Habitus is socially acquired. Its socially constituted dispositions are derived from cultural conditioning. It is manifest in outlooks, opinions and embodied phenomena. These (habitual) schemes trammel options for actions and thoughts, setting limits to thoughts and behaviour which are considered meaningful or proper to specific situations or occurrences.

In identifying the relationship between habitus, configured around acquired habits or socially acquired and conditioned embodied systems of dispositions, and its manifestation as practical or common-sense cognition, the middle ground between individual agency and structural determinacy is made apparent. Through analysis of interpersonal discussions – about things which people have in common, or shared understanding (systems of dispositions, predispositions, tendencies or inclinations) – attributes of specifically owned habitus can be clearly determined. What is taken for granted? What suppositions underpin social transactions? How is the culture of lived experience perceived and understood?

In investigating responses to change we were interested in the extent to which that which had been 'unconscious' had become 'conscious'. Generally Bourdieu was dismissive of qualitative interviewing as a research technique to access people's understandings of what they do and why they do it. However, he did recognize that periods of great structural change open up habitus and engender rational self-reflection: 'Times of crisis, in which the routine adjustment of subjective and objective structures is brutally disrupted, constitute a class of circumstances when . . . "rational choice" may take over, at least among those agents who are in a position to be rational' (in Bourdieu and Wacquant 1992: 131).

Whereas people do not think about what they are doing while life runs on in its usual way, when things change they are forced to reflect on their own particular place in the world. They are also forced to reflect on the place of collectives of people to which they have belonged in the past, and to which they may still belong in the present and future. This reflection can be seen in its social context as well as as an individual act. In other words, people reflect on issues of identity in conversation with others about this identity. Our method was based on getting people talking about change. The images expressed what had been and what is. They indicated change.

The conventional wisdom among those who consider the use of images in social research is that research is done *by people,* who work in terms of written text as a way of describing things, *on people,* whose main way of understanding the world is through visual images of it. We were particularly interested in the way in which images might describe a situation of change and we wanted to use images of what had been and of the absence of things, as well as of the presence of things, in order to see what people felt about the way their lives had changed in the very recent past.

Pictures and groups

The actual conduct of the research was straightforward. We set up twelve group discussions. The exhibition was held in the sports pavilion of the Harton and Westoe Colliery Miners' Welfare. We invited the groups to the venue, showed them the exhibition in an informal way, and then asked them to talk about whatever it prompted them to consider. The final group of 'rapporteurs' met in the North East Institute of Mining and Mechanical Engineers in Newcastle, where the project was based. The discussions were taped and transcribed, and our research is based on an analysis of the transcriptions in relation to a reconsideration by ourselves of the significance of the images we presented.

The images

Originally our intention was that the images would serve primarily as the basis of group discussions. In the preparation of the images we realized that they represented important research objects in their own right precisely because they were visual records of change. Coincidentally, one of us (see Byrne 1998) was working on ideas to do with the use of chaos/complexity theory in the social sciences. Central to these perspectives is the idea of non-linear transformation, of phase shifts. Adam

(1994, 1995) has been explicitly influenced by ideas from chaos/complexity theory, and we were able to draw on her discussion of time. The images began to serve as the foundation of an understanding which was based around two conceptions of the 'time of coal'. The first is of an overall time of coal, as had been illustrated by our diagrammatic representation of historical changes in mining employment in South Shields. Within this there is a time of 'modern coal', which begins after the Second World War. This time of modern coal was not a concept we had before we began the research. It emerged from our own 'researching' of the images as they were prepared for the purposes of stimulating group discussion. We deliberately prepared a time sequence for Westoe Colliery but realized that other images could be ordered, in fact had an intrinsic order, which represented more than a simple continuous chronology. The preparation of the research became research in itself: the images are objects of qualitative research. The illustrations for this chapter (Plates 1–3) are the third, fourth and fifth in a series of six images of Westoe Colliery which showed it under construction, in existence, being demolished, demolished, the bare cleared site, and a commemorative plaque marking the location of the colliery. This was a very slow movie in six frames across nearly forty years.

Another 'emergent' characteristic was that as we worked with the images we realized that we should distinguish between the 'visible' and 'invisible' landscapes they represented. A series of images of the last phase of this hidden world had been prepared for exhibition, but we had not realized quite how hidden it was. The authors had both 'seen' this world, although not to the extent that a photograph portrays it, but most people had not, certainly not in its 'modern' form. All our respondents had direct experience of the visible side of coal, the fruiting body of the hidden mycellae which literally undermined the place in which they lived (just as a mushroom is only the visible part of a much larger organism, the bulk of which remains unseen, the workings at the pit-head represent only a fraction of what lies underground). The images of 'below' for many of them represented a confrontation with new experience. Even for experienced miners the image in a well-lit photograph went beyond what they had previously seen.

The groups

The twelve groups were: a group of ex-miners who manage the colliery welfare; a group of former mining officials – pit deputies and overmen who had worked in the South Shields collieries; a group from a women's health project in South Shields; a group of students attending a business studies course; a group of people with interest in the arts; a group selected at random from the ward; a group from an adult arts course; a group from a local arts project; a group who primarily were amateur artists; a group drawn from users of the colliery welfare; a group of friends of a local hospital porter; a group of people involved in an industrial archaeology preservation scheme; and finally a group drawn from people who had participated in other focus groups and had indicated that they would be willing to come back and discuss with us what we thought we had found out. This last group was the immediate reflexive element of the project.

Plates 1–3 Crown Tower sequence, Westoe Colliery.

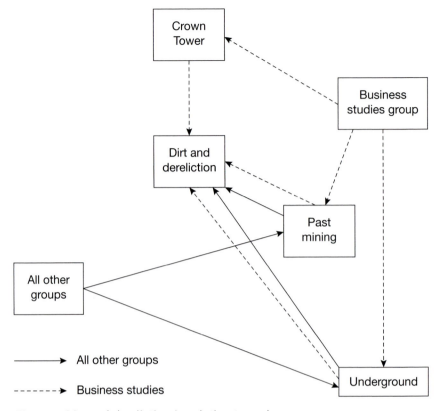

Figure 1 Dirt and dereliction in relation to socioscape.

In Figure 1 the direction of 'understanding' is indicated by the flow of the arrows. Thus it shows that the business studies students associated all representations of mining with dirt and dereliction – with a gone and good riddance past – whereas the other groups did not have this view of the 'modern' Crown Tower images. It is important to note that the visual sources of this understanding seem to help the visualization of the model we have generated of it in Figure 1. Pictorial models of this kind seem a useful link between representations in the form of images and causal accounts generated from textual interpretations.

The concept of socioscape is a useful tool in articulating an understanding of the products of research based primarily around visual representations of landscape. We had conceived the whole project as one addressing the significance of landscape. This reflects the 'policy significance' of the transformation of the landscape through the physical elimination of the structures of mining. The idea of socioscape can contain this visual element and we can see how changes in the experience of the visual everyday matter in relation to 'structures of feeling'. Figure 1 shows how the temporal dimension seems crucial to the formation of interpretations as a basis for action – in essence that socioscape must be a temporal as well as spatial construct. The comments of the 'post-coal' group suggest that the policy makers who removed the mining structures had succeeded in their objective of 'restructuring' identities beyond coal. We have no documentary evidence of this direct intention in relation to mining structures but the Tyne and Wear Development Corporation explicitly stated that it demolished a very modern shipyard in Sunderland with the exact intention of demonstrating that the industrial past was gone and was not going to return. Again, the time ordering – historicity – of images seems to offer a format which stimulates focus group members to express – literally to give forth – complex understandings of their worlds.

We will conclude by asserting the value of the approach described here. The project was funded primarily as a way of assessing the utility of the method. We think it works very well.

References

Adam, B. (1994) *Time and Social Theory*, Cambridge: Polity.
—— (1995) *Timewatch*, Cambridge: Polity.
Albrow, M. (1997) 'Travelling beyond local cultures: socioscapes in a global city', in J. Eade (ed.) *Living the Global City*, London: Routledge.
Bourdieu, Pierre and Wacquant, Loïc J.D. (1992) *An Invitation to Reflexive Sociology*, Chicago: University of Chicago Press.
Byrne, D. (1998) *Complexity Theory and the Social Sciences*, London: Routledge.
Caunce, Stephen (1994) *Oral History and the Local Historian*, London: Longman.
Doyle, Aidan (2001) *Aidan's Beamish Mining Photos Book*.
Harper, D. (1998) 'An argument for visual sociology', in J. Prosser (ed.) *Image Based Research*, Brighton: Falmer Press.
Hudson, Mark (1994) *Coming Back Brockens: A Year in a Mining Village*, London: Cape.
Jenkins, R. (1992) *Pierre Bourdieu*, London: Routledge.
Kaye, H.J. (1991) *The Power of the Past*, Hemel Hempstead: Harvester Wheatsheaf.
Said, E.W. (1993) *Culture and Imperialism*, London: Chatto & Windus.
Thompson, E.P. (1978) *The Poverty of Theory and Other Essays*, London: Merlin Press.

Chapter 10

Ana Maria Mauad and Alicia J. Rouverol

With photographs by Cedric N. Chatterley

TELLING THE STORY OF LINDA LORD THROUGH PHOTOGRAPHS

IN MAY 2002 ALICIA ROUVEROL was invited to a conference
to discuss her co-authored book, *'I Was Content and Not Content': The Story of
Linda Lord and the Closing of Penobscot Poultry* (Chatterley and Rouverol 2000). The
book explores the closing of Maine's last broiler-processing plant and the effects of
plant closure on one of the plant workers, Linda Lord, using oral history text and
photographs to retell her story.[1] Rouverol suggested showing slides, in addition to
reading text from the book, to depict Linda Lord's experience, and urged the
conference organizers to invite Lord to participate, as well as project photographer
and co-author Cedric Chatterley since his images were crucial to the book. The
organizers asked how the presentation might fit into the existing conference format.
A folklorist by training, Rouverol's research on workers and plant closure meant
that she was paired ordinarily with labour and/or social historians at academic
conferences.[2] In the end, our panel was granted an evening programme slot alongside other slide and video presentations, largely because the organizers seemed
nonplussed by an academic presentation that was so visually driven. Because the
historical analysis included – in fact, relied upon – visual documentation to expli-
cate its points, the presentation was relegated to a segment of the programme
designed for 'visuals' and not for 'content' or analysis.

   We raise this point not to criticize the conference organizers, but to raise an
underlying theme of our chapter: visual methods of presenting historical research
are a legitimate, and not a secondary, tool for historical interpretation. As Caroline
Knowles and Paul Sweetman have noted, 'Visual methods provide an alternative
means of formulating, conducting and disseminating research, and – more particularly – a productive and evocative means of uncovering and demonstrating links
between the general and the particular, the global and the local, society and the

individual, biography and place' (personal communications, December 2001). Not a lesser alternative, simply different. Text and images taken together, as we will argue in this chapter, can have a particular kind of effect. 'When experienced social scientists who are also skilled photographers aim to produce images which have both documentary reach and aesthetic quality, these can – in combination with verbal text – generate a type of social science understanding which is very rich' (Chaplin 1994: 221–2). We would argue further that, through text and images, historians can tell a historical narrative, in this case, a 'narrative of deindustrialization'. What emerges is a 'dialogue' between the words (written analysis and/or oral history text) and photographs, in which neither medium is privileged but rather both build collectively to tell a cohesive narrative. Through this kind of intertextuality between text and images, historians, sociologists and documentarians can gain particular insights and create new kinds of knowledge and understanding.

Our chapter explores this new way of making history as reflected in *'I Was Content and Not Content': The Story of Linda Lord and the Closing of Penobscot Poultry*. The book involved multiple collaborators in a polyphonic approach, and in a different, and rather creative, form of building historical contexts, conveying our understanding of larger processes through particular cases – as in the trajectory of one woman worker, Linda Lord, whose narrative is 'told' through words and photographs. We will analyse here not only the story of Linda Lord as told in this narrative of deindustrialization, but also the ways in which images, in combination with text, can be used to 'visualize' deindustrialization and other social and economic phenomena.

Economies of scale

In 1976 the Italian historian Carlo Ginsburg wrote a book telling the story of Menocchio, an Italian peasant from a small community located in the hills of the Friuli region, who was convicted for heresy by the Holy Inquisition in the sixteenth century (1976: 309). Ginsburg rescued this obscure peasant from the past through a very original analysis. While rebuilding the order of facts that determined the condemnation of Menocchio, he narrated the story of a man and his experiences of faith and religious sensibility in a world ordered by dogmas and threatened by religious wars. In this narrative appears the daily life of the common people: their reaction to facing their fears and their ability to create other possibilities of belief. All of this research was based on substantive documentation and a precise sense that history can deal with different kinds of scale. As the English historian Eric J. Hobsbawm comments, it doesn't matter whether you use the telescope or the microscope, you are seeing the same cosmos (1998: 336). Ginsburg and other Italians historians, such as Giovanni Levi and Edoardo Grendi, called it 'micro-history' (1991: 354). They defend their project as an alternative scale for historical analysis, in which the historical generalizations are considered not as an immutable frame that involves all singular cases, but as a dimension that has to deal dialectically with the specificity of particular stories. Historian Steven Biel argues the point from another direction: it is the individual stories, uncovered through oral history, that often challenge our historical generalizations (1995: 704–9).

In '*I Was Content and Not Content*', Chatterley, Cole and Rouverol developed a project that dealt with a general problem in the US economy: the process of deindustrialization in a globalized world. This process affected not only the state of Maine but also many other regions of the country, representing a massive problem that ideally should be faced by those in power as a social and collective matter. Analyses have been made of this process on a quantitative level, as the co-authors knew; but they wanted more than statistics of unemployment. They wanted to reach readers through a 'narrative of deindustrialization', not by an economic approach, but by exploring the daily life of individuals: workers losing their jobs, facing their fears and trying to survive.

To address the problem the co-authors reduced the scale: by telling the story of Linda Lord, through tape-recorded interviews and photographs – a 'close-up history', to use a photographic metaphor. Oral history is no longer radical to historians; its methodology has been integrated into the problematics of social history over the past thirty years. Today it is impossible to work with issues such as historical memory, contemporary history or the history of urban cultures, among others, without dealing with visual and oral sources, through an intertextual approach (Vilches 1992).

Using images to develop a research agenda

'*I Was Content and Not Content*', and its project beginnings, are noteworthy precisely because images played a central role from the start. The book grew out of a modest

Plate 1 Workers transferring poultry from one conveyor to another.

documentary project developed initially in 1988 by Stephen Cole and Cedric Chatterley. Penobscot Poultry Inc. – Maine's last broiler processor and a mainstay of Belfast, Maine (population 6,200) – would be closing shortly, and Cole thought the project should be documented visually, as well as through tape-recorded interviews. Ten days before Penobscot was to close they toured the hatcheries and grain mill; a week later they toured the plant. The photographs Chatterley made on those two shoots would become the core of a travelling exhibit and the book. But in that moment, as he now describes it, Chatterley had to 'photograph first, think later'. It was a tense time: at least 400 plant workers would be losing their jobs and prospects for future employment looked bleak.[3]

On Penobscot's closing day, Chatterley returned to the plant in the hope of photographing one last time. Management could not provide him an escort, as they had for the original tour. Chatterley slipped into the back entrance of the plant, where he found himself in the heart of Penobscot's slaughtering area. It was there that he discovered Linda Lord for the first time. The photographs he made of her, just hours before the plant's closing, would become the centrepiece of the book. They met later that afternoon at Rollie's Cafe in Belfast, when he and Steve attended Penobscot's closing day party. Lord recognized Chatterley and called them over to her table. She told them her story and agreed to be interviewed the following week. Chatterley's photography had already become the driving force of the project, leading them to their chief interviewee.

Born in 1948, in Waterville, Maine, Linda Lord had grown up in a family intimately linked to poultry. Her father had been a pollorum (poultry blood) tester for the University of Maine, and the family had raised laying hens. 'I was the type

Plate 2 Linda Lord at work in the 'blood tunnel' on the last day of Penobscot Poultry, 24 February 1988.

of kid growing up that nothing bothered me – blood or anything like that', Lord commented. 'I guess just being a country girl and being brought up on the farm and stuff. Blood never bothered me.' After high school, she went on to take a job at Penobscot Poultry, where she worked for twenty years. When Lord started at the plant, she worked in 'transferring', hanging poultry on the plant's mechanized lines. After five years, she moved into the 'blood tunnel', not only because of the pitfalls of blood poisoning associated with 'transferring' but because the pay was far better.[4] 'At the time I was going through a divorce,' she said, 'so I was out to get as much money as I could to support myself', Lord would lose the sight of her right eye on the job; participate in the 1984 strike for higher wages and benefits; face sexual harassment; and address (much later still) the challenge of trying to care for her ailing and ageing parents in the midst of losing her job at Penobscot Poultry.[5] Though Lord's edited oral history text was the book's central vehicle for her story, the photographs remained integral to the process.[6] Some aspects of Lord's experience could only, or perhaps best, be 'told' visually.

A story of contrasts told through text and photographs

Cole: Would you say you were discontent, though, during the years you worked at Penobscot?

Lord: I really wasn't happy. When I first went to work there, my hands were awful sore. They would swell up. You'd go home and you'd soak them and try to get so you could move them. And about when you got up in the morning so you could move your hands, you were back in there and you had to go through it again. Oh, it might take two or three months, and finally your hands got used to it. But it was a job. It was a fairly good paying job for around this area at that time. So, in some ways, I was content and not content.

To understand better how Chatterley's images helped 'tell' the story of Linda Lord, it may be useful to lay out some of the book's substantive arguments: namely, the effects of plant closure generally on workers, pointing to the social impact of industrial decline (or 'deindustrialization');[7] the question of whether Penobscot Poultry actually had to close; and Linda Lord's ambivalence about her work at Penobscot. Lord's 'content and not contented-ness' would become the central point of Rouverol's analysis, as well as of labour historian Michael Frisch's subsequent interpretation of her story.[8] The selection and placement of the photographs would only reinforce that interpretation.

The book aims to use Lord's experience as a window (or telescope) onto workers' experience more broadly. Through text and images, the authors illustrate the social and human costs of deindustrialization, which economists and historians have only recently begun to consider. By charting Lord's experience of plant closure, the reader can understand just what Penobscot's closing meant for her – indeed, what plant closure means for laid-off workers anywhere. The effects of a plant shutdown have a kind of 'fanning out' effect from the initial plant closure itself. What begins as job loss, producing short-term unemployment at a minimum, can lead to longer-term difficulties. Often subsequent jobs, workers find, do not provide comparable income (Wallace and Rothschild 1988: 19–20). (In Lord's case, the loss of sight in her right eye at Penobscot significantly impaired her ability to secure work in other industries, so that she had even fewer options than the other workers.) Losing seniority on the job can also make workers especially vulnerable to lay-offs on their new jobs. During times of severe recession or in areas where there are few employment opportunities – like Belfast, Maine, where Penobscot was located – plant closure has a more significant impact still. Studies reveal that at least one-third of those affected by a plant closing will experience long-term unemployment (Bluestone and Harrison 1982: 51–3). Women, displaced older workers, and minorities are especially hard hit.[9] Chatterley's photographs, depicting Belfast's relatively impoverished environs, and showing the large number of women and older workers in the plant, drive home this point. We know as readers that the plant's closure will significantly affect their lives.

Lord's experience after Penobscot's closing illustrates the unique effects of industrial decline on women workers. Her job retraining course – touted as a means by which workers can start anew – did not enable Lord to retool easily for the post-industrial age. Because of the loss of sight in her eye, she was ill-equipped to maintain the reading load for the oil burner course she had enrolled in. Equally discouraging was the experience of being shoved aside, literally, by the men in the class as all the students gathered around the oil burner for instruction. Lord dropped out of the course and continued her job search, but felt hampered by her lack of higher education. As she said of her oldest brother, 'He's got the education behind him, so he can probably step out and get another good job somewhere.' The photo-graph of Lord taking a test at Champion Paper Company most keenly illustrates Lord's disadvantage as a woman worker. We see her surrounded by men; in the foreground is the large, imposing shoulder of the man who administered the test that day.

Yet Lord, it seemed initially, defied the statistics; within six months of losing her job, she found work at a local rope-making factory employing 30–35 workers. With a solid medical benefits package but no retirement benefits, Lord felt that she had improved her work situation, despite the job's insecurity (linked, as it was, to the defence industry). The work was a lot cleaner and she got a better hourly wage, although she was paid piece-rate. As she put it, 'Well, I'll tell you, looking at ten miles of rope goes a lot faster than watching chickens go by on a line.' Most impor-tantly, Lord felt the job enabled her to stay in her home community and tend to her family. Chatterley's photographs of Lord at her new rope-making job are both dark and ambiguous. One image in particular (the last image in the book depicting Lord at work) shows her gazing into the rope-making machine towards the viewer, as if looking into her future, implying the uncertainty of her new circumstances.

In 2001, after suffering a fire in her home – and moving between various friends' homes until a settlement could be made and she could rebuild her house – Lord was laid off from her job. She was hired by a local fish-packing firm, then laid off once more. In March 2002, she suffered a stroke that kept her in rehabilitation for over a year. Lord does not blame Penobscot's closing for the subsequent events in her life; but there's no question that its closing resulted in a series of less stable employment situations for her.

Whether Penobscot might have avoided closure is another key question posed in the book.[10] Most attribute Penobscot's and the industry's decline to competition from southern markets, which offered cheaper labour, as well as to the high costs of fuel and especially the expense of shipping grain to the state. But other factors also contributed to the industry's failure: poor management, problematic government policies and unsustainable loans. Some argue that the industry might have survived if the grain predicament alone had been adequately handled; others claim that the younger family members had no real interest in carrying the industry forward. Regardless of the reasons, the industry did fail or, as some critics claim, actually fled the state, presumably for more 'business-friendly' environs.[11] The fate of Penobscot Poultry, Rouverol concludes in the book, is an example of capital mobility.[12]

What does this mean in human, social terms? What did it mean for Linda Lord and other plant workers at Penobscot, indeed any plant workers facing lay-offs? Lord's experience at Penobscot and thereafter points to how individuals cope with change, hardship and uncertain times to create possibilities where few exist. Perhaps most importantly, her story reveals some of the challenges and complexities that most human beings share. Regardless of how and why she lost her position, Lord still expressed considerable ambivalence about her work at Penobscot. 'I was content and not content', she says of her job there; and this seeming paradox proved central to Lord's story. During the interviews, she spoke frequently in what seemed to be paradoxical terms on a variety of topics: her relationship with her employers, her perspectives on business, but most especially her feelings about her work life; she was 'content and not content'. Rouverol went on to interview and develop an ongoing dialogue with Lord to address this key question about her relationship to her work. This final collaboration with Lord became a central part of the book, as it enabled the authors to deepen her involvement in the project and helped shape the final product.[13] 'I was content and not content' had become the book's unifying theme. Lord's comments in that final interview reinforced the authors' assessment that being 'content and not content' did not reflect a kind of 'divided consciousness' but rather a more complete understanding of Lord's life experience. Her seemingly contradictory perspectives were in fact integrated. Lord's reasons for working at Penobscot and staying in her home community became apparent: economics, gender, rural values, family dynamics, commitment to home, commitment to family, all played a role. Her words ('I was content and not content') imply paradox or contradiction; but her story (what she actually tells us throughout the narrative) implies polyphony, expressing multiple threads and perspectives simultaneously (Rouverol 1995). Lord's ability to embrace all aspects of her experience, her willingness to acknowledge conflicting needs and desires, concerns and interests, might well be an example for us all. By presenting the range of Lord's experience at Penobscot – her appreciation of her employers, as well as her anger at their unjust behaviour – the authors sought to bring all sides to dialogue. For it is through dialogue that political and economic crises such as deindustrialization can perhaps begin to be addressed.

And it was precisely through the dialogue between text and images in the book that the authors drove home their points about Lord's 'content and not contentedness' and the effects of deindustrialization on workers like Linda Lord. The photographs Chatterley made – and, more critical still, their selection and place-ment – give the reader a visual sense of Lord's ambivalence. A key example would be the placement of the image of the foreman, standing in the dark, with his back to the light, opposite Lord's text about the workers' mixed prospects after closing (see Plate 3). In a broader sense, the images depicting Lord's experience at the plant, in comparison to the photographs of life at home and in her community, illustrate a life of contrast: the dirtiness of the 'blood tunnel', the relative harmony of her home and community life; cutting chickens' throats, at one end of the spectrum, playing drums in a country and western band, at the other. The particular difficul-ties Lord faced due to her job loss are amply illustrated through the book's words and images. At the same time, the text and photographs show Lord struggling to secure subsequent work and succeeding – against the odds – if only for a time.

Visualizing deindustrialization

Although the process of editing and selecting the images creates, alongside the inter-views, a narrative of the book, the very act of taking pictures also anticipates what is worth being shown by the photographs:

> On a cold and clear February morning in 1998, accompanied by oral historian Steve Cole and a plant manager, I [Chatterley] walked the entire length and width of Penobscot Poultry, photographing as much as I could, stopping only to wipe the steam from my camera lens or to change the film. A week earlier, Steve and I had been given a one-day

Plate 3 Foreman standing next to a window overlooking Penobscot Bay.

tour of the grain mill, hatchery, and poultry barns outside Belfast in the
midst of a blinding snowstorm, but nothing could have prepared me for
what I saw and heard during the three-hour tour inside the plant itself.
People everywhere worked in a steady rhythm. . . . The motion, the
noise, the blood, and the stench stick vividly in my memory today.

(Chatterley and Rouverol 2000: xv)

As an eyewitness of a plant closing, Chatterley's photographic message reveals
a contradictory world. In dialogue not only with the consolidated tradition of documentary photography but also with his vivid experience of the plant, and with the
feelings from the workers' community, especially Lord (whom he interviewed),
Chatterley built a visual narrative that integrates multiple glances and sensibilities.
This is why in his photographs the sense of revelation and testimony is mixed with
a strong feeling of contradiction, expressed by Lord's statement: 'I was content and
not content'. Yet it is not only the content of the photos, but also the way he has
photographed these scenes, that captures the entire meaning of their expressiveness.

In total, the book featured fifty-seven photographs, including the image used
on its cover (Plate 4), in which Lord is showing the picture of when she left high
school. Memory is condensed in this photograph and the contrast of two different
times gives us the first clue for the rest of the narrative – the process of closing the
plant and the contradictory feelings that surrounded the closure.

In the second photograph, we enter into the region, the scenery of the history
that the book is about to tell. It is the foreigner's point of view that gives a sense

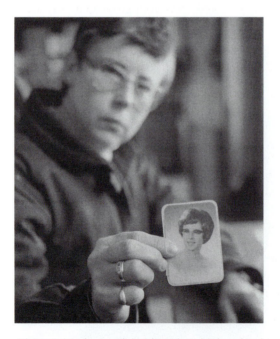

Plate 4 Linda Lord holding her high school
graduation photograph – Rollie's Cafe, Belfast,
Maine (USA), 15 March 1988.

of the beginning of the narrative. In the foreground is the road, followed by a general view of the town with the fields covered in snow in the background. We encounter the town from the outside; but as the narrative develops we get closer and closer, and the photographs allow us to see what we are not accustomed to seeing.

The following thirty-four pictures are all about the interior of the plant and the poultry work in the mechanized lines, taken in March 1988. All the steps of the process are photographed in detail: hangers shackling poultry; Lord working in the 'blood tunnel'; the defeathering machine; the removal of small hairs and feathers by the fire of several singeing machines; workers transferring poultry from one conveyor to the other; the eviscerating line; and further processing and packing. It is Penobscot's closing day, the last time all of these workers will be doing their jobs. Throughout the day, Chatterley has not only photographed the work, but also the break time, when people talk about what is going on, and the commotion before leaving on closing day.

Of the twenty-one photographs that follow the interviews with Lord, only two are landscapes from Belfast, Maine; seventeen are about the daily life of Lord and her new job in a rope factory, six months after she left Penobscot Poultry. The two remaining photographs are from different periods in time: the summer of 1992, and the summer of 1994. On both of these occasions, Lord is in the garden of her father's home (and what will later be her home). At this time, we are no longer strangers; we have gained exposure to her feelings, her fight to get a new job, her opinions about politics, and her tastes in having fun. We know more about Lord from her words and the images that she allowed us to see. The narrative also enabled us to know other aspects of the deindustrialization process.

It is interesting to remark that of fifty-seven photographs, 63 per cent were taken in the plant. The remainder are from a variety of places, in which the story of Lord is traced. The places relating to the work were, in the great majority, clean and large; only in the photos of the 'blood tunnel' were they narrow and dirty. At no time are the places where the people work reflecting waste, degeneration or even disorganization. Nothing shows that the machinery or plant is out-of-date, or the workers are not fully occupied; they all work hard. The photos show the steady rhythm of the plant. So why close it? This question lies within the images.

Labour is the main subject of the photos, as 74 per cent of the pictures published are about people working and working conditions; Lord searching for a job or working as a volunteer at the Brooks Fire Department. In these pictures, men and women had been equally represented; men appeared in 45 per cent of the photographs and women in 49 per cent, as the central focus of the image. Today in the labour world, gender plays a significant role, often determining the kind of work reserved for men and women, although, as the photograph of Linda Lord working in the 'blood tunnel' shows, such prejudices can sometimes be overcome. The goal is to get a job, to be employed. In her interviews, Lord stresses the import-ance of having a job that could support her and allow her to help her parents, confirming the weight of labour in community daily life and explaining why collective unemployment of this kind is so traumatic.

The majority of the photographs follow the pattern of contemporary photo-journalism: medium-sized; square; instantaneous; horizontal; centralized; parallel to the ground; varying between two planes and one plane; with equal distribution

Plate 5 Linda signing up for unemployment benefits for the first time in her life –
American Legion, Post 43, Belfast, Maine, 1 March 1988.

of the figures organized in lines; the whole scenery in focus, with well-defined lines and an acute sense of light and dark. Options that express a direct message about what was going on, a message that goes straight to the point, showing with sharp images the contradiction of being employed one day and unemployed the next; working hard one day, and searching for a chance on the next. But these photographic messages also translate a desire: a more stable and fair labour world.

Conclusion

The images selected for the book, as the authors acknowledge, were designed to change the readers' understanding and perceptions. Chatterley's vision of the plant as 'mechanized death' shaped the images he shot, and the ways in which the co-authors interedited the photographs and text to tell a story of contradiction, heightened the theme of paradox within the book (Chatterley and Rouverol 2000). The photographs illustrate aspects of deindustrialization that could only have been captured through visual means. Images matter – in some cases are even necessary – to the telling of a historical narrative, because new kinds of understandings can emerge through the dialogue between images and text. It is not simply that photographs make accessible (and therefore democratize) the reading and making of history. It is also that photographs – by revealing multiple stories, contrasts and contradictions, ambiguities and uncertainties – enrich the analysis, deepen and complicate the story we can tell through words. The photographs, like Lord's text,

Plate 6 Playing drums with the Golden Nuggets at a campground in Dixmont, Maine, June 1988.

imply contrast and paradox, but instead reveal polyphony, a multiplicity of perspectives: as in being 'content and not content'. By breaking open Lord's story through visual means, the authors aimed to challenge their readers, but now also aim to challenge the writers and makers of history: to 'visualize' new kinds of knowledge, to 'visualize' new forms of history.

Notes

1   All three co-authors of the book, Alicia J. Rouverol, Cedric N. Chatterley and Stephen A. Cole, in addition to the project interviewee, Linda Lord, participated in the Yale conference on *The Chicken: Its Biological, Social, Cultural, and Industrial History*, 17–19 May 2002. Rouverol notes Chatterley's presence because the decision to place the presentation in the video/film section of the programme may have been linked to his participation, or that of Linda Lord (conference organizers sometimes shy away from placing interviewees on formal paper panels). It should be noted that Brazilian historian Ana Maria Mauad, co-author of this chapter, was not involved in the creation of *'I Was Content and Not Content'* or the project's original research. Mauad analyses the use of photographs in historical research and has commented elsewhere on the use of images in this book (see Mauad 2000). The authors of this article wish to thank Caroline Knowles and Paul Sweetman for their editorial assistance, and Cedric Chatterley for his insights.

2   Rouverol had presented this material previously at the Oral History Association, the Berkshire Conference on the History of Women, and the International Oral History Association, all settings in which she had shown slides in addition to presenting the

paper. But conferences that draw heavily on oral history may also be more open to the use of visual methods.

3 Less conservative estimates suggest that more than 1,000 workers throughout the county were affected.

4 In the 'blood tunnel', Lord manually cut the chickens' throats until the company installed an automatic neck-cutting device, which she then backed up. Lord's starting pay at Penobscot in 1967 was around $3.25 an hour. Over twenty years later, when Penobscot closed in 1988, she was earning $5.69 an hour. At that time, the highest-paying positions at the plant included truck driving, weighing and sticking (Linda Lord's position).

5 Lord's story – a gendered analysis of her work at Penobscot and her role in the community – are explored elsewhere in greater detail (see Rouverol 2000, 1998).

6 In the book, the authors aimed to tell Lord's narrative through multiple 'voices': Lord's oral history text; Rouverol's historical and methodological essays; writer Carolyn Chute's literary essay about working in a poultry plant; Cole's epilogue; and Chatterley's photographs.

7 See Bluestone and Harrison (1982). While political economist Barry Bluestone has defined deindustrialization as a 'systematic decline in the industrial base', economists increasingly understand the phenomenon to encompass far more than the loss of our nation's manufacturing base (1982: 6). It is not simply an issue of job loss, since jobs are being created in the United States. Rather it is the type of jobs created and their geographical locale. Job growth is predominantly in the retail and service sectors, generally offering low pay with few benefits (Browne and Sims 1993: 16, 18).

8 For a discussion of paradox in Linda Lord's story, and the polyphonic nature of her testimony, see Chatterley and Rouverol (2000: esp. 125–8). Linda's own narrative is not paradoxical but polyphonic, revealing a range of perspectives, and implying multiple identities. In his foreword to the book, Frisch calls this 'multivalence' or 'multi-valents, many values, the holding of different values at the same time without implying confusion, contradiction, or even paradox' (2000: xxi).

9 Women are twice as likely to be found unemployed a year after job loss (Bluestone and Harrison 1982: 54). Displaced older workers also encounter long periods of unemployment and declines in earnings trajectories (Folbre et al. 1987: 294).

10 See Chatterley and Rouverol (2000: 95–116) for the history of the company and its role in the state's economy. Though Maine never led the nation in poultry produc-tion, poultry was central to the state's economy; and Belfast had long been the state's 'broiler capital' (Hanke et al. 1973: 771; 'Waldo County' 1973). For Belfast, chicken was indeed big business: by the early 1970s, when the industry peaked, Penobscot and Maplewood, the other major broiler processor in town, together employed 2,500 people (Barringer 1989: 6; Caldwell 1971: 9D).

11 See Chatterley and Rouverol (2000: 98–104). Rouverol argues that the decline of poultry in the state was in fact an exodus (see also Bailey 1981: 3; and Brown 1980: 23). The implication, here, is capital migration, with the decline of the industry fitting the generalized pattern of businesses relocating to regions that offer a better 'busi-ness climate'. (This term usually implies an environment that offers low-wage and non-unionized labour, as well generous tax incentives, to attract businesses.)

12 For a nuanced discussion of capital mobility, see Cowie (1999). In his book, *Capital Moves: RCA's Seventy-Year Quest for Cheap Labor*, Cowie examines a series of relocations of the company's radio and television manufacturing across three states and finally to Mexico, '[r]evealing a much longer and more complicated history of capital migra-tion than we tend to hear about in the "global era"' (1999: 1–2). Mexico alone has seen a dramatic rise in US-owned, export-oriented assembly plants (called *maquiladoras*). In 1968, there were 112 *maquiladoras*; by 1992, there were over 2,000 (Browne and Sims 1993: 21–2). Statistics also show that while the share of

manufactured exports produced in the US slipped from 1955 to 1985, the percentage of global production held by US-owned corporations has actually increased (Kwan 1991: 7). US corporate managers are still investing, but not in this country's basic industries. Capital mobility has become a key strategy for lowering costs, with redirection of investment from basic manufacturing becoming fundamental to increased profits (Bluestone and Harrison 1982: 15–19).

13   For an examination of the collaborative dimensions of this project, see Rouverol (2000: 66–78). For a broader discussion on collaborative oral history, see Rouverol (2003).

References

Bailey, Denise (1981) 'The great poultry failure', *Maine Times*, 17 July, pp. 1–7.

Barringer, Richard E. (1989) 'Waldo County: historical profile', unpublished manuscript.

Biel, Steven (1995) 'The left and public memory', *Reviews in American History* 23: 704–9.

Bluestone, Barry and Harrison, Bennett (1982) *The Deindustrialization of America: Plant Closings, Community Abandonment, and the Dismantling of Basic Industry*, New York: Basic Books.

Brown, Dennis O. (1980) 'Poultry firm is "forced" to expand in Southland', *Bangor Daily News*, 17 January, p. 23.

Browne, Harry and Sims, Beth (1993) *Runaway America: U.S. Jobs and Factories on the Move*, Albuquerque: The Resource Center.

Caldwell, Bill (1971) 'Belfast's battle of chicken guts', *Maine Sunday Telegram*, 12 September, p. 9D.

Chaplin, Elizabeth (1994) *Sociology and Visual Representation*, London: Routledge.

Chatterley, C. and Rouverol, A., with Cole, S. (2000) *'I Was Content and Not Content': The Story of Linda Lord and the Closing of Penobscot Poultry*, Carbondale: Southern Illinois University Press.

Cowie, Jefferson (1999) *Capital Moves: RCA's Seventy-Year Quest for Cheap Labor*, Ithaca: Cornell University Press.

Folbre, N., Leighton, J. and Roderick, M. (1987) 'Legislation in Maine', in Paul D. Staudohar and Holly E. Brown (eds) *Deindustrialization and Plant Closure*, Lexington, Mass.: D.C. Heath.

Ginsburg, Carlo (1976) *Il formaggio e i vermi: il cosmo di un mugnaio de '500*, Turin: Giulio Einaudi Editore.

Hanke, O., Skinner, J. and Florea, J. (eds) (1973) *American Poultry History, 1823–1973*, Madison, Wis.: American Poultry Historical Society, Inc.

Hobsbawm, Eric (1998) *Sobre História*, São Paulo: Ediotra Companhia das Letras.

Kwan, Ronald (1991) 'Footloose and country free: mobility key to capitalists' power', *Dollars & Sense* (March).

Levi, Giovanni (1991) 'About micro-history', in Peter Burke (ed.) *New Perspectives on Historical Writing*, Oxford: Basil Blackwell.

Mauad, A.M. (2000) *Commentarios sobre o painel 'Identidade da classe trabalhadora em uma economia global'. Historia Oral: desafios para o seculo XXI*, Rio de Janeiro: Editora Fiocruz/Casa de Oswaldo Cruz/CPDOC – Fundacao Getulio Vargas.

Rouverol, A. (1995) 'The story of Linda Lord and the closing of Penobscot Poultry: an ethnography in process', master's thesis, University of North Carolina at Chapel Hill.

—— (1998) 'The closing of Penobscot Poultry and the story of Linda Lord: one woman's experience of deindustrialization', *Journal of Applied Folklore* 4: 5–21.

—— (2000) '"I was content and not content": oral history and the collaborative process', *Oral History* 28(2): 66–78.

—— (2003) 'Collaborative oral history in a correctional setting: promise and pitfalls', *Oral History Review* 30(1): 61–85.

Vilches, Lorenzo (1992) *La lectura de la imagen: Prensa, cine, televisión*, Barcelona, Ed. Paidós Ibérica, 4th edn.

'Waldo County: an area where industry, agriculture, recreational industries complement each other' (1973) *Maine Sunday Telegram*, 4 March.

Wallace, Michael and Rothschild, Joyce (1988) 'Plant closings, capital flight, and worker dislocation: the long shadow of deindustrialization', in Michael Wallace and Joyce Rothschild (eds) *Deindustrialization and the Restructuring of American Industry, Research in Politics and Society*, vol. 3, Greenwich, Conn.: JAI Press.

Howard S. Becker

AFTERWORD
Photography as evidence, photographs as exposition

Anthropologists and sociologists have been using photographs ever since the beginnings of both disciplines, but have never been able to agree on just how these images should be used or to what ends. It's as though we social scientists have a feeling that this is somehow a good thing to do, something everyone else is doing and we ought to be doing too, but we can't communicate to ourselves or anyone else exactly why and how that is so. The chapters in this volume speak to this problem in many ways.

In sociology's beginnings, photographs were an integral part of the disciplinary project of repairing a society that wasn't working well. They provided what in those innocent days we took to be concrete, 'objective' evidence of bad things going on: substandard housing that afflicted the poor, the evil consequences of inbreeding among 'mentally defective' people, the vicious circumstances of child labour, the condition of immigrant populations. Anthropological uses were typically not reform-oriented, most often serving as a warrant for the authenticity of anthropological accounts of the societies observed, providing evidence of the researcher's physical presence on the scene and thus of the trustworthiness of the account offered. Anthropologists used images in a greater variety of ways than sociologists did. Their photographic work often consisted of nothing more than simple recordings of the physical appearance of peoples and artefacts studied. A major work of visual social science, far more ambitious both theoretically and methodologically, Bateson and Mead's *Balinese Character* (1942) appeared in the early 1940s but was essentially ignored both within and beyond anthropology. No one knew what to do with this incredible example of the possibilities of using visual material in our work.

Sociologists lost interest in the reformist uses of photography as they shifted their attention from reform to scientific generalization. Photography's standing declined because of its association with the 'unscientific' business of social reform and very few photographs accompanied sociological articles and books. Anthropologists complained that their colleagues made photographs that were no different from the ones tourists made of exotic places and that served no better purpose than those amateur works.

The social science failure to see the uses of imagery was all the more surprising because during this same period the natural sciences, in both biology and physics, came to rely on visual images for much of their work. Astronomy could not have been carried on as it was without the photographs made through radio telescopes. Biologists routinely relied on visual inspection to assess the results of their experiments. Nuclear physics would not have been possible without the photographic records of what happened when you bombarded atoms. It was only the social sciences, poor backward things, that ignored these possibilities or failed to make good use of these resources.

Beginning in the 1960s – we can date these developments crudely to that period – new generations of visually oriented social scientists arrived with new, more ambitious ideas about what visual materials could accomplish. They were more aware of the extensive body of work by photographers and filmmakers that overlapped their own concerns and showed that methods of recording and analysing and working with visual materials already existed. No need for social scientists to invent these things. Many members of this generation of social scientists had experience in visual work, having worked professionally as photographers or filmmakers, or just having been serious picture makers for a long time. They brought a double sensibility to the field, seeing the visual disciplines as lacking in complex ideas about society, and the social science disciplines as lacking in a minimum of what had come to be called 'visual literacy'. Some of the authors in this volume contributed work in this genre.

The arrival of these new visual social scientists coincided with the appearance of visual artists whose work, while not social science in any conventional sense, was informed by a sensitivity to class, race and the usual social science concerns and to the problems of visual representation of complex ideas about society. Some of this work – Robert Frank's *The Americans* (1969) is my favourite example – approached the concerns of social science obliquely and implicitly. Other works – I think here primarily of the explicitly political and theoretical works of John Berger and Jean Mohr (1982a, 1982b) – looked more like social science: not the kind of thing you could publish in the professional journals of sociology and anthropology, but nevertheless explicitly addressed to the body of ideas social scientists were at home with.

These developments spawned durable professional organizations in both sociology and anthropology, which published journals, elected presidents and held annual meetings. The journals, especially, went some way towards solving what seemed to be an endemic problem for professional academics who wanted to do serious visual work: having the visual work they did – so unlike the conventional social science analyses published in the major sociological and anthropological journals – taken seriously as scholarly work and 'counting' in the constant assessments of one's worth conducted by colleagues and administrators. Would these articles filled with photographs, or this film, improve your job security or help you get a salary increase? A great deal of theoretical and methodological writing about visual representation seemed to have these as underlying concerns.

Into this mélange of ideas and professional unease, the rise of postmodern concerns introduced an avenue that led away, unfortunately in my opinion, from image making and serious consideration of the problems associated with bringing the images you made into some kind of dialogue with the traditional concerns of social science. People who might otherwise have done solid empirical work (yes, my prejudices are showing) devoted themselves to detailed exegeses of mostly hypothetical data, or of visual materials made by others. So social scientists diagnosed the ills of modern society by analysing popular films or the photographs that appeared in popular magazines.

I don't mean to disparage all this work. You clearly could use advertising photographs, as Goffman (1979) did, to work out gender relations as those were expressed in habitual postures. But you always had to allow for the influence of the professional standards and concerns of the photographers and publicists who oversaw the making of the images, because what you saw there might express no more than their work-related interests.

But the analysis of already existing imagery did not make the full use of visual material towards which the natural sciences had pointed the way. We now need to find ways of using visual imagery that will be as natural and as acceptable to our colleagues as other forms of data – and other ways of presenting what we know – are now. Here are some things that stand in the way of that happy situation. Keep in mind that, as I will suggest, some of these problems afflict every variety of data gathering and representation, and are in no way unique to visual materials.

The 'subjectivity' of the inevitable choices involved in making photographs bothers many people. There is no doubt about this: every paper on the subject dutifully lists the choices (framing, film, focus, etc.) and as dutifully confesses that these are not made in any 'scientific' way. All true, but likewise true, with the appropriate translations for other cases, of survey research and its tabular and statistical reporting, and of interviews and field observations and their recording, transcribing and interpretation. To say that does not excuse us from having to deal with these questions. It does mean that we don't have to feel any more burdened by them than our colleagues who use other methods.

Many people who work with visual materials have not realized that there are real skills involved and that you have to learn them, practise them, and keep them in mind as you do your research and prepare it for public presentation. Most people who work with statistical methods learn something about what they are doing, though they often misuse the methods, fail to satisfy their requirements for data, and so on. Many people have failed to master the mechanics of writing clearly and unambiguously (I'm not talking about literary flourishes here, only about telling people what you think you know in a way that won't mislead them) and of making a logical argument. Ask the editor of any social science journal. And, similarly, most people do not know how to make a visual image that communicates clearly what's to be said (see Edward Tufte's books on graphical displays 1983, 1990) and certainly do not know how to deliberately control the many aspects of such images. Most of us, as Jay Ruby (1973) complained years ago about anthropologists who used photographs in their work, are just making holiday or family pictures without realizing that there is more to it.

Reproducing visual materials is a continuing problem. It's expensive to print photographs in a way that gives them a chance to be seen properly, and most social science journals are not as equipped to handle them as they ought to be. Presenting materials on film is of course a much greater problem. A possible solution lies in the increasing availability of computers with enough memory and speed to incorporate still photographs and film clips into a verbal presentation. PowerPoint has many sins to answer for, but does present a simple and efficient way to incorporate visual evidence and exposition.

This brings us to the core of the problem, the part that will not change when more ephemeral technical and organizational problems are solved or at least become the site of durable compromise: how do you use photographs and film to elaborate an argument and how do you deploy them as evidence for the argument you want to make?

We should recognize, to begin, that no way of deploying these arguments is really sound. No forms of argument supporting social science conclusions can withstand all the logical and epistemological and practical arguments that might be brought against them. All our ways of doing business – of presenting arguments and adducing evidence in their favour – are flawed. Nevertheless, we continue to use them. We use them because all of us who make and use them, or some significant portion of those people, have agreed to treat them as good, reliable and workable enough to let us go ahead with our work as though they were the epistemological wonders they are not. And our methods of arguing and adducing evidence do work. That is, they produce results reliable enough, at least for a while, not to produce any knowledge disasters.

Such a happy situation does not last for ever, of course, and eventually the flaws we had agreed to ignore pay us back and produce troubles: our hypotheses aren't confirmed, we can no longer quite believe our theories or persuade our colleagues to believe them, and we experience all the other troubles knowledge is heir to. And then it's time to do the thinking and arguing that will create a new provisional consensus about how work good enough to believe in can be done. This is the life of science that such colleagues as Max Weber (1946), Thomas Kuhn (1970) and Bruno Latour (1987) described.

This suggests that the problem about visual materials is that we have not found that minimal agreement which lets work proceed, which provides the guidelines we can observe and orient ourselves by as we produce and consume the products of a visual social science. What we have now is a variety of proposals, put forward in the form of theoretical essays, methodological arguments, but most importantly as finished pieces of work which vie for our attention.

I think – it's just a thought – that the way to proceed is not to reason from methodological principles but to look at books and articles that seem to be what we would like to produce and work out what they have done right. I've already mentioned some likely candidates for such analysis, works of visual social science that seem to have done it right: Bateson and Mead's *Balinese Character* and the books by John Berger and Jean Mohr, particularly *A Seventh Man*. I'd add Doug Harper's *Working Knowledge* (1987) to that list. And I think we'd do well to look also at the work of photographers who never pretended to be social scientists but who we would do well to claim as our own. Robert Frank's *The Americans* (1969) and Walker

Evans's *American Photographs* (1975) are obvious choices here (I made a start on the Evans book in a piece on what we can learn about analytic categories from it. See Becker 1998–9.)

Even though visual social science is almost as old as photography, as I remarked when I began, we are really still at the beginning, with a lot of work yet to do.

References

Bateson, Gregory and Mead, Margaret (1942) *Balinese Character: a Photographic Analysis*, New York: New York Academy of Sciences.

Becker, Howard S. (1998–9) 'Categories and comparisons: how we find meaning in photographs', *Visual Anthropology Review* 14: 3–10.

Berger, John and Mohr, Jean (1982a [1975]) *A Seventh Man*, London: Writers and Readers Publishing Cooperative.

—— (1982b) *Another Way of Telling*, New York: Pantheon Books.

Evans, Walker (1975 [1938]) *American Photographs*, New York: East River Press.

Frank, Robert (1969 [1959]) *The Americans*, New York: Aperture.

Goffman, Erving (1979) *Gender Advertisements*, Cambridge, Mass.: Harvard University Press.

Harper, Douglas (1987) *Working Knowledge*, Chicago: University of Chicago Press.

Kuhn, Thomas (1970) *The Structure of Scientific Revolutions*, Chicago: University of Chicago Press.

Latour, Bruno (1987) *Science in Action*, Cambridge, Mass.: Harvard University Press.

Ruby, Jay (1973) 'Up the Zambesi with notebook and camera or being an anthropologist without doing anthropology . . . with pictures', *PIEF Newsletter* 4: 12–14.

Tufte, Edward R. (1983) *The Visual Display of Quantitative Information*, Cheshire, Conn.: Graphics Press.

—— (1990) *Envisioning Information*, Cheshire, Conn.: Graphics Press.

Weber, Max (1946) 'Science as a vocation', in H.H. Gerth and C. Wright Mills (trans. and eds) *From Max Weber: Essays in Sociology*, New York: Oxford University Press.

Index

Note: page numbers in *italics* denote plate references.